
Mirror for Man

CLASSICS OF ANTHROPOLOGY
Ashley Montagu, Editor

Mirror for Man

The Relation of Anthropology to Modern Life

CLYDE KLUCKHOHN

Foreword by Ashley Montagu

UNIVERSITY OF ARIZONA PRESS
Tucson, Arizona

About the Author

CLYDE KLUCKHOHN (1905–1960) was one of this nation's most distinguished anthropologists. A specialist in Navajo Indian culture, Kluckhohn taught at the University of New Mexico in Albuquerque, and later joined the faculty of Harvard University, where he taught until his death. Kluckhohn was the author of numerous professional articles and monographs, among them *To the Foot of the Rainbow* (1927), *Navaho Witchcraft* (1944), and *Anthropology and the Classics* (1961).

THE UNIVERSITY OF ARIZONA PRESS
First Printing 1985

Manufactured in the U.S.A.

Library of Congress Cataloging in Publication Data

Kluckhohn, Clyde, 1905-1960.
Mirror for man.

Reprint. Originally published: New York: Whittlesey House, c1949.
Bibliography: p.
Includes index.
1. Anthropology. 2. United States—Civilization.
I. Title.
GN31.K53 1985 301 85-1120

ISBN 0-8165-0919-0 (pbk. : alk. paper)

To

H. G. Rockwood

and

R. J. Koehler

Contents

Anthropology is often considered a collection of curious facts, telling about the peculiar appearance of exotic people and describing their strange customs and beliefs. It is looked upon as an entertaining diversion, apparently without any bearing upon the conduct of life of civilized communities.

This opinion is mistaken. More than that, I hope to demonstrate that a clear understanding of the principles of anthropology illuminates the social processes of our own times and may show us, if we are ready to listen to its teachings, what to do and what to avoid.

—Franz Boas (1928)*

Foreword

CLYDE KAY MABEN KLUCKHOHN was born in LeMars, Iowa, in 1905, and died in Santa Fe, New Mexico, on 29 July 1960. His early death deprived the world of one of its most distinguished anthropologists, a great teacher and friend to all his students, as well as to his colleagues in many fields. The early death of such a man is truly calamitous, for everyone who knew him knew that his greatest contributions to humanity were yet to come. I emphasize *humanity* because it was not simply theory that interested him, but more importantly the value of the field he had chosen as his life's work for the benefit of the human being and human society, and beyond that the cooperation of the world's peoples in one great harmony by mutual understanding. That, indeed, was the contribution Kluckhohn hoped to make through the volume the reader has before him, written during the years 1945 and 1946. The title, *Mirror for Man*, explains itself. It enables the reader not only to take a good look at himself, but also at how he and all his fellow human beings have come to be the way they are now; and the practical purpose of the book is further emphasized in the subtitle: "The Relation of Anthropology to Modern Life." Never was a book better realized in what it set out to do than *Mirror for Man*.

It so happened that when Kluckhohn had finally put the book into shape, Whittlesey House, a division of the McGraw-Hill Book Company, announced a competition for a $10,000 prize for the book that most contributed to man's understanding of the world of the day. Over 250 manuscripts were submitted for the prize. The judges were Harlow Shapley, professor of astronomy at Harvard University; Waldemar Kaempffert, science editor of *The New York Times*; Donald Culross Peattie, a botanist and natural-history writer; and Gerald Wendt, a popular-science writer. It was the unanimous decision of the four judges that of the many excellent books that were submitted, *Mirror for Man* far outranked them all. Shapley was impressed by its "great imagination and scholarship," and Kaempffert by its authoritativeness and the clarity with which it was written.

When the book was published in 1949 it received accolades everwhere, and especially from professional anthropologists. Margaret Mead summed it all up with the words, "the best contemporary introduction to modern anthropology," and with a few unimportant modifications it so remains. It is in the best sense of the word a classic, a model of its kind. As the classic it is, I believe it will always hold a high place as an introduction to anthropological science, to the study of humanity. Written for the layman, the book has been valued not only by a generation of lay readers, but also by the author's professional peers for his ability to act as a spokesman for them, and as a refreshing reminder of their high calling, and what they are about, the students and expositors of the art and science of humanity. The reader, therefore, need not worry as to whether *Mirror for Man* is an up-to-date introduction to anthropology and its practical applications. I can assure the reader that it is. Not only does the book retain its contemporaneity to the present day, but it also has, in a very real sense, become even more relevant in its concerns, and in the recommendations which Kluckhohn wisely leaves the reader to draw for himself.

Kluckhohn graduated from the University of Wisconsin at Madison with a major in classics. Shortly thereafter he was elected a Rhodes Scholar and took up residence at Corpus Christi College in the University of Oxford, where in 1932 he was awarded the M.A. degree. At Oxford he studied both Greek and anthropology under Sir Gilbert Murray and other members of their departments. Traveling in Spain, France, and Italy, Kluckhohn began his formal study of anthropology at the University of Vienna, where he came under the influence of the *Kulturkreise* school, which held that it was possible to trace the diffusion of clusters or complexes of basic cultural elements over space and time. Though he did not embrace the school's ideas, he nevertheless wrote an appreciative article on them.[1]

Kluckhohn's interest in anthropology began when he visited the Indian and Spanish-speaking peoples of the American Southwest. He took extensive trips into Navajo country, exploring unknown territory and learning to speak the language. He tells of this in his two books *To the Foot of the Rainbow* (1927) and *Beyond the Rainbow* (1933). It seemed only natural that he should commence his teaching career at the University of New Mexico, in Albuquerque, in 1932. Invited by the Department of Anthropology at Harvard as a visiting lecturer some two years later, I remember very clearly the head of the department, Ernest Hooton, saying to me, "When I heard him speak, I said to myself, 'We must get that man.'" And so they did. Kluckhohn joined the Harvard faculty in 1935 and remained there until his death.

Kluckhohn was not a flamboyant speaker, but always a very impressive one. He was modest, never striving for effect, concerned always with the sound statement and the appropriate question. As a teacher he was much appreciated and admired by his students, for his great learning and his ability to make complicated ideas comprehensible; not only that, but his interest in and friendship with his students is still remembered by them all, especially those he helped over the hurdles of personal and academic problems.

Kluckhohn's publications were many, in both periodicals and books. In 1938, with Leland C. Wyman he wrote *Navaho Classification and Their Song Ceremonials*, and in 1940, with the same coauthor, he wrote *An Introduction to Navaho Chant Practice*. In 1944 he produced a classic study, *Navaho Witchcraft*, followed by two books in collaboration with Dorothea Leighton, *The Navaho* (1946) and *Children of the People* (1947). With Henry R. Murray, Kluckhohn edited the pioneer anthology *Personality: In Nature, Society, and Culture* (1948; rev. 1953). In 1951, with Leonard Macombe and E. Z. Vogt, he wrote *Navaho Means People*, followed in 1952 by a collaborative work with A. L. Kroeber, *Culture: A Critical Review of Concepts and Definitions*. In 1956, while serving as director of Harvard's Russian Research Center, with Raymond Bauer and Alex Inkeles he wrote *How the Soviet System Works*. And in 1959 Kluckhohn delivered the Colver Lectures at Brown University, which were published in 1961 as *Anthropology and the Classsics*. The lectures were delivered in April 1960, just three months before his death, and *Anthropology and the Classics*, an utterly delightful book of seventy-six pages, is surely one of the best accounts in English on the nature of Greek culture.

Throughout *Mirror for Man* the evidences of Kluckhohn's classical knowledge are generously peppered. The route from the classics to anthropology was a natural one, and was followed by many classicists who later became distinguished anthropologists: Sir James Frazer, Franz Boas, Andrew Lang, J. L. Myres, R. R. Marett, Ernest Hooton, and others. It is evident, however, from his writings that Kluckhohn's classical training exerted a powerful influence not alone upon his intellect, but also upon his spirit. He was a gentleman in Aristotle's sense of that word, as set out in the *Nicomachean Ethics*, and by that *eutrapelia*, as Pericles used the word, to describe the Athenian's lucidity of thought, cleanness and propriety of language, freedom from prejudice and from stiffness, openness of mind, amiability of manners, accompanied by a happy flexibility of nature. Kluckhohn possessed all these qualities, in addition to which he was utterly charming, and especially and most strikingly delightful with children at a time when most men were awkward with them. This fetching trait of Kluckhohn's is well seen in his book with Dorothea Leighton on Navajo children. In the technological world in which, as Bruno Bettelheim has said, the fascination with technical competence has dulled our concern for human feelings, Kluckhohn remained to the last deeply involved—this, too, is evident in his writings. It was he who organized Harvard's Russian Research Center in the hope that by the work done there a better understanding might come about between the USSR and the USA. This involvement took him to Washington during the Second World War, where he served in various capacities. From 1942 on he was actively engaged in the Office of War Information and the Overseas Administration, and he was expert consultant to the Secretary of War in 1946 and 1947. He was later a consultant to the Research and Development Board and the State Department's Foreign Service Committee, as well as to the Indian Service of the Department of the Interior.

After the war Kluckhohn worked with Talcott Parsons,

then a professor of sociology at Harvard, to organize a wholly new conception of the behavioral sciences with the Department of Social Relations, which continues to flourish at Harvard.

For his distinguished work in anthropology, Kluckhohn was elected president of the American Anthropological Association in 1948, and he was awarded the Viking Fund Medal in 1950. He was made a member of the National Academy of Sciences, a fellow of the American Philosophical Society, and an honorary fellow of the Anthropological Institute of Great Britain and Ireland.

Let me return to the classical influence so evident in Kluckhohn's writings. This seems to me particularly necessary in an age in which the gray shadow of specialization that has fallen like a cloud over what we miscall "education," but which is in fact for the most part instruction, training in techniques and skills. In the western world, with its passion for pigeonholing, the humanities have been slighted and Greek and Latin regarded as very dead languages with a collective literature that is in any event available in translation. But this is to miss the point, for the study of these "dead" languages opens up not only the royal road to an understanding of societies that have long ceased to be, but also a vista of experience which is never-ending, for, as Kluckhohn says, every language is, among other things, a means of categorizing experience, the human enterprise. Furthermore, the best way of understanding one's own language is to understand Greek and Latin, for the origins of many our words are found in those sources. (As Goethe said, those who know only their own language do not know even that.) And what better way is there to the understanding of a people than through the study of its language? Nothing, indeed, better expresses the genius of a people than its tongue, as Kluckhohn makes abundantly clear in this book. Here we see language in action, and that the meaning of a word is the action it produces, or, as Kluckhohn puts it, "the difference its utterance brings about in a situation." Speaking from personal experience and wide knowledge, Kluckhohn tells us what a great influence the anthropologist has had upon the teaching and learning of human tongues. The vagaries of languages are dealt with with wit and wisdom; this is especially true of nonliterate languages. Language, Kluckhohn shows, is not only a means of categorizing experience but also of interpreting it.

In a world in which nothing alien is human to so many of the world's leaders, Kluckhohn more than ever thought it necessary to teach the meaning of those sterling words of the Latin playwright Terence (ca.190–159 B.C.): "I am a man; nothing human is alien to me." And although he nowhere makes reference to him, Kluckhohn writes as if he had taken to heart other of Terence's words: "I bid him look into the lives of men as though into a mirror, and from others to take an example for himself." Although he was the leading authority on one people, the Navajo, Kluckhohn took the whole of humanity as his province, and in *Mirror for Man* he provides much more than a guided tour through what the anthropologist calls "culture." It is the genius of this book that he combines the interactive processes of the biological evolution of humanity with its cultural evolution (it is of interest to note that he once thought of becoming a biological anthropologist, for which discipline he maintained an active interest). As an illustration of his understanding of what almost all biological anthropologists in the 1940s took the concept of "race" to be as a basic axiom of their trade, Kluckhohn saw its many fallacies, and he therefore entitled the fifth chapter of this book "Race: A Modern

Myth." As Kluckhohn makes clear, "human populations are too mongrel and too variable to be grouped into races as meaningful as animal varieties." In the course of his discussion Kluckhohn shows how popular and scientific errors concerning "race" came into being, and in so doing he writes a chapter that will always remain a model of its kind. As he points out, "the biological oneness of mankind is far more significant than the relatively superficial differences."[2]

The concept of race is really a zoological idea which in pro-slavery days was converted into social doctrine. Physical differences were made to serve as proof of basic behavioral differences—a view still urged by certain academic racists to this day. With the rise of genetics, of which most racists were remarkably ill-informed, it was argued that there was a genetic relationship between the physical appearance of an individual, his ability, and the ability of the "race" to which he belonged for great cultural achievement. The fact is that no such relationship exists; there are greater differences within human populations than between them, and it is no argument against the overwhelming likeness to point out differences. Whatever differences do exist between and within human populations, they do not render equality of opportunity a contemptible principle. The whole matter will depend simply upon the answer we give to the question "is this person a human being?" If the answer is yes, then it should follow, as night follows day, that he or she has the right to develop fully his or her potentialities, that to the increase of achievement through the improvement of environment the influence of heredity offers no barrier.

When Kluckhohn writes that "the tendency to rate biological groups as inferior or superior to one another is due in part to a holdover from Darwinian thinking," it is not

Darwin of whom he is speaking, but of his followers who had a propensity for ranking everything on a "scale of evolution." Darwin was of a very different frame of mind.[3]

Among the other eight chapters of *Mirror for Man*, "An Anthropologist Looks at the United States" is surely one of the most valuable. As Kluckhohn says, the preceding chapters rest on well-documented data and theory that have proved their predictive powers. However, in an analysis of American culture one can go only a shade beyond impressionism; it was F. Scott Fitzgerald who summed up America as "a willingness of heart." Kluckhohn agrees, and he writes one of the most insightful and sympathetic analyses of this country ever written by an American. This chapter, more than anything else, will give the reader a view of the kind of illuminations an anthropologist can bring to the study of a society. It was such insight that Kluckhohn brought to bear, when he became a principal advisor to General Douglas MacArthur, upon the problem of pacifying and democratizing the Japanese after World War II. His, too, was among the most powerful voices to advise against the shortsighted "unconditional surrender" and forced abdication of Emperor Hirohito, on the grounds that the first condition would stiffen Japanese resistance, while the second would be even more unacceptable to the Japanese, who regarded the Emperor as a deity. But with the atom bomb, the first admonition was disregarded, the second approved. It is just this sort of thing that makes anthropology relevant to the problems of modern life on a national and international scale in the important task of reconciling domestic conflict, as well as conflict between cultures. We are shown how knowledge of the past and of nonliterate cultures can help us with the solutions to contemporary world problems, that, indeed, anthropology has predictive power in the realm of politics, social attitudes, and above all in human relations of every sort.

As Alexander Pope said, and as Clyde Kluckhohn makes so enchantingly clear, all our knowledge is ourselves to know in all our wonderful variety.

ASHLEY MONTAGU

NOTES

1. Clyde Kluckhohn, "Some Reflections on the Method and Theory of the *Kulturkreislehre*." *American Anthropologist*, vol. 38 (1936), 157–96.

2. See Ashley Montagu, *Man's Most Dangerous Myth: The Fallacy of Race* (New York: Oxford University Press, 1974).

3. See Charles Darwin, *The Descent of Man* (London: John Murray, 1901), pp. 187–88.

Preface

THIS BOOK is intended for the layman, not for the carping professional. The latter is humbly begged to remember that if I had put in all the documentation he could wish, this book would have grown into several volumes. Had I entered all the qualifications and reservations required in a technical study, the intelligent layman would stop before the end of the first chapter.

There is no claim that every statement is "proved." Anthropology is a young subject, and there is still much work to be done, both gathering and sifting of data. This is an honest and a careful assessment of the evidence I have been able to cover. In certain instances others have, with equal honesty and perhaps with better judgment, drawn different conclusions from the same materials. But I have tried ordinarily to follow the present consensus of the profession. Where I have expressed heterodox or personal opinions, the phrasing gives some warning to the reader. Similarly, by the use of such words as, "some authorities say," "perhaps," "probably," and "maybe," I have indicated my tentative choice between controversial findings or interpretations. For all save a few statements and my own gazings into the crystal ball of the future there is some evidence that I consider hard. Speculations of others or of my own are labeled or are clear as such from context.

CLYDE KLUCKHOHN

CHAPTER I

Queer Customs, Potsherds, and Skulls

ANTHROPOLOGY PROVIDES a scientific basis for dealing with the crucial dilemma of the world today: how can peoples of different appearance, mutually unintelligible languages, and dissimilar ways of life get along peaceably together? Of course, no branch of knowledge constitutes a cure-all for the ills of mankind. If any statement in this book seems to support such messianic pretensions, put this absurd claim down as a slip of an enthusiast who really knows better. Anthropology is, however, an overlapping study with bridges into the physical, biological, and social sciences and into the humanities.

Because of its breadth, the variety of its methods, and its mediating position, anthropology is sure to play a central role in the integration of the human sciences. A comprehensive science of man, however, must encompass additional skills, interests, and knowledge. Certain aspects of psychology, medicine and human biology, economics, sociology, and human geography must be fused with anthropology in a general science which must likewise embrace the tools of historical and statistical methods and draw data from history and the other humanities.

Present-day anthropology, then, cannot pretend to be the whole study of man, though perhaps it comes closer than any other branch of science. Some of the discoveries that will here be spoken of as anthropological have been made possible only by collaboration with workers in other fields. Yet even the traditional anthropology has a special right to be heard by those who are deeply concerned with the problem of achieving one world.

This is because it has been anthropology that has explored the gamut of human variability and can best answer the questions: what common ground is there between human beings of all tribes and nations? What differences exist? what is their source? how deep-going are they?

By the beginning of the twentieth century the scholars who interested themselves in the unusual, dramatic, and puzzling aspects of man's history were known as anthropologists. They were the men who were searching for man's most remote ancestors; for Homer's Troy; for the original home of the American Indian; for the relationship between bright sunlight and skin color; for the origin of the wheel, safety pins, and pottery. They wanted to know "how modern man got this way": why some people are ruled by a king, some by old men, others by warriors, and none by women; why some peoples pass on property in the male line, others in the female, still others equally to heirs of both sexes; why some people fall sick and die when they think they are bewitched, and others laugh at the idea. They sought for the universals in human biology and in human conduct. They proved that men of different continents and regions were physically much more alike than they were different. They discovered many parallels in human customs, some of which could be explained by historical contact. In other words, anthropology had become the science of human similarities and differences.

In one sense anthropology is an old study. The Greek historian, Herodotus, sometimes called the "father of anthropology" as well as the "father of history," described at length the physique and customs of the Scythians, Egyptians, and other "barbarians." Chinese scholars of the Han dynasty wrote monographs upon the Hiung-Nu, a light-eyed tribe wandering near China's northwestern frontier. The Roman historian, Tacitus, produced his famous study of the Germans. Long before Herodotus, even, the Babylonians of the time of Hammurabi collected in museums objects made by the Sumerians, their predecessors in Mesopotamia.

Although ancients here and there showed that they thought types and manners of men worth talking about, it was the voyages and explorations from the fifteenth century onward that stimulated the study of human variability. The observed contrasts with the tight little medieval world made anthropology necessary. Useful though the writings of this period are (for example, the travelogues of Peter Martyr) they cannot be ranked as scientific documents. Often fanciful, they were written to amuse or for narrowly practical purposes. Careful accounts of firsthand observation were mixed up with embellished and frequently secondhand anecdotes. Neither authors nor observers had any special training for recording or interpreting what they saw. They looked at other peoples and their habits through crude and distorting lenses manufactured of all the prejudices and preconceptions of Christian Europeans.

It was not until the late eighteenth and nineteenth centuries that scientific anthropology began to develop. The discovery of the relationship between Sanskrit, Latin, Greek, and the Germanic languages gave a great impetus to the comparative point of view. The first systematic anthropologists were gifted amateurs—physicians, natural historians, lawyers, businessmen to whom anthropology was a hobby. They applied common sense, the habits they had learned in their professions, and the fashionable scientific doctrines of their day to growing knowledge about "primitive" peoples.

What did they study? They devoted themselves to oddities, to matters which appeared to be so trivial or so specialized that the fields of study which had been established earlier failed to bother with them. The forms of human hair, the variations in skull formation, shades of skin color did not seem very important to anatomists or to practicing physicians. The physical remains of cultures other than the Greco-Roman were beneath the notice of classical scholars. Languages unrelated to Greek and Sanskrit had no interest for the comparative linguists of the nineteenth century. Primitive rites interested only a few of the curious until the elegant prose and respectable classical scholarship of Sir James Frazer's *Golden Bough* won a wide audience. Not without justification has anthropology been termed "the science of leftovers."

It would be going too far to call the nineteenth-century anthropology "the investigation of oddments by the eccentric." The English Tylor, the American Morgan, the German Bastian, and other leading figures were respected citizens. Nevertheless, we shall understand the growth of the subject better if we admit that many of the first anthropologists were, from the point of view of their contemporaries, eccentrics. They were interested in bizarre things with which the average person had no serious concern and even the ordinary intellectual felt to be inconsequential.

If one does not confuse the results of intellectual activities with the motives leading to these activities, it is useful to ask what sort of people would be curious about these questions. Archaeology and museum anthropology provide an obvious happy hunting ground for those who are driven by that passion for finding and arranging which is common to collectors of everything from stamps to suits of armor. Anthropology has also always had with it the romantics, those who have taken it up because the lure of distant places and exotic people was strong upon them. The lure of the strange and far has a peculiar appeal for those who are dissatisfied with themselves or who do not feel at home in their own society. Consciously or unconsciously, they seek other ways of life where their characteristics are understood and accepted or at any rate, not criticized. Like many historians, the historical anthropologist has an urge to escape from the present by crawling back into the womb of the cultural past. Because the study had something of the romantic aroma about it and because it was not an easy way to make a living, it drew an unusual number of students who had independent means.

The beginnings do not sound very promising, either from the point of view of the students who were attracted to the subject or of what they were drawn to study. Nevertheless these very liabilities provided what are the greatest advantages of anthropology as compared with other approaches to the study of human life. Because nineteenth-century anthropologists studied the things they did out of pure interest and not either to earn a living or to reform the world, a tradition of relative objectivity grew up. The philosophers were shackled by the weighty history of their subject and by the vested interests of their profession. Auguste Comte, the founder of sociology, was a philosopher, but he tried to model sociology after the natural sciences. However, many of his followers, who were only slightly disguised philosophers of history, had a bias in favor of reasoning as opposed to observation. Many of the first American sociologists were Christian ministers, more eager to improve the world than to study it with detachment. The field of political science was also tinged with the philosophic point of view and with reformist zeal. The psychologists became so absorbed in brass instruments and the laboratory that they found little time to study man as one really wants to know him—not in the laboratory but in his daily life. Because anthropology was the science of leftovers and because leftovers were many and varied, it avoided the preoccupation with only one aspect of life that stamped, for instance, economics.

The eagerness and energy of the amateurs gradually won a place for their subject as an independent science. A museum of ethnology was established in Hamburg in 1850; the Peabody Museum of Archaeology and Ethnology at Harvard was founded in 1866; the Royal Anthropological Institute in 1873; the Bureau of American Ethnology in 1879. Tylor was made Reader in Anthropology at Oxford in 1884. The first American professor was appointed in 1886. But in the nineteenth century there were not a hundred anthropologists in the whole world.

The total number of anthropological Ph.D.'s granted in the United States prior to 1920 was only 53. Before 1930 only four American universities gave the doctorate in anthropology. Even today there are a bare dozen. Nor has anthropology become in any sense a staple of the undergraduate curriculum. In only two or three secondary schools is instruction regularly given.

The astonishing thing, considering the trifling number of anthropologists and the minute fraction of the population that has been exposed to formal instruction in the subject is that during the last decade or so the word "anthropology" and some of its terms have come out of hiding in recondite literature to appear with increasing frequency in *The New Yorker, Life, The Saturday Evening Post,* detective stories, and even in moving pictures. It is also symptomatic of a trend that many colleges and universities and some secondary schools have indicated their intention of introducing anthropology in their revised courses of study. Although anthropologists—like psychiatrists and psychologists—are still regarded with a bit of suspicion, present-day society is beginning to feel they have something useful as well as diverting to offer.

In the American Southwest one of the signs of summer is the arrival of many "-ologists" who disrupt the quiet of the countryside. They dig up ruins with all the enthusiasm of small boys hunting for "Indian curios" or of delayed adolescents seeking buried treasure. They pry into the business of peaceful Indians and make a nuisance of themselves generally with a lot of queer-looking gadgets. The kind who dig into ruins are technically called "archaeologists," those who dig into the minds of Indians, "ethnologists" or "social anthropologists," those who measure heads, "physical anthropologists," but all are varieties of the more inclusive breed term "anthropologists."

Now what are they really up to? Is it just sheer curiosity about "ye beastly devices of ye heathen" or do the diggings, questionings, and measurings really have something to do with the world today? Do anthropologists merely produce exotic and amusing facts which have nothing to do with the problems of here and now?

Anthropology is something more than brooding over skulls or hunting for "the missing link," and it has a greater usefulness than providing means to tell one's friends from the apes. Seen from the outside, anthropological activities look, at best, harmlessly amusing, at worst, pretty idiotic. No wonder many a Southwesterner quips, "The Indians are going to start putting a bounty on you fellows." The lay reaction is well summed up by the remark of an army officer. We had met socially and were getting along very well until he asked me how I made my living. When I told him I was an anthropologist he drew away and said, "Well, you don't have to be crazy to be an anthropologist, but I guess it helps."

An anthropologist is a person who is crazy enough to study his fellow man. The scientific study of ourselves is relatively new. In England in 1936 there were over 600 persons who earned their living as students of one specialized branch (biochemistry) of the science of things, but fewer than 10 were employed as anthropologists. There are less than a dozen jobs for physical anthropologists in the United States today.

Yet nothing is more certain than that men ought to see

whether the scientific methods which have given such stupendous results in unlocking the secrets of the physical universe might not help them understand themselves and their neighbors in this rapidly shrinking world. Men build machines that are truly wonderful, only to find themselves next to helpless when it comes to treating the social disorders that often follow the introduction of these machines.

Ways of making a living have changed with such bewildering rapidity that we are all a bit confused most of the time. Our ways of life have altered too—but not symmetrically. Our economic, political, and social institutions have not caught up with our technology. Our religious beliefs and practices and our other idea systems have much in them that is not appropriate to our present way of life and to our scientific knowledge of the physical and biological world. Part of us lives in the "modern" age—another part in medieval or even Greek times.

In the realm of treating social ills we are still living in the age of magic. We often act as if revolutionary and disturbing ideas could be exorcised by a verbal rite—like evil spirits. We hunt for witches to blame for our troubles: Roosevelt, Hitler, Stalin. We resist changing our inner selves even when altered conditions make this clearly necessary. We are aggrieved if other peoples misunderstand us or our motives; but if we try to understand them at all, we insist on doing so only in terms of our own assumptions about life which we take to be infallibly correct. We are still looking for the philosopher's stone—some magic formula (perhaps a mechanical scheme for international organization) that will make the world orderly and peaceful without other than external adaptions on our part.

We don't know ourselves very well. We talk about a rather vague thing called "human nature." We vehemently assert that it is "human nature" to do this and not to do that. Yet anybody who has lived in the American Southwest, to cite but one instance, knows from ordinary experience that the laws of this mysterious "human nature" do not seem to work out exactly the same way for the Spanish-speaking people of New Mexico, for the English-speaking population, and for the various Indian tribes. This is where the anthropologists come in. It is their task to record the variations and the similarities in human physique, in the things people make, in ways of life. Only when we find out just how men who have had different upbringing, who come from different physical stocks, who speak different languages, who live under different physical conditions, meet their problems, can we be sure as to what all human beings have in common. Only then can we claim scientific knowledge of raw human nature.

It will be a long job. But perhaps before it is too late we will come close to knowing what "human nature" really is—that is, what the reactions are that men inevitably have as human beings, regardless of their particular biological or social heritage. To discover human nature, the scientific adventurers of anthropology have been exploring the byways of time and of space. It is an absorbing task—so absorbing that anthropologists have tended to write only for each other or for scholars in other professions. Most of the literature of anthropology consists of articles in scientific journals and of forbidding monographs. The writing bristles with strange names and unfamiliar terms and is too detailed for the general reader. Some anthropologists may have had an obsession for detail as such. At any rate there are many whole monographs devoted to such subjects as "An Analysis of Three Hair-nets from the Pachacamac Area." Even to other students of man the great mass of anthropological endeavor has appeared, as Robert Lynd says, "aloof and preoccupied."

Though some research thus appears to leave the "anthropos" (man) off to one side, still the main trends of anthropological thought have been focused on a few questions of broad human interest, such as: what has been the course of human evolution, both biologically and culturally? Are there any general principles or "laws" governing this evolution? What necessary connections, if any, exist between the physical type, the speech, and the customs of the peoples of past and present? What generalizations can be made about human beings in groups? How plastic is man? How much can he be molded by training or by the necessity to adapt to environmental pressures? Why are certain personality types more characteristic of some societies than of others?

To most people, however, anthropology still means measuring skulls, treating little pieces of broken pottery with fantastic care, and reporting the outlandish customs of savage tribes. The anthropologist is the grave robber, the collector of Indian arrowheads, the queer fellow who lives with unwashed cannibals. As Sol Tax remarks, the anthropologist has had a function in society "something between that of an Einstein dealing with the mysterious and that of an entertainer." His specimens, his pictures, or his tales may serve for an hour's diversion but are pretty dull stuff compared to the world of grotesque monsters from distant ages which the paleontologist can recreate, the wonders of modern plant and animal life described by the biologist, the excitement of unimaginably far-off universes and cosmic processes roused by the astronomer. Surely anthropology seems the most useless and impractical of all the "-ologies." In a world of rocket ships and international organizations, what can the study of the obscure and primitive offer to the solution of today's problems?

"The longest way round is often the shortest way home." The preoccupation with insignificant nonliterate peoples that is an outstanding feature of anthropological work is the key to its significance today. Anthropology grew out of experience with primitives and the tools of the trade are unusual because they were forged in this peculiar workshop.

Studying primitives enables us to see ourselves better. Ordinarily we are unaware of the special lens through which we look at life. It would hardly be fish who discovered the existence of water. Students who had not gone beyond the horizon of their own society could not be expected to perceive custom which was the stuff of their own thinking. The scientist of human affairs needs to know as much about the eye that sees as the object seen. *Anthropology holds up a great mirror to man and lets him look at himself in his infinite variety.* This, and not the satisfaction of idle curiosity nor romantic quest, is the meaning of the anthropologist's work in nonliterate societies.

Picture the field worker in a remote island of the South Seas or among a tribe of the Amazon jungle. He is usually alone. But he is expected to bring back a report on both the physique and the total round of the people's activities. He is forced to see human life as a whole. He must become a Jack-of-all-trades and acquire enough diverse knowledge to describe such varying things as head shape, health practices, motor habits, agriculture, animal husbandry, music, language, and the way baskets are made.

Since there are no published accounts of the tribe, or only spotty or inadequate ones, he depends more on his eyes and his ears than upon books. Compared with the average sociologist, he is almost illiterate. The time that the sociologist spends in the library, the anthropologist spends in the field. Moreover, his seeing and his listening take on a special character. The ways of life he observes are so unfamiliar that it is next to impossible to interpret them through his own values. He cannot analyze in terms of the things he had decided in advance were important, because everything is out of pattern. It is easier for him to view the scene with detachment and relative objectivity just because it is remote and unfamiliar, because he himself is not emotionally involved. Finally, since the language has to be learned or interpreters found, the anthropologist is compelled to pay more attention to deeds than to words. When he cannot understand what is being said, the only thing he can do is devote himself to the humble but very useful task of noting who lives with whom, who works with whom in what activities, who talks loudly and who talks softly, who wears what when.

A perfectly legitimate question at this point would be: "Well, perhaps anthropologists in working in nonliterate societies did happen to pick up some skills that have given good results when applied to studies of our society. But in the name of everything, why, if you anthropologists are really interested in modern life, do you keep on bothering with these inconsequential little tribes?"

The anthropologist's first answer would be that the life ways of these tribes are part of the human record and that it is his job to see that these things get recorded. Indeed anthropologists have felt this responsibility very keenly. They have felt that they had no time to write general books when each year saw the extinction of aboriginal cultures that had not yet been described. The descriptive character of most anthropological literature and the overpowering mass of detail are to be traced to the anthropologist's obsession with getting down the facts before it is too late.

The traditional scientific attitude is that knowledge is an end in itself. There is much to be said for this point of view. Probably the applications that have been made possible by pure science have been richer and more numerous because scientists did not narrow their interests to fields that promised immediate practical utility. But in these troublous times many scientists are also concerned about the social justification of their work. There is such a thing as scientific dilettantism. It is nice that a few rich museums can afford to pay a few men to spend their lives in the intensive study of medieval armor, but the life careers of some anthropologists do remind one of Aldous Huxley's character who consecrated his existence to writing the history of the three-tined fork. Society cannot afford, in a period like the present, to support many specialists in highly esoteric studies unless they show promise of practical usefulness. Fortunately, the detailed study of primitive peoples falls into the useful category.

I may decide that what is really needed is knowledge of urban communities like Cambridge, Massachusetts. But, in the present situation of social science, a host of practical difficulties confront me. In the first place, to do a comprehensive job, I should need more collaborators than could be paid for under existing arrangements for the support of research on human behavior. Then I should have to ask: in terms of actual human interactions, where does Cambridge leave off and where do Boston, Watertown, and Somerville begin? Many people living in Cambridge grew up in different parts of the United States and in foreign countries. I should always be in danger of attributing to conditions in Cambridge ways of behavior which in fact should be explained as results of upbringing in far-distant places. Finally, I should be dealing with dozens of different biological stocks and mixtures between them. L. J. Henderson used to say, "When I go into my laboratory and try an experiment in which there are five or six unknowns, I can sometimes solve the problem if I work long enough. But I know better than even to try when there are twenty or more unknowns."

This is not to argue that it is useless to study Cambridge at the present time. Far from it. Certain small problems can be defined and answers of a high degree of validity obtained. Something of scientific and practical benefit could be learned about the workings of the whole community. The issue is not Shall the scientific student of man work in our own society *or* among primitives? It is rather: Does the anthropologist by working in the simpler scene isolate certain crucial factors which can then be investigated more effectively in the complex picture? The right questions to ask and the right techniques for getting the answers to them can best be discovered by work on smaller canvases, that is, in more homogeneous societies that have been by-passed by civilization.

The primitive society is the closest to laboratory conditions the student of man can ever hope to get. Such groups are usually small and can be studied intensively by few people at slight expense. They are ordinarily rather isolated so that the question does not arise as to where one social system begins and another ends. The members of the group have lived their lives within a small area and have been exposed continually to the pressure of the same natural forces. They have had an almost identical education. All of their experiences have much more in common than is the case with members of complex societies. Their ways of life are comparatively stable. Commonly there is a high degree of biological inbreeding so that any member of the society chosen at random has about the same biological inheritance as any other. In short, many factors can be regarded as more or less constant, and the anthropologist is free to study a few variables in detail with real hope of ferreting out the connections between them.

This can be made clearer by an analogy. How much would we know today of human physiology if we had been able to study the physiological processes only among human beings? The fact that we would have been blocked at every turn is due partly to the humanitarian limitations we place upon using humans as guinea pigs, but it must also be traced to the complexity of the human organism. There are so many variables that it would have been enormously difficult to isolate the decisive ones had we not been able to study physiological processes in simpler settings. A reflex could be speedily isolated in the frog, then studied with more complications in the simpler mammals. Once these complexities had been mastered, it was possible to go successfully to monkeys and apes and then to mankind. This is, of course, the essential method of science: the method of successive steps, the method of going from the known to the unknown, from the simple to the ever more and more complex.

Nonliterate societies represent the end results of many different experiments carried out by nature. Groups that have largely gone their way without being absorbed in the great civilizations of the West and the East show us the variety of solutions which men have worked out for perennial human problems and the variety of meanings that peoples attach to the same and to different cultural forms. Contemplation of this vast tableau gives us perspective and detachment. By analyzing the results of these experiments, the anthropologist also gives us practical information on what works and what doesn't.

A nonanthropologist, Grace de Laguna, has luminously summed up the advantages of a view of ourselves from the anthropological angle:

> It is indeed precisely with regard to standards of life and thought that the intimate studies of primitive peoples have cast more light on human nature than all the reflections of sages or the painstaking investigations of laboratory scientists. On the one hand, they have shown concretely and vividly the universal kinship of mankind, abstractly recognized by the Stoics and accepted as an article of Christian faith; on the other hand, they have revealed a wealth of human diversity and a variety of human standards and of modes of feeling and thinking hitherto unimagined. The horrid practices of the savage have shown themselves to the intimate and unprejudiced

study of the field ethnologist at once more amazing and more understandable than romance had painted them. The wider sympathy with men and the deeper insight into human nature which these studies have brought have done much to shake our complacent estimate of ourselves and our attainments. We have come to suspect that even our own deepest beliefs and our most cherished convictions may be as much the expression of an unconscious provincialism as are the fantastic superstitions of the savage.

CHAPTER II

Queer Customs

Why do the Chinese dislike milk and milk products? Why would the Japanese die willingly in a Banzai charge that seemed senseless to Americans? Why do some nations trace descent through the father, others through the mother, still others through both parents? Not because different peoples have different instincts, not because they were destined by God or Fate to different habits, not because the weather is different in China and Japan and the United States. Sometimes shrewd common sense has an answer that is close to that of the anthropologist: "because they were brought up that way." By "culture" anthropology means the total life way of a people, the social legacy the individual acquires from his group. Or culture can be regarded as that part of the environment that is the creation of man.

This technical term has a wider meaning than the "culture" of history and literature. A humble cooking pot is as much a cultural product as is a Beethoven sonata. In ordinary speech a man of culture is a man who can speak languages other than his own, who is familiar with history, literature, philosophy, or the fine arts. In some cliques that definition is still narrower. The cultured person is one who can talk about James Joyce, Scarlatti, and Picasso. To the anthropologist, however, to be human is to be cultured. There is culture in general, and then there are the specific cultures such as Russian, American, British, Hottentot, Inca. The general abstract notion serves to remind us that we cannot explain acts solely in terms of the biological properties of the people concerned, their individual past experience, and the immediate situation. The past experience of other men in the form of culture enters into almost every event. Each specific culture constitutes a kind of blueprint for all of life's activities.

One of the interesting things about human beings is that they try to understand themselves and their own behavior. While this has been particularly true of Europeans in recent times, there is no group which has not developed a scheme or schemes to explain man's actions. To the insistent human query "why?" the most exciting illumination anthropology has to offer is that of the concept of culture. Its explanatory importance is comparable to categories such as evolution in biology, gravity in physics, disease in medicine. A good deal of human behavior can be understood, and indeed predicted, if we know a people's design for living. Many acts are neither accidental nor due to personal pecularities nor caused by supernatural forces nor simply mysterious. Even those of us who pride ourselves on our individualism follow most of the time a pattern not of our own making. We brush our teeth on arising. We put on pants—not a loincloth or a grass skirt. We eat three meals a day—not four or five or two. We sleep in a bed—not in a hammock or on a sheep pelt. I do not have to know the individual and his life history to be able to predict these and countless other regularities, including many in the thinking process, of all Americans who are not incarcerated in jails or hospitals for the insane.

To the American woman a system of plural wives seems "instinctively" abhorrent. She cannot understand how any woman can fail to be jealous and uncomfortable if she must share her husband with other women. She feels it "unnatural" to accept such a situation. On the other hand, a Koryak woman of Siberia, for example, would find it hard to understand how a woman could be so selfish and so undesirous of femine companionship in the home as to wish to restrict her husband to one mate.

Some years ago I met in New York City a young man who did not speak a word of English and was obviously bewildered by American ways. By "blood" he was as American as you or I, for his parents had gone from Indiana to China as missionaries. Orphaned in infancy, he was reared by a Chinese family in a remote village. All who met him found him more Chinese than American. The facts of his blue eyes and light hair were less impressive than a Chinese style of gait, Chinese arm and hand movements, Chinese facial expression, and Chinese modes of thought. The biological heritage was American, but the cultural training had been Chinese. He returned to China.

Another example of another kind: I once knew a trader's wife in Arizona who took a somewhat devilish interest in producing a cultural reaction. Guests who came her way were often served delicious sandwiches filled with a meat that seemed to be neither chicken nor tuna fish yet was reminiscent of both. To queries she gave no reply until each had eaten his fill. She then explained that what they had eaten was not chicken, not tuna fish, but the rich, white flesh of freshly killed rattlesnakes. The response was instantaneous—vomiting, often violent vomiting. A biological process is caught in a cultural web.

A highly intelligent teacher with long and successful experience in the public schools of Chicago was finishing her first year in an Indian school. When asked how her Navaho pupils compared in intelligence with Chicago youngsters, she replied, "Well, I just don't know. Sometimes the Indians seem just as bright. At other times they just act like dumb animals. The other night we had a dance in the high school. I saw a boy who is one of the best students in my English class standing off by himself. So I took him over to a pretty girl and told them to dance. But they just stood there with their heads down. They wouldn't even say anything." I inquired if she knew whether or not they were members of the same clan. "What difference would that make?"

"How would you feel about getting into bed with your brother?" The teacher walked off in a huff, but, actually, the two cases were quite comparable in principle. To the Indian the type of bodily contact involved in our social dancing has a directly sexual connotation. The incest taboos between members of the same clan are as severe as between true brothers and sisters. The shame of the Indians at the suggestion that a clan brother and sister should dance and the indignation of the white teacher at the idea that she should share a bed with an adult brother represent equally nonrational responses, culturally standardized unreason.

All this does not mean that there is no such thing as raw human nature. The very fact that certain of the same institutions are found in all known societies indicates that at bottom all human beings are very much alike. The files of the Cross-Cultural Survey at Yale University are organized according to categories such as "marriage ceremonies," "life crisis rites," "incest taboos." At least seventy-five of these categories are represented in every single one of the hundreds of cultures analyzed. This is hardly surprising. The members of all human groups have about the same biological equipment. All men undergo the same poignant life experiences such as birth, helplessness, illness, old age, and death. The biological potentialities of the species are the blocks with which cultures are built. Some patterns of every culture crystallize around focuses provided by the inevitables of biology: the difference between the sexes, the presence of persons of different ages, the varying physical strength and skill of individuals. The facts of nature also limit culture forms. No culture provides patterns for jumping over trees or for eating iron ore.

There is thus no "either-or" between nature and that special form of nurture called culture. Culture determinism is as one-sided as biological determinism. The two factors are interdependent. Culture arises out of human nature, and its forms are restricted both by man's biology and by natural laws. It is equally true that culture channels biological processes—vomiting, weeping, fainting, sneezing, the daily habits of food intake and waste elimination. When a man eats, he is reacting to an internal "drive," namely, hunger contractions consequent upon the lowering of blood sugar, but his precise reaction to these internal stimuli cannot be predicted by physiological knowledge alone. Whether a healthy adult feels hungry twice, three times, or four times a day and the hours at which this feeling recurs is a question of culture. *What* he eats is of course limited by availability, but is also partly regulated by culture. It is a biological fact that some types of berries are poisonous; it is a cultural fact that, a few generations ago, most Americans considered tomatoes to be poisonous and refused to eat them. Such selective, discriminative use of the environment is characteristically cultural. In a still more general sense, too, the process of eating is channeled by culture. Whether a man eats to live, lives to eat, or merely eats and lives is only in part an individual matter, for there are also cultural trends. Emotions are physiological events. Certain situations will evoke fear in people from any culture. But sensations of pleasure, anger, and lust may be stimulated by cultural cues that would leave unmoved someone who has been reared in a different social tradition.

Except in the case of newborn babies and of individuals born with clear-cut structural or functional abnormalities we can observe innate endowments only as modified by cultural training. In a hospital in New Mexico where Zuñi Indian, Navaho Indian, and white American babies are born, it is possible to classify the newly arrived infants as unusually active, average, and quiet. Some babies from each "racial" group will fall into each category, though a higher proportion of the white babies will fall into the unusually active class. But if a Navaho baby, a Zuñi baby, and a white baby—all classified as unusually active at birth—are again observed at the age of two years, the Zuñi baby will no longer seem given to quick and restless activity—*as compared with the white child*—though he may seem so as compared with the other Zuñis of the same age. The Navaho child is likely to fall in between as contrasted with the Zuñi and the white, though he will probably still seem more active than the average Navaho youngster.

It was remarked by many observers in the Japanese relocation centers that Japanese who were born and brought up in this country, especially those who were reared apart from any large colony of Japanese, resemble in behavior their white neighbors much more closely than they do their own parents who were educated in Japan.

I have said "culture channels biological processes." It is more accurate to say "the biological functioning of individuals is modified if they have been trained in certain ways and not in others." Culture is not a disembodied force. It is created and transmitted by people. However, culture, like well-known concepts of the physical sciences, is a convenient abstraction. One never sees gravity. One sees bodies falling in regular ways. One never sees an electromagnetic field. Yet certain happenings that can be seen may be given a neat abstract formulation by assuming that the electromagnetic field exists. Similarly, one never sees culture as such. What is seen are regularities in the behavior or artifacts of a group that has adhered to a common tradition. The regularities in style and technique of ancient Inca tapestries or stone axes from Melanesian islands are due to the existence of mental blueprints for the group.

Culture is a *way* of thinking, feeling, believing. It is the group's knowledge stored up (in memories of men; in books and objects) for future use. We study the products of this "mental" activity: the overt behavior, the speech and gestures and activities of people, and the tangible results of these things such as tools, houses, cornfields, and what not. It has been customary in lists of "culture traits" to include such things as watches or lawbooks. This is a convenient way of thinking about them, but in the solution of any important problem we must remember that they, in themselves, are nothing but metals, paper, and ink. What is important is that some men know how to make them, others set a value on them, are unhappy without them, direct their activities in relation to them, or disregard them.

It is only a helpful shorthand when we say "The cultural patterns of the Zulu were resistant to Christianization." In the directly observable world of course, it was individual Zulus who resisted. Nevertheless, if we do not forget that we are speaking at a high level of abstraction, it is justifiable to speak of culture as a cause. One may compare the practice of saying "syphilis caused the extinction of the native population of the island." Was it "syphilis" or "syphilis germs" or "human beings who were carriers of syphilis?"

"Culture," then, is "a theory." But if a theory is not contradicted by any relevant fact and if it helps us to understand a mass of otherwise chaotic facts, it is useful. Darwin's contribution was much less the accumulation of new knowledge than the creation of a theory which put in order data already known. An accumulation of facts, however large, is no more a science than a pile of bricks is a house. Anthropology's demonstration that the most weird set of customs has a consistency and an order is comparable to modern psychiatry's showing that there is meaning and purpose in the apparently incoherent talk of the insane. In fact, the inability of the older psychologies and philosophies to account for the strange behavior of madmen and heathens was the principal factor that forced psychiatry and anthropology to develop theories of the unconscious and of culture.

Since culture is an abstraction, it is important not to confuse culture with society. A "society" refers to a group of people who interact more with each other than they do with other individuals—who cooperate with each other for the attainment of certain ends. You can see and indeed count the individuals who make up a society. A "culture" refers to the distinctive ways of life of such a group of people. Not all social events are culturally patterned. New types of circumstances arise for which no cultural solutions have as yet been devised.

A culture constitutes a storehouse of the pooled learning of the group. A rabbit starts life with some innate responses. He can learn from his own experience and perhaps from observing other rabbits. A human infant is born with fewer instincts and greater plasticity. His main task is to learn the answers that persons he will never see, persons long dead, have worked out. Once he has learned the formulas supplied by the culture of his group, most of his behavior becomes almost as automatic and unthinking as if it were instinctive. There is a tremendous amount of intelligence behind the making of a radio, but not much is required to learn to turn it on.

The members of all human societies face some of the same unavoidable dilemmas, posed by biology and other facts of the human situation. This is why the basic categories of all cultures are so similar. Human culture without language is unthinkable. No culture fails to provide for aesthetic expression and aesthetic delight. Every culture supplies standardized orientations toward the deeper problems, such as death. Every culture is designed to perpetuate the group and its solidarity, to meet the demands of individuals for an orderly way of life and for satisfaction of biological needs.

However, the variations on these basic themes are numberless. Some languages are built up out of twenty basic sounds, others out of forty. Nose plugs were considered beautiful by the predynastic Egyptians but are not by the modern French. Puberty is a biological fact. But one culture ignores it, another prescribes informal instructions about sex but no ceremony, a third has impressive rites for girls only, a fourth for boys and girls. In this culture, the first menstruation is welcomed as a happy, natural event; in that culture the atmosphere is full of dread and supernatural threat. Each culture dissects nature according to its own system of categories. The Navaho Indians apply the same word to the color of a robin's egg and to that of grass. A psychologist once assumed that this meant a difference in the sense organs, that Navahos didn't have the physiological equipment to distinguish "green" from "blue." However, when he showed them objects of the two colors and asked them if they were exactly the same colors, they looked at him with astonishment. His dream of discovering a new type of color blindness was shattered.

Every culture must deal with the sexual instinct. Some, however, seek to deny all sexual expression before marriage, whereas a Polynesian adolescent who was not promiscuous would be distinctly abnormal. Some cultures enforce lifelong monogamy, others, like our own, tolerate serial monogamy; in still other cultures, two or more women may be joined to one man or several men to a single woman. Homosexuality has been a permitted pattern in the Greco-Roman world, in parts of Islam, and in various primitive tribes. Large portions of the population of Tibet, and of Christendom at some places and periods, have practiced completely celibacy. To us marriage is first and foremost an arrangement between two individuals. In many more societies marriage is merely one facet of a complicated set of reciprocities, economic and otherwise, between two families or two clans.

The essence of the cultural process is selectivity. The selection is only exceptionally conscious and rational. Cultures are like Topsy. They just grew. Once, however, a way of handling a situation becomes institutionalized, there is ordinarily great resistance to change or deviation. When we speak of "our sacred beliefs," we mean of course that they are beyond criticism and that the person who suggests modification or abandonment must be punished. No person is emotionally indifferent to his culture. Certain cultural premises may become totally out of accord with a new factual situation. Leaders may recognize this and reject the old ways in theory. Yet their emotional loyalty continues in the face of reason because of the intimate conditionings of early childhood.

A culture is learned by individuals as the result of belonging to some particular group, and it constitutes that part of learned behavior which is shared with others. It is our social legacy, as contrasted with our organic heredity. It is one of the important factors which permits us to live together in an organized society, giving us ready-made solutions to our problems, helping us to predict the behavior of others, and permitting others to know what to expect of us.

Culture regulates our lives at every turn. From the moment we are born until we die there is, whether we are conscious of it or not, constant pressure upon us to follow certain types of behavior that other men have created for us. Some paths we follow willingly, others we follow because we know no other way, still others we deviate from or go back to most unwillingly. Mothers of small children know how unnaturally most of this comes to us—how little regard we have, until we are "culturalized," for the "proper" place, time, and manner for certain acts such as eating, excreting, sleeping, getting dirty, and making loud noises. But by more or less adhering to a system of related designs for carrying out all the acts of living, a group of men and women feel themselves linked together by a powerful chain of sentiments. Ruth Benedict gave an almost complete definition of the concept when she said, "Culture is that which binds men together."

It is true any culture is a set of techniques for adjusting both to the external environment and to other men. However, cultures create problems as well as solve them. If the lore of a people states that frogs are dangerous creatures, or that it is not safe to go about at night because of witches or ghosts, threats are posed which do not arise out of the inexorable facts of the external world. Cultures produce needs as well as provide a means of fulfilling them. There exists for every group culturally defined, acquired drives that may be more powerful in ordinary daily life than the biologically inborn drives. Many Americans, for example, will work harder for "success" than they will for sexual satisfaction.

Most groups elaborate certain aspects of their culture far beyond maximum utility or survival value. In other words, not all culture promotes physical survival. At times, indeed, it does exactly the opposite. Aspects of culture which once were adaptive may persist long after they have ceased to be useful. An analysis of any culture will disclose many features which cannot possibly be construed as adaptations to the total environment in which the group now finds itself. However, it is altogether likely that these apparently useless features represent survivals, with modifications through time, of cultural forms which were adaptive in one or another previous situation.

Any cultural practice must be functional or it will disappear before long. That is, it must somehow contribute to the survival of the society or to the adjustment of the individual. However, many cultural functions are not manifest but latent. A cowboy will walk three miles to catch a horse which he then rides one mile to the store. From the point of view of manifest function this is positively irrational. But the act has the latent function of maintaining the cowboy's prestige in the terms of his own subculture. One can instance the buttons on the sleeve of a man's coat, our absurd English spelling, the use of capital letters, and a host of other apparently nonfunctional customs. They serve mainly the latent function of assisting individuals to maintain their security by preserving continuity with the past and by making certain sectors of life familiar and predictable.

Every culture is a precipitate of history. In more than one sense history is a sieve. Each culture embraces those aspects of the past which, usually in altered form and with altered meanings, live on in the present. Discoveries and inventions, both material and ideological, are constantly being made available to a group through its historical contacts with other peoples or being created by its own members. However, only those that fit the total immediate situation in meeting the group's needs for survival or in promoting the psychological adjustment of individuals will become part of the culture. The process of culture building may be regarded as an addition to man's innate biological capacities, an addition providing instruments which enlarge, or may even substitute for, biological functions, and to a degree compensating for biological limitations—as in ensuring that death does not always result in the loss to humanity of what the deceased has learned.

Culture is like a map. Just as a map isn't the territory but an abstract representation of a particular area, so also a culture is an abstract description of trends toward uniformity in the words, deeds, and artifacts of a human group. If a map is accurate and you can read it, you won't get lost; if you know a culture, you will know your way around in the life of a society.

Many educated people have the notion that culture applies only to exotic ways of life or to societies where relative simplicity and relative homogeneity prevail. Some sophisticated missionaries, for example, will use the anthropological conception in discussing the special modes of living of South Sea Islanders, but seem amazed at the idea that it could be applied equally to inhabitants of New York City. And social workers in Boston will talk about the culture of a colorful and well-knit immigrant group but boggle at applying it to the behavior of staff members in the social-service agency itself.

In the primitive society the correspondence between the habits of individuals and the customs of the community is ordinarily greater. There is probably some truth in what an old Indian once said, "In the old days there was no law; everybody did what was right." The primitive tends to find happiness in the fulfillment of intricately involuted cultural patterns; the modern more often tends to feel the pattern as repressive to his individuality. It is also true that in a complex stratified society there are numerous exceptions to generalizations made about the culture as a whole. It is necessary to study regional, class, and occupational subcultures. Primitive cultures have greater stability than modern cultures; they change—but less rapidly.

However, modern men also are creators and carriers of culture. Only in some respects are they influenced differently from primitives by culture. Moreover, there are such wide variations in primitive cultures that any black-and-white contrast between the primitive and the civilized is altogether fictitious. The distinction which is most generally true lies in the field of conscious philosophy.

The publication of Paul Radin's *Primitive Man as a Philosopher* did much toward destroying the myth that an abstract analysis of experience was a peculiarity of literate societies.

Speculation and reflection upon the nature of the universe and of man's place in the total scheme of things have been carried out in every known culture. Every people has its characteristic set of "primitive postulates." It remains true that critical examination of basic premises and fully explicit systematization of philosophical concepts are seldom found at the nonliterate level. The written word is an almost essential condition for free and extended discussion of fundamental philosophic issues. Where dependence on memory exists, there seems to be an inevitable tendency to emphasize the correct perpetuation of the precious oral tradition. Similarly, while it is all too easy to underestimate the extent to which ideas spread without books, it is in general true that tribal or folk societies do not possess competing philosophical systems. The major exception to this statement is, of course, the case where part of the tribe becomes converted to one of the great proselytizing religions such as Christianity or Mohammedanism. Before contact with rich and powerful civilizations, primitive peoples seem to have absorbed new ideas piecemeal, slowly integrating them with the previously existing ideology. The abstract thought of nonliterate societies is ordinarily less self-critical, less systematic, nor so intricately elaborated in purely logical dimensions. Primitive thinking is more concrete, more implicit—perhaps more completely coherent than the philosophy of most individuals in larger societies which have been influenced over long periods by disparate intellectual currents.

No participant in any culture knows all the details of the cultural map. The statement frequently heard that St. Thomas Aquinas was the last man to master all the knowledge of his society is intrinsically absurd. St. Thomas would have been hard put to make a pane of cathedral glass or to act as a midwife. In every culture there are what Ralph Linton has called "universals, alternatives, and specialties." Every Christian in the thirteenth century knew that it was necessary to attend mass, to go to confession, to ask the Mother of God to intercede with her Son. There were many other universals in the Christian culture of Western Europe. However, there were also alternative cultural patterns even in the realm of religion. Each individual had his own patron saint, and different towns developed the cults of different saints. The thirteenth-century anthropologist could have discovered the rudiments of Christian practice by questioning and observing whomever he happened to meet in Germany, France, Italy, or England. But to find out the details of the ceremonials honoring St. Hubert or St. Bridget he would have had to seek out certain individuals or special localities where these alternative patterns were practiced. Similarly, he could not learn about weaving from a professional soldier or about canon law from a farmer. Such cultural knowledge belongs in the realm of the specialties, voluntarily chosen by the individual or ascribed to him by birth. Thus, part of a culture must be learned by everyone, part may be selected from alternative patterns, part applies only to those who perform the roles in the society for which these patterns are designed.

Many aspects of a culture are explicit. The explicit culture consists in those regularities in word and deed that may be generalized straight from the evidence of the ear and the eye. The recognition of these is like the recognition of style in the art of a particular place and epoch. If we have examined twenty specimens of the wooden saints' images made in the Taos valley of New Mexico in the late eighteenth century, we can predict that any new images from the same locality and period will in most respects exhibit the same techniques of carving, about the same use of colors and choice of woods, a similar quality of artistic conception. Similarly, if, in a society of 2,000 members, we record 100 marriages at random and find that in 30 cases a man has married the sister of his brother's wife, we can anticipate that an additional sample of 100 marriages will show roughly the same number of cases of this pattern.

The above is an instance of what anthropologists call a behavioral pattern, the practices as opposed to the rules of the culture. There are also, however, regularities in what people say they do or should do. They do tend in fact to prefer to marry into a family already connected with their own by marriage, but this is not necessarily part of the official code of conduct. No disapproval whatsoever is attached to those who make another sort of marriage. On the other hand, it is explicitly forbidden to marry a member of one's own clan even though no biological relationship is traceable. This is a regulatory pattern—a Thou Shalt or a Thou Shalt Not. Such patterns may be violated often, but their existence is nevertheless important. A people's standards for conduct and belief define the socially approved aims and the acceptable means of attaining them. When the discrepancy between the theory and the practice of a culture is exceptionally great, this indicates that the culture is undergoing rapid change. It does not prove that ideals are unimportant, for ideals are but one of a number of factors determining action.

Cultures do not manifest themselves solely in observable customs and artifacts. No amount of questioning of any save the most articulate in the most self-conscious cultures will bring out some of the basic attitudes common to the members of the group. This is because these basic assumptions are taken so for granted that they normally do not enter into consciousness. This part of the cultural map must be inferred by the observer on the basis of consistencies in thought and action. Missionaries in various societies are often disturbed or puzzled because the natives do not regard "morals" and "sex code" as almost synonymous. The natives seem to feel that morals are concerned with sex just about as much as with eating—no less and no more. No society fails to have some restrictions on sexual behavior, but sex activity outside of marriage need not necessarily be furtive or attended with guilt. The Christian tradition has tended to assume that sex is inherently nasty as well as dangerous. Other cultures assume that sex in itself is not only natural but one of the good things of life, even though sex acts with certain persons under certain circumstances are forbidden. This is implicit culture, for the natives do not announce their premises. The missionaries would get further if they said, in effect, "Look, our morality starts from different assumptions. Let's talk about those assumptions," rather than ranting about "immorality."

A factor implicit in a variety of diverse phenomena may be generalized as an underlying cultural principle. For example, the Navaho Indians always leave part of the design in a pot, a basket, or a blanket unfinished. When a medicine man instructs an apprentice he always leaves a little bit of the story untold. This "fear of closure" is a recurrent theme in Navaho culture. Its influence may be detected in many contexts that have no explicit connection.

If the observed cultural behavior is to be correctly understood, the categories and presuppositions constituting the implicit culture must be worked out. The "strain toward consistency" which Sumner noted in the folkways and mores of all groups cannot be accounted for unless one grants a set of systematically interrelated implicit themes. For example, in American culture the themes of "effort and optimism," "the common man," "technology," and "virtuous materialism" have a functional interdependence, the origin of which is historically known. The relationship between themes may be that of conflict. One may instance the competition between Jefferson's theory of democracy and Hamilton's "government by the rich, the wellborn, and the able." In other cases most themes may be integrated under a single dominant theme. In Negro cultures of West Africa the mainspring of social life is religion; in East Africa almost all cultural behavior seems to be oriented toward certain premises and categories centered on the cattle economy. If there be one master principle in the implicit culture, this is often called the "ethos" or *Zeitgeist.*

Every culture has organization as well as content. There is nothing mystical about this statement. One may compare ordinary experience. If I know that Smith, working alone, can shovel 10 cubic yards of dirt a day, Jones 12, and Brown 14, I would be foolish to predict that the three working together would move 36. The total might well be considerably more; it might be less. A whole is different from the sum of its parts. The same principle is familiar in athletic teams. A brilliant pitcher added to a nine may mean a pennant or may mean the cellar; it depends on how he fits in.

And so it is with cultures. A mere list of the behavioral and regulatory patterns and of the implicit themes and categories would be like a map on which all mountains, lakes, and rivers were included—but not in their actual relationship to one another. Two cultures could have almost identical inventories and still be extremely different. The full significance of any single element in a culture design will be seen only when that element is viewed in the total matrix of its relationship to other elements. Naturally, this includes accent or emphasis, as well as position. Accent is manifested sometimes through frequency, sometimes through intensity. The indispensable importance of these questions of arrangement and emphasis may be driven home by an analogy. Consider a musical sequence made up of three notes. If we are told that the three notes in question are A, *B*, and G, we receive information which is fundamental. But it will not enable us to predict the type of sensation which the playing of this sequence is likely to evoke. We need many different sorts of relationship data. Are the notes to be played in that or some other order? What duration will each receive? How will the emphasis, if any, be distributed? We also need, of course, to know whether the instrument used is to be a piano or an accordion.

Cultures vary greatly in their degree of integration. Synthesis is achieved partly through the overt statement of the dominant conceptions, assumptions, and aspirations of the group in its religious lore, secular thought, and ethical code; partly through habitual but unconscious ways of looking at the stream of events, ways of begging certain questions. To the naïve participant in the culture these modes of categorizing, of dissecting experience along these planes and not others, are as much "given" as the regular sequence of daylight and darkness or the necessity of air, water, and food for life. Had Americans not thought in terms of money and the market system during the depression they would have distributed unsalable goods rather than destroyed them.

Every group's way of life, then, is a structure—not a haphazard collection of all the different physically possible and functionally effective patterns of belief and action. A culture is an interdependent system based upon linked premises and categories whose influence is greater, rather than less, because they are seldom put in words. Some degree of internal coherence which is felt rather than rationally constructed seems to be demanded by most of the participants in any culture. As Whitehead has remarked, "Human life is driven forward by its dim apprehension of notions too general for its existing language."

In sum, the distinctive way of life that is handed down as the social heritage of a people does more than supply a set of skills for making a living and a set of blueprints for human relations. Each different way of life makes its own assumptions about the ends and purposes of human existence, about what human beings have a right to expect from each other and the gods, about what constitutes fulfillment or frustration. Some of these assumptions are made explicit in the lore of the folk; others are tacit premises which the observer must infer by finding consistent trends in word and deed.

In our highly self-conscious Western civilization that has recently made a business of studying itself, the number of assumptions that are literally implicit, in the sense of never having been stated or discussed by anyone, may be negligible. Yet only a trifling number of Americans could state even those implicit premises of our culture that have been brought to light by anthropologists. If one could bring to the American scene a Bushman who had been socialized in his own culture and then trained in anthropology, he would perceive all sorts of patterned regularities of which our anthropologists are completely unaware. In the case of the less sophisticated and less self-conscious societies, the unconscious assumptions characteristically made by individuals brought up under approximately the same social controls bulk even larger. But in any society, as Edward Sapir said, "Forms and significances which seem obvious to an outsider will be denied outright by those who carry out the patterns; outlines and implications that are perfectly clear to these may be absent to the eye of the onlooker."

All individuals in a culture tend to share common interpretations of the external world and man's place in it. To some degree every individual is affected by this conventional view of life. One group unconsciously assumes that every chain of actions has a goal and that when this goal is reached tension will be reduced or will disappear. To another group, thinking based upon this assumption is meaningless—they see life not as a series of purposive sequences, but as a complex of experiences which are satisfying in and of themselves, rather than as means to ends.

The concept of implicit culture is made necessary by certain eminently practical considerations. Programs of the British Colonial services or of our own Indian service, which have been carefully thought through for their continuity with the overt cultural patterns, nevertheless fail to work out. Nor does intensive investigation reveal any flaws in the setup at the technological level. The program is sabotaged by resistance which must be imputed to the manner in which the members of the group have been conditioned by their implicit designs for living to think and feel in ways which were unexpected to the administrator.

What good is the concept of culture so far as the contemporary world is concerned? What can you do with it? Much of the rest of this book will answer these questions, but some preliminary indications are in order.

Its use lies first in the aid the concept gives to man's endless quest to understand himself and his own behavior. For example, this new idea turns into pseudo problems some of the questions asked by one of the most learned and acute thinkers of our age, Reinhold Niebuhr. In his recent book *The Nature and Destiny of Man* Niebuhr argues that the universally human sense of guilt or shame and man's capacity for self-judgment necessitate the assumption of supernatural forces. These facts are susceptible of self-consistent and relatively simple explanation in purely naturalistic terms through the concept of culture. Social life among human beings never occurs without a system of conventional understandings which are transmitted more or less intact from generation to generation. Every individual is familiar with some of these and they constitute a set of standards against which he judges himself. To the extent that he fails to conform he experiences discomfort because his childhood training put great pressure on him to follow the accepted pattern, and his now unconscious tendency is to associate deviation with punishment or withdrawal of love and protection. This and other issues which have puzzled philosophers and scientists for countless generations become understandable through this fresh concept.

The principal claim which can be made for the culture concept as an aid to useful action is that it helps us enormously toward predicting human behavior. One of the factors limiting the success of such prediction thus far has been the naïve assumption of a minutely homogeneous "human nature." In the framework of this assumption all human thinking proceeds from the same premises; all human beings are motivated by the same needs and goals. In the cultural framework we see that, while the ultimate logic of all peoples may be the same (and thus communication and understanding are possible), the thought processes depart from radically different premises—especially unconscious or unstated premises. Those who have the cultural outlook are more likely to look beneath the surface and bring the culturally determined premises to the light of day. This may not bring about immediate agreement and harmony, but it will at least facilitate a *more* rational approach to the problem of international understanding and to diminishing friction between groups within a nation.

Knowledge of a culture makes it possible to predict a good many of the actions of any person who shares that culture. If the American Army was dropping paratroopers into Thailand in 1944, under what circumstances would they be knifed, under what circumstances would they be aided? If one knows how a given culture defines a certain situation, one can say that the betting odds are excellent that in a future comparable situation people will behave along certain lines and not along others. If we know a culture, we know what various classes of individuals within it expect from each other—and from outsiders of various categories. We know what types of activity are held to be inherently gratifying.

Many people in our society feel that the best way to get people to work harder is to increase their profits or their wages. They feel that it is just "human nature" to want to increase one's material possessions. This sort of dogma might well go unchallenged if we had no knowledge of other cultures. In certain societies, however, it has been found that the profit motive is not an effective incentive. After contact with whites the Trobriand Islanders in Melanesia could have become fabulously rich from pearl diving. They would, however, work only long enough to satisfy their immediate wants.

Administrators need to become conscious of the symbolic nature of many activities. American women will choose a job as hostess in a restaurant rather than one as waitress at a higher salary. In some societies the blacksmith is the most honored of individuals while in others only the lowest class of people are blacksmiths. White children in schools are motivated by grades; but children from some Indian tribe will work less hard under a system that singles the individual out from among his fellows.

Understanding of culture provides some detachment from the conscious and unconscious emotional values of one's own culture. The phrase, "some detachment," must be emphasized. An individual who viewed the designs for living of his group with complete detachment would be would be disoriented and unhappy. But I can prefer (*i.e.*, feel affectively attached to) American manners while at the same time perceiving certain graces in English manners which are lacking or more grossly expressed in ours. Thus, while unwilling to forget that I am an American with no desire to ape English drawing-room behavior, I can still derive a lively pleasure from association with English people on social occasions. Whereas if I have no detachment, if I am utterly provincial, I am likely to regard English manners as utterly ridiculous, uncouth, perhaps even immoral. With that attitude I shall certainly not get on well with the English, and I am likely to resent bitterly any modification of our manners in the English or any other direction. Such attitudes clearly do not make for international understanding, friendship, and cooperation. They do, to the same extent, make for a too rigid social structure. Anthropological documents and anthropological teachings are valuable, therefore, in that they tend to emancipate individuals from a too strong allegiance to every item in the cultural inventory. The person who has been exposed to the anthropological perspective is more likely to live and let live both within his own society and in his dealings with members of other societies; and he will probably be more flexible in regard to needful changes in social organization to meet changed technology and changed economy.

Perhaps the most important implication of culture for action is the profound truth that you can never start with a clean slate so far as human beings are concerned. Every person is born into a world defined by already existing culture patterns. Just as an individual who has lost his memory is no longer normal so the idea of a society's becoming completely emancipated from its past culture is inconceivable. This is one source of the tragic failure of the Weimar constitution in Germany. In the abstract it was an admirable document. But it failed miserably in actual life partly because it provided for no continuity with existent designs for acting, feeling, and thinking.

Since every culture has organization as well as content, administrators and lawmakers should know that one cannot isolate a custom to abolish or modify it. The most obvious example of failure caused by neglect of this principle was the Eighteenth Amendment. The legal sale of liquor was forbidden, but the repercussions in law enforcement, in family life, in politics, in the economy were staggering.

The concept of culture, like any other piece of knowledge, can be abused and misinterpreted. Some fear that the principle of cultural relativity will weaken morality. "If the Bugabuga do it why can't we? It's all relative anyway." But this is exactly what cultural relativity does *not* mean.

The principle of cultural relativity does not mean that because the members of some savage tribe are allowed to behave in a certain way that this fact gives intellectual warrant for such behavior in all groups. Cultural relativity means, on the contrary, that the appropriateness of any positive or negative custom must be evaluated with regard to how this habit fits with other group habits. Having several wives makes economic sense among herders, not among hunters. While breeding a healthy skepticism as to the eternity of any value prized by a particular people, anthropology does not as a matter of theory deny the existence of moral absolutes. Rather, the use of the comparative method provides a scientific means of discovering such absolutes. If all surviving societies have found it necessary to impose some of the same restrictions upon the behavior of their members, this makes a strong argument that these aspects of the moral code are indispensable.

Similarly, the fact that a Kwakiutl chief talks as if he had delusions of grandeur and of persecution does not mean that paranoia is not a real ailment in our cultural context. Anthropology has given a new perspective to the relativity of the normal that should bring greater tolerance and understanding of socially harmless deviations. But it has by no means destroyed standards or the useful tyranny of the normal. All cultures recognize some of the same forms of behavior as pathological. Where they differ in their distinctions, there is a relationship to the total framework of cultural life.

There is a legitimate objection to making culture explain too much. Lurking, however, in such criticisms of the cultural point of view is often the ridiculous assumption that one must be loyal to a single master explanatory principle. On the contrary, there is no incompatibility between biological, environmental, cultural, historical, and economic approaches. All are necessary. The anthropologist feels that so much of history as is still a living force is embodied in the culture. He regards the economy as a specialized part of the culture. But he sees the value in having economists and historians, as specialists, abstract out their special aspects—so long as the complete context is not entirely lost to view. Take the problems of the American South, for example. The anthropologist would entirely agree that biological (social visibility of black skin, etc.), environmental (water power and other natural resources), historical (South settled by certain types of people, somewhat different governmental practices from the start, etc.), and narrowly cultural (original discrimination against Negroes as "heathen savages," etc.) issues are all inextricably involved. However, the cultural factor is involved in the actual working out of each influence—though culture is definitely not the whole of it. And to say that certain acts are culturally defined does not always and necessarily mean that they could be eliminated by changing the culture.

The needs and drives of biological man, and the physical environment to which he must adjust, provide the stuff of human life, but a given culture determines the way this stuff is handled—the tailoring. In the eighteenth century a Neapolitan philosopher, Vico, uttered a profundity which was new, violent—and unnoticed. This was simply the discovery that "the social world is surely the work of man." Two generations of anthropologists have compelled thinkers to face this fact. Nor are anthropologists willing to allow the Marxists or other cultural determinists to make of culture another absolute as autocratic as the God or Fate portrayed by some philosophies. Anthropological knowledge does not permit so easy an evasion of man's responsibility for his own destiny. To be sure, culture is a compulsive force to most of us most of the time. To some extent, as Leslie White says, "Culture has a life and laws of its own." Some cultural changes are also compelled by economic or physical circumstances. But most of an economy is itself a cultural artifact. And it is men who change their cultures, even if—during most of past history—they have been acting as instruments of cultural processes of which they were largely unaware. The record shows that, while situation limits the range of possibility, there is always more than one workable alternative. The essence of the cultural process is selectivity; men may often make a choice. Lawrence Frank probably overstates the case:

> In the years to come it is probable that this discovery of the human origin and development of culture will be recognized as the greatest of all discoveries, since heretofore man has been helpless before these cultural and social formulations which generation after generation have perpetuated the same frustration and defeat of human values and aspirations. So long as he believed this was necessary and inevitable, he could not but accept this lot with resignation. Now man is beginning to realize that his culture and social organization are not unchanging cosmic processes, but are human creations which may be altered. For those who cherish the democratic faith this discovery means that they can, and must, undertake a continuing assay of our culture and our society in terms of its consequences for human life and human values. This is the historic origin and purpose of human culture, to create a human way of life. To our age falls the responsibility of utilizing the amazing new resources of science to meet these cultural tasks, to continue the great human tradition of man taking charge of his own destiny.

Nevertheless, to the extent that human beings discover the nature of the cultural process, they can anticipate, prepare, and —to at least a limited degree—control.

Americans are now at a period in history when they are faced with the facts of cultural differences more clearly than they can take with comfort. Recognition and tolerance of the deeper cultural assumptions of China, Russia, and Britain will require a difficult type of education. But the great lesson of culture is that the goals toward which men strive and fight and grope are not "given" in final form by biology nor yet entirely by the situation. If we understand our own culture and that of others, the political climate can be changed in a surprisingly short time in this narrow contemporary world providing men are wise enough and articulate enough and energetic enough. The concept of culture carries a legitimate note of hope to troubled men. If the German and Japanese peoples behaved as they did because of their biological heredity, the outlook for restoring them as peaceful and cooperative nations would be hopeless. But if their propensities for cruelty and aggrandizement were primarily the result of situational factors and their cultures, then something can be done about it, though false hopes must not be encouraged as to the speed with which a culture can be planfully changed.

CHAPTER III

Potsherds

WHAT SERVICE do the scientific diggers and collectors render the community beyond filling the cases of museums and supplying material for the rotogravure sections of the Sunday papers? These describers and recorders are anthropological historians. That is, they are concerned mainly with answering the questions about man: what? who? where? when? in what patterns?

The study of biological evolution as history is carried out from the same point of view and with basically the same tools as is the attempt to discover the succession of flint industries in the Old Stone Age. Could the fossil gibbons found in Egypt be ancestral to human beings or only to modern gibbons? Is the Neanderthal species of the Europe and Palestine of 50,000 years ago completely extinct, or is modern man the result of a cross between the Neanderthal and the Cro-Magnon types? Was pottery independently invented in the New World or were pots or the idea of pottery brought from the Eastern Hemisphere? Did Polynesians cross the Pacific and bring the concept of social classes to Peru? Is the language of the Basques of Spain related to languages spoken in parts of north Italy in pre-Roman times?

These studies in archaeology, ethnology, historical linguistics, and human evolution give us a long-term perspective upon ourselves and help to free us from transitory values. Indeed, to consider human history on the basis of only those peoples who left written records is like trying to understand a whole book from reading the last chapter. All of historical anthropology widens the scope of general history. As curtain after curtain has been raised, deeper areas of the human stage have been revealed. The enormous interdependence of all men upon each other stands out clearly. The Ten Commandments, for example, are seen to be derived from the earlier code of Hammurabi, a Babylonian king. Some of the *Book of Proverbs* is taken from the wisdom of Egyptians who lived more than two thousands years before Christ.

Ortega y Gasset has written, "Man has no nature; he has history." This, as we saw in the last chapter, is an overstatement. Cultures are the products of history, yes; but they are the results of history as influenced by man's biological nature and conditioned by environing situations. Nevertheless our view of the world as nature must be supplemented by a view of the world as history. The historical anthropologists have performed a great service in emphasizing the concrete and the historically unique.The facts of chance, of historical accident, must be understood as well as the universals of sociocultural process. As Tylor wrote long ago, "Much learned nonsense is due to attempting to explain by the light of reason what must be understood by the light of history." As the archaeologists inject chronology into a confusing mass of descriptive facts, one gets a sense not only of the cumulative nature of culture but also of pattern in history.

There is admittedly little about archaeology that is immediately practical. Archaeological research does enrich present-day life through rediscovery of art motifs and other inventions of past times. It provides a healthy intellectual interest manifested in the archaeological National Monuments and Parks of the United States and in local archaeological societies. Lancelot Hogben has termed archaeology "a powerful intellectual vitamin for the democracies and dictatorships alike." Mussolini poured money into the excavation of Roman ruins to stimulate the pride of the Italians in their past. New states created by the treaty of Versailles, such as Czechoslovakia, developed archaeology as a means of nation building and self-expression. However, diggings have been related to contemporary issues in ways more socially useful than that of supplying spurious foundations for unhealthy nationalism. Archaeological work helped to explode the politically dangerous Nordic myth by proving that this physical type had not, as the Nazis claimed, been resident from time immemorial in Germany.

It is easy to poke fun at archaeologists as "relic hunters" whose intellectual activity is on about the same level as stamp collecting. Wallace Stegner voices a common attitude:

> The things archaeologists find in their erudite picking-over of the garbage dumps of vanished civilizations are pretty disappointing, really. They give us only the most tantalizing glimpses; they make us judge of a culture by the contents of a small boy's overalls pockets. Time sucks the meaning from many things, and the future finds the rind.

Yet to the archaeologist who is truly an anthropologist each kind of stone tool, for example, represents a human problem which some individual, conditioned by the culture of his group, has solved. The archaeologist does not treat each potsherd so seriously because he is interested in pottery as such but because he has so little material he must make the most of it. Pottery types offer the archaeologist a way of recognizing that the products of human behavior fall into patterns.

There is, of course, always the danger of being taken in by the unique products of human eccentricity. I remember once walking through a village of thatch-covered cottages in Oxfordshire. Almost everything conformed beautifully to pattern. Suddenly, however, I saw a miniature replica of a Maya Indian pyramid in one garden, the product of a farmer's odd reading and his

Sunday leisure. If all written records were destroyed and the standard wooden objects of the village dissolved in dust, what outlandish theories might not the archaeologist of a thousand years hence build on this solitary pyramid in southern England! A 1947 newspaper announced that a retired schoolteacher in Oklahoma had built a seventy-foot concrete totem pole—"just to confuse erudite investigators." Actually, the days of sweeping explanations supported by only a single specimen are over. Intensive and extensive excavations in each area quickly sort out the unique from the regular. Those who still say that no prediction is possible in the human scene should watch a Southwestern archaeologist scan the surface of an undug site. He looks at a handful of potsherds and, if they come from a now well-known archaeological culture, he can predict not only what other types of pottery will be found on excavation but also the style of masonry, the techniques of weaving, the arrangement of rooms, and the kinds of stone and bone work. He knows the pattern.

The essential method of modern archaeology is that of the jig-saw puzzle. Take the matter of the domestication and use of the horse. At present we have scattered pieces of the total pattern. The earliest known site in which horse bones occur in large numbers but do not appear to be those of game animals is in Russian Turkestan and dates from the fourth millennium before Christ. But were the horses ridden or used to draw carts or kept for their milk or to be eaten? In the Battle-ax culture of Northern Europe at about 2000 B.C. horses were buried like people. Again there is no information as to the use to which they were put. Certain artistic representations from Persia at about the same period may depict men on horses—or on asses? It is about 1000 B.C. before there is definite proof that horses were used for riding. There are some indications that horses were used to draw carts or chariots about 1800 B.C. We know that the Scythians were fighting on horseback by about 800 B.C. We know that the Chinese did not develop cavalry until they were forced in self-protection to do so in the third century B.C. Present data indicate two tentative conclusions. First, the horse was domesticated later than such animals as the sheep and pig. Second, domestication of the horse probably took place off the main Near Eastern stage where the inventions basic to modern civilization were produced—perhaps in a wing to the north. This particular jig-saw puzzle will almost certainly be filled in eventually, even though knowledge of exactly how the domestication of the horse occurred and who first used the horse remains unknown.

Archaeology has become immensely technical. The chemist and the metallurgist assist in analyzing certain specimens. The archaeologist himself must be a skilled mapper and photographer. Dating may involve the study of the tree rings in building timbers, microscopic identification of the minerals in potsherds, analysis of the pollens in the layers deposited, identification of the bones of fossil animals found, tracing the strata to link up with a geologically established sequence of river terraces. A promising technique, now in an experimental phase, is based upon new knowledge of radiation and atomic physics. Carbon 14, present in all organic matter, disappears at a fairly constant rate. This may make it possible to take a fragment of bone from men who died ten or twenty thousand years ago and say with some precision the date of their death.

As W. H. Holmes said, "Archaeology is the great retriever of history . . . it reads and interprets that which was never meant to be read or interpreted . . . revealer of vast resources of history of which no man had previously taken heed." So the modern archaeologist does not think well of his precursors in the Romantic Period who tore thousands of pages of history to bits for the price of a few objects prized only for their aesthetic or antiquarian interest. Nor is the archaeologist today obsessed with the quest for ultimate origins. He knows we shall never discover who first invented the making of fire or what the first human language was like.

The interest of modern archaeology is focused upon helping to establish the principles of culture growth and change. The significance of the archaeological proof that the Hopi Indians mined and used coal before Columbus is not that of a startling or curious fact. Rather, its meaning is as one important bit of evidence bearing on the principles of psychic unity of mankind and independent invention. Although certain psychological aspects of these principles can be discovered only by work with living peoples, archaeology can, by the study of material remains of past peoples, put a chronological backbone into our theories. Grahame Clarke well says, "To see big things whole they must be seen from a distance, and that is precisely what archaeology enables one to do." When we see the whole panorama of inventions and borrowings on the vast scale of space and time which archaeology alone can provide, we realize the tremendous interdependence of cultures and the essential cultural brotherhood of man.

So the diggers and collectors look forward as well as back. When the archaeologist scrupulously compares his specimens with ones found at other times and places and plots on maps and graphs by space and time sequence the occurrence of similar traits or combinations of traits, he is looking for regularities. Have different peoples who lived in the same region at various time periods shown certain common features in their ways of life? In other words, how potent is the physical environment in shaping the development of human institutions? Do modes of economic production in the long run determine the ideas of a people? How can we learn from the lessons of history, avoiding the mistakes of the past?

By extending in time as well as in space the comparisons that can be made as to how different peoples have solved or failed to solve their problems, the chances for testing scientifically certain theories about human nature and the course of human progress are much improved. For example, the question as to whether American Indian cultures developed independently without borrowing major inventions or ideas from the Old World is no mere academic argument. Pottery, weaving, domestic plants and animals, metal working, writing, and the conception of mathematical zero were current in certain areas of the New World by the time of Columbus. The social classes that had developed in Middle America and Peru had some points of resemblance to feudal social structure in Europe. The view of conservative American anthropologists is that the emigrants to America from Asia brought with them only a rude culture and that there were no significant contacts between the Old and New Worlds after the peoples of Eastern Asia had acquired such techniques as weaving and metallurgy. If the archaeologists, ethnologists, and linguists can prove that these inventions were made all over again in the Americas, then we must assume that if you let human beings alone long enough their inherited biological equipment is such that they will go through about the same successive steps in building their ways of life. On this assumption social planning and the orderly preservation and transmission of knowledge do not seem too important. Progress will occur anyway, and not much can be done about the course of human development. If, on the other hand, it is demonstrated that at least the ideas of pottery, weaving, metallurgy, and the like were borrowed from the Old World, one's crucial assumptions about human nature become importantly different. Man is seen as extraordinarily imitative and only rarely profoundly creative. If that should prove to be the case, then one must ask what peculiar combination of conditions produced once and only once the economic techniques basic to city life and inventions such as writing that made modern civilization possible.

Archaeological materials reveal a great deal about the economy, subsistence, technology, environmental adjustment, and even the social organization of a people:

> The stone axe, the tool distinctive of part at least of the Stone Age, is the home-made product that could be fashioned and used by anybody in a self-contained group of hunters or peasants. It implies neither specialization of labour nor trade beyond the group. The bronze axe which replaces it is not only a superior implement, it also presupposes a more complex economic and social structure. The casting of bronze is too difficult a process to be carried out by anyone in the intervals of growing or catching his food or minding her babies. It is a specialist's job, and these specialists must rely for such primary necessities as food upon a surplus produced by other specialists. Again, the copper and tin of which the bronze axe is composed are comparatively rare, and very seldom occur together. One or both constituents will almost certainly have to be imported. Such importation is possible only if some sort of communications and trade have been established and if there is a surplus of some local product to barter for the metals. —GORDON CHILDE

And so a vast sifting of the archaeological evidence is one sound way of testing some of the theories of the Marxists on correlations between types of technology, economic structure, and social life.

In principle, archaeology is identical with the work of the anthropological describers who deal with living peoples. Archaeology is the ethnography and culture history of past peoples. Indeed someone has said that "the ethnographer is an archaeologist who catches his archaeology alive." The record of cultures set down by the ethnographer is analyzed by the ethnologist in historical terms, sometimes with the use of statistical tools as well as maps. The ethnologist also studies the relationship between culture and physical environment and deals with such topics as primitive art, primitive music, and primitive religion. The folklorist follows the tangled skein of motives in and out of both literate and nonliterate cultures.

These activities have their impact upon modern life. Modern music and the graphic arts received a genuine stimulus from the comparative outlook. Once the primitive arts were well described and taken seriously, their counterparts in our civilization had enlarged possibilities for development. The knowledge ethnographers had collected on the geography, resources, and native customs of out-of-the-way places was put to practical use during the war when these areas became of military importance. In January, 1942, an anthropologist who happened to be the only person in the United States who had ever spent any time on a certain obscure little island in the Pacific was hardly allowed to sleep for weeks, so badly did the Navy and the Marine Corps need to quiz him on the beaches, water courses, and population of this island. Anthropologists wrote "survival manuals," dealing with problems of food, clothing, dangerous insects and animals, water supply, and proper ways of securing native cooperation in the areas they knew best. During the Versailles Peace Conference ethnographers were present as expert advisers on cultural boundaries in Europe. Perhaps it would have been well if the cultural lines had been taken as seriously as the political lines.

Once again, however, the notebooks of historical anthropologists are only means to broader objectives. Description is never an end in itself. The first aim is that of filling in the blank pages of world history for the living peoples who do not have written languages. A number of well-documented conclusions have been reached on specific points. For example, Polynesia was settled relatively late. Social units, such as clans, appear in human history after a long period when the family and the band were the bases of social organization. Certain peoples of Siberia represent a backwash from North America. Other migrations have been approximately traced.

Sometimes historical linguistics is of crucial importance in these reconstructions. For example, we find groups of tribes in Alaska and Canada, the coast of Oregon and California, and in the Southwest who speak languages that are closely related. Presumably all the tribes at one time lived in the same area. But was the migration from north to south or from south to north? A comparison of certain words used by one of the southern tribes with similar words in the West Coast and northern tongues indicates a northern origin. The Navaho word for corn breaks down into "food of the Pueblo Indians." Apparently the Navaho did not themselves raise maize when they came into the Southwest. Their word for a gourd ladle had an earlier meaning of "horn of an animal." Gourds are native to the Southwest; horns are important to hunting peoples of the North Woods. A Navaho word for sowing seed has the basic meaning "the snow lies in particles on the ground." An obscure Navaho ceremonial expression actually signifies "sleep paddles away from me"—which all too clearly points to Canadian rivers and lakes rather than to the deserts of New Mexico and Arizona. So does the ritual description of the owl—"he who brings darkness back in his canoe."

Such putting together of descriptive bits into coherent historical reconstruction is also, however, only a means to answering more general questions. For example, archaeologists and ethnologists join hands in depicting the natural history of warfare. Freud and Einstein, in their famous exchange of letters, argued the question of the inevitability of war. A more scientific approach would be to discover whether in fact war has always and everywhere been part of the human scene. If it has, this does not prove that Freud was right for all time since some persistent institutions, such as chattel slavery, have been successfully eliminated. Also, the existence of present types of destructive instruments is a new element in the picture. However, if the data favor Freud's assumption of an aggressive instinct, planning for a speedy abolition of warfare would appear a waste of time. Constructive energies would better go into the redirection of aggressive impulses and the gradual achieving of a certain measure of control over outbreaks of armed hostility between groups.

The necessary evidence is not yet all in. Facts now known do indicate that Freud's view was needlessly pessimistic, biased presumably by exclusive contemplation of recent centuries of European history. It is not certain that warfare existed during the Old Stone Age. The indications are that it was unknown during the earlier part of the New Stone Age in Europe and the Orient. Settlements lack structures that would have defended them against attack. Weapons seem to be limited to those used in hunting animals. Some prominent ethnologists read the record of more recent times to mean that war is not endemic but a perversion of human nature. Organized, offensive warfare was unknown in aboriginal Australia. Certain areas of the New World seem to have been completely free from war in the pre-European period. All the above statements are to greater or lesser degree disputed among the specialists, though most of them are capable of settlement in terms of obtainable data. What is absolutely certain at present is that different types of social order carry with them varying degrees of propensity for war. The continuum ranges from groups like the Pueblo Indians who for many centuries have almost never engaged in offensive warfare to groups like some Plains Indians who made fighting their highest virtue. Even in societies that exalt aggression, the variation in approved outlets is enormous.

Just as a culture that centers on wealth may elect to prove wealth by hoarding or by distribution, so an aggressive culture may emphasize war against neighbors, hostility within the group, or competitive activities like sports or the mastery of the natural environment.

How do cultures change and grow? What proportion of their cultures have peoples created and what proportion have they borrowed from others? Does history in any sense repeat itself or is history, as Henry Adams once complained to a friend, like a Chinese play—without end and without lesson? Are there true cycles in history? Is "progress" a reality?

In the opinion of one anthropologist, R. B. Dixon, who carefully studied these matters, a triad of factors is always in the background of each new trait: opportunity, need, and genius. Basic additions to the total inventory of human culture arise either from accidental discovery or from conscious invention. The phenomenon of large numbers of men systematically and planfully seeking inventions is peculiar to our times. Invention of improvements, at least, is accelerating at a tremendous rate. The totality of human culture is cumulative. Increasingly, we stand on the shoulders of those who have gone before us. The achievements of Einstein rest upon a substructure built up by at least 5,000 years of collective effort. The theory of relativity traces its genealogy from an unknown hunter who discovered abstract numbers by notching his stick, from Mesopotamian priests and traders who invented multiplication and division, from Greek philosophers and Moslem mathematicians.

There are few proved instances of totally independent invention. A familiar illustration is the development of one form of mathematical calculus by Newton and Leibniz in the seventeenth century. Often cited examples from recent times, such as the wireless and the airplane, appear on examination to be cases of a somewhat different order because they involve primarily the assembling of a number of basic inventions that, under modern conditions of communication, were equally known to both parties.

The appearance of the idea of mathematical zero in India and in Central America would be a dramatic example but must be regarded as still unsettled. The Hopi use of coal seems more certain. There are a few instances where convergence appears to have developed out of two totally distinct cultural backgrounds. The fire piston appears to have been known in Southeast Asia in relatively ancient times. In Europe it was produced in the nineteenth century on the basis of experiments in physics. Apparent resemblances need to be scrutinized carefully. It is easy to say "there are pyramids in both Egypt and the New World." Yet Egyptian pyramids are peaked and were used exclusively as tombs. Maya pyramids were flat-topped as foundations for temples or altars.

What happens to a discovery or invention, once made, depends on the total cultural milieu and all sorts of situational demands. Doubtless many discoveries have perished with their discoverers because they did not fit the necessities of the times or because the discoverers were regarded as crackpots. The momentous findings of Gregor Mendel on the principles of heredity were neglected for many years, buried in an obscure journal. Had Mendel not lived in a literate culture, the fact of his discovery would be unknown today. A finding may now be preserved by publication until an important use for it turns up. DDT was discovered in 1874 but not utilized as an insecticide until 1939. Similarly, an invention may survive but not be exploited to its limits. The Greeks of the Hellenistic period knew the principle of the steam engine, but it was utilized only in a toy. The social and economic conditions did not favor its development. Moreover, Greek culture in general was interested in people—not in machines.

Many culture traits which we call by a single name actually show only a rather vague resemblance in general function, not in specific structure. In certain instances (*e.g.*, clan, the mother-in-law taboo, feudalism, totemism) multiple causes and multiple historical origins are probable. It is all too tempting to dramatize culture growth, singling out one date and one inventor. A great intellectual achievement, like writing, is probably born out of the subconscious mind of many individuals and is perhaps first actualized in random activity or play. In a fortunate context of situation a particular individual's spontaneous innovation is accepted by others. Only after many acceptances and many successive "inventions" does writing progress slowly toward the full realization of its inherent potentialities and attain such regularity that the observer would say, "Yes, here, we have a written language."

The spread of an invention beyond the group where it originated is called by anthropologists diffusion. The diffusion of tobacco, the alphabet, and other cultural elements has been traced in considerable detail. The adoption or rejection of a trait depends upon a variety of factors, once contact has been established through trade, missionaries, or the printed word. The most obvious factor is, of course, need. The Chinese had rice and so were not particularly attracted by the potato. The English eat the leaves of the beet and throw the root to swine and oxen. Europeans adopted maize as a food for animals; Africans quickly became fond of corn on the cob and integrated corn meal into their ritual. Then there is the factor of general suitability to preexisting culture patterns. A religion centered around a male deity is not easily established among a people that has traditionally worshipped female figures. Some cultures are much more resistant than others to all types of borrowing. However, a culture that has had a tradition of being self-contained will become much more receptive if the group is disorganized by famine or by military conquest. Then all the forces making for resistance to change are weakened. Similarly, it may be noted that within a well-integrated society those individuals who are disgruntled or maladjusted are ordinarily more likely to accept foreign patterns. If, on the other hand, a chief or king happens to find a new religion psychologically congenial to his temperament, culture change can be much accelerated.

Borrowing is always selective. When the Natchez Indians of Mississippi came into contact with French traders they readily adopted knives, cooking pots, and firearms. They learned to shake hands in European fashion. They took at once to chicken raising even though not attracted by European methods of farming. Contrary to folklore, they refused liquor. A tribe in Western Canada took over a well-known folktale, "The Ant and the Grasshopper," but completely altered the moral to fit its own established pattern.

Sometimes the outward form is kept unaltered, but the trait is given a completely different set of meanings. A kind of visionary experience, called the Guardian Spirit Complex, spread among many tribes of Western North America. In one tribe it was part of the ceremonies of adolescence, in another it was made the basis for training as a *shaman,* in still another it was fitted into clanship practices. Sometimes the culture trait is modified by improving inventions. Thus the Greeks took over a consonantal alphabet from the Phoenicians but added vowels.

Some cultural elements characteristically spread much more rapidly than others. In general, material objects spread more rapidly than ideas because the linguistic factor is not involved and because ideas demand sharper alterations of established value patterns. There are exceptions, however. The Indians of the Plateau region were more receptive to Catholicism than to European material culture. In general, women are more resistant to culture change than men, perhaps because in most societies, until recently, they had much less contact with the outside world.

Dixon has compared cultural diffusion to the spread of a forest fire. Depending on the direction of the winds, the relative dryness of different kinds of timber, and the existence of water or other barriers, a fire does not develop evenly from its origin. It may leap over a whole wood and rage with undiminished fury beyond. In the same way, seaborne diffusion is often discontinuous. If a people migrates, it will diffuse whole complexes of traits that have been united merely by historical accidents. If traits are spread merely by the contact of individuals or by books, bundles of traits may still be diffused, but they are likely to be logical trait complexes like the horse, saddle, bridle, spurs, and quirt.

Ralph Linton has estimated that not more than 10 per cent of the material objects used by any people represents its own invention. This proportion is steadily shrinking under present-day conditions of communication. A week's menu in an American home may well include chicken, which was domesticated in Southeast Asia; olives, which originated in the Mediterranean region; corn bread, the meal of an American Indian plant, baked in an aboriginal fashion; rice and tea from the Far East; coffee, which was probably domesticated in Ethiopia; citrus fruits, which were first cultivated in Southeast Asia but reached Europe by way of the Middle East; and perhaps chili from Mexico. A particular food habit gets established through the historical accidents of original contact: Indians in Canada drink tea; Indians in the United States drink coffee.

The course of cultural evolution both resembles and differs from that of biological evolution. In culture change there are sudden spurts reminiscent of those abrupt alterations in hereditary materials that biologists call mutations. In fact, Childe maintains that these sudden cultural advances have the same sort of biological effect as organic mutations. The invention of a food-producing economy made possible not only settled village life and specialization of labor but also great increase of population. Childe sees no less than fifteen basic cultural mutations underlying what he calls the "urban revolution." No set of events in known history is so dramatic as this burst of creativity. The achievements of Egypt and Babylonia which our schoolbooks still portray as the bases of modern civilization pale into relative insignificance, for they contributed only two first-rate discoveries: decimal notation and aqueducts.

Exactly when and where the momentous inventions of domestic plants and animals, pottery, the plough, weaving, the sickle, the wheel, metallurgy, the sailing ship, architecture, and the rest of the complex occurred is still in doubt. They appear together by about 3000 B.C. in Egypt, Palestine, Syria, North Mesopotamia, and Iran. The earliest definitely established dates for domestic animals and pottery are about 5000 B.C. Metallurgy appears about 4000 B.C., the sailing ship between 4000 and 3000. The wheel is not known to be earlier than about 3000 B.C. All of these dates may be pushed further back by new discoveries. In the opinion of some authorities the whole complex will eventually be proved to have been originated around 7000 B. C.—plus or minus a thousand years. When first encountered in these sites, this new technology and economy seem already to have passed through their formative stages. The transition from food collecting to food producing is perhaps the most significant revolution in human history. It was a genuine addition ("mutation")—not just a development.

This same tendency to sudden bursts has been demonstrated through the course of the major civilizations in Kroeber's great book *Configurations of Culture Growth*. The famous names of philosophy, science, sculpture, painting, drama, literature, and music tend to cluster in periods which range in length from thirty or forty years to as much as a thousand. To present an example not given by Kroeber, the following important publications all appeared in the single year, 1859: Darwin's *Origin of Species*, Marx's *Critique of Political Economy*, Virchow's *Cellular Pathology*, Littré's *Paroles de Philosophie Positive*, Bain's *Emotions and the Will*, Whately's *Lessons on the Mind*. It could be added that this was the year of the discovery of spectrum analysis, of the founding of the Great Atlantic and Pacific Tea Company, and of the publication of three novels by Trollope. "Cultures appear to grow in patterns and to fulfill or exhaust these." There is thus a cyclical element in human history.

Of the causes of culture growth and decay little more can be said at present than that they are complicated. As A. V. Kidder has written:

> A thousand explanations have been offered. The geneticist attributes slumps to bad genes and recoveries to happy combinations of good ones; the nutritionist sees things in terms of vitamins; the medical man in terms of diseases; the sociologist perceives faults or virtues in this or that aspect of social organization. The theologian blames heresies. And if all else fail, we can always appeal to climatic changes or economic determinism.

The anthropologist insists that an appeal to any one factor is always wrong. And this negative generalization is important in a world where man is always trying to simplify his environment by pointing to *the* cause: race, climate, economics, culture, or whatever. Kroeber says, "No amount or type of external influence will produce a burst of cultural productivity unless the internal situation is ripe." He adds, however, that in most cases a direct relationship can be shown to external stimulation, notably that of new ideas.

In an intellectual climate dominated by economic and biological notions the role of ideas has been underplayed. It has been fashionable to maintain that such movements as the Reformation and the Crusades were primarily economic. Yet the fact that during the wars of the Reformation people thought they were fighting about religion and were directly motivated by sentiments involving religion cannot be explained away. In any case it must not be forgotten that labels like "economics" and "religion" are abstractions—not clear-cut categories given directly by experience. Here is the main error of those Communists who claim that economic phenomena are primary. They are making an abstraction come alive—what Whitehead has called "the fallacy of misplaced concreteness." Actually, the Marxist position is amusing in view of the history of Russia since 1917. Does anyone seriously think that the industrialization of Russia would have proceeded so rapidly had not Russia been under the sway of Marxist ideas? Were economic need alone sufficient to produce a communistic revolution, all of China would have become totally communistic long ago.

There are some regularities in the historical process as in organic development. The fixity of the stages of cultural evolution is exaggerated by the Marxist anthropologists, for some peoples seem to have gone directly from hunting and collecting to agriculture without passing through an epoch of pastoralism. Other tribes have gone directly from stone tools to iron tools. Nevertheless, in general, culture developments have followed about the same series of steps. There seem even to be some more or less irreversible trends. For example, there is only a single known instance of a society's moving from patrilineal to matrilineal institutions. The breakdown of cultural isolation is followed sooner or later by increased secularization and individualization. Cities breed heresies; a cosmopolitan society is never a homogeneous society. Cultural climaxes are followed by periods of disintegration and confusion.

Culture development resembles organic evolution, then, in its uneven character and in its following certain directional trends. On the other hand, as Kroeber says:

> The tree of life is eternally branching, and never doing anything fundamental but branching, except for the dying away of branches. The tree of human history, on the contrary, is constantly branching and at the same time having its branches grow together again. Its plan is therefore much more complex and difficult to trace. Even its basic patterns can in some degree blend; which is contrary to all experience in the merely organic realm, where patterns are irreversible in proportion as they are fundamental.

If one defines progress as the gradual enrichment of human ideas and subjects, there can be no question that the potential resources of human culture in general and of most individual cultures have steadily increased. The amount of energy harnessed per person per year has increased from an estimated 0.05 horsepower per day at the beginning of culture history to 13.5 in the United States in 1939. The number of ideas and of forms of artistic expression is also vastly greater. Any argument as to whether the intellectual and aesthetic life of classical Greece was "superior" to ours is essentially futile. Yet we do not need scientific proof that human misery and degradation are evil. Our culture certainly represents an advance over the Greek to the extent that slavery is abolished, the position of women more nearly approaches that of equality, and our ideal is that of equal access to education and comfort for all, rather than for a tiny minority. Progress, however, has a spiral character rather than that of an unbroken climb. Childe writes:

> Progress is real if discontinuous. The upward curve resolves itself into a series of troughs and crests. But in those domains that archaeology as well as written history can survey, no trough ever declines to the low level of the preceding one, each crest outtops its last precursor.

The historical approach thus leads to important conclusions of some generality. In this connection one ghost must be laid. During the twenties and thirties anthropologists spilled a good deal of ink on a controversy over "history" versus "function." This is now almost universally regarded as a false issue. One anthropologist may legitimately emphasize descriptive synthesis in which the historical context is preserved in all its details. Another may emphasize the role that a given pattern plays in meeting the physical or psychological needs of the group. Both approaches are necessary; they supplement each other. Nor is any watertight isolation practical in actuality. The historical anthropologist can never completely avoid questions of meaning and function. The archaeologist, in contrast to the geologist, can never stop with the description of what is present in a stratum. He is compelled to ask: what is it for? Similarly, the social anthropologist is forced to realize that the processes that determine events are imbedded in time as well as in situation.

Let us take the example of the Ghost Dance cult among the Sioux Indians sixty years ago when they were beset on all sides by the White Man. The more general features of this predominantly native religion can probably be explained in functional terms. In fact, one of the best established generalizations of social anthropology is that when the pressure of whites upon aborigines reaches a certain point there will be a revival of the ancient religion or a partially new cult of messianic type will arise. In either case the nativistic faith preaches the old values and prophesies the withdrawal or destruction of the invaders. This has occurred in Africa and Oceania as well as in the Americas. The emotional appeal of such doctrine is not hard to understand. But once we try to understand specific traits of the Ghost Dance religion, psychology and function lead us only to confusion unless we bring in history. Why are certain symbolic acts directed always toward the west? Not because the west is the land of the setting sun, nor because it is the place of the nearest ocean, nor for any other reason that might be deduced from general psychological principles. The west is significant because of a specific historical fact—the founder of the cult came to the Sioux from Nevada.

Could a Martian visitor to the United States in 1948 make a sensible interpretation of States Rights on the basis of the contemporary facts? Surely they could be comprehended only if he were able to project himself back into the circumstances of 1787 when small Rhode Island had good reason to fear large Massachusetts and Virginia. Any given culture trait can be fully understood only if seen as the end point of specific sequences of events reaching back into the remote past. Forms persist; functions change.

The complex historical events that have led to the diversification of cultures cannot be accounted for by any simple formula. The stimulus of foreign objects and ideas and of environmental changes has been important. Crowded conditions due to population increases have forced new social and material inventions. Populational pressures have also led to migrations which have been significant because of their selective character. Emigrants are never a random biological, temperamental, or cultural sample of the home people. While many patterned ways of reacting unquestionably represent almost inevitable responses to an external environment in which the group lives or once lived, there are certainly also many cases where the conditions merely limit the possibility of response rather than eventually compel one and only one mode of adaptation. These are the "accidents of history."

Let me give an example or two. In a society where the chief really has great power one particular chief happens to be born with a glandular disorder which brings about an unusual personality. By virtue of his position, he is able to bring about changes, congenial to his temperament, in the way of life of his group. Such a circumstance has been known to be followed by relatively temporary or relatively enduring changes in culture patterns.

Or suppose that in the same group a chief dies as a relatively young man, leaving an infant as his heir. This has been observed to result in a marked crystallization of two factions around two rival older relatives, each of whom has about equally valid claims to act as "regent." A schism occurs. Each group thereafter pursues its own separate destiny, and the end result is the formation of two distinguishable variants of what was at one time a homogeneous culture. Now, to be sure, it is likely that the original factional lines had their bases in economic, populational, or other conditions. In short, the form and the mesh of the "sieve which is history" must be seen as shaped not only by the total environment at any given point in time but also by individual psychological and accidental factors.

One of the diagnostic features of a culture is its selectivity. Most specific needs can be satisfied in a wide variety of ways, but the culture selects only one or a very few of the organically and physically possible modes. "The culture selects" is, to be sure, a metaphorical way of speaking. The *original* choice was necessarily made by one or more individuals, and then followed by other individuals (or it wouldn't have become culture). But from the angle of those individuals who later learn the culture the existence of this element in a design for living has the *effect* not of a selection made by these human beings as a reaction to their own particular situation but rather of a choice which still binds, though made by individuals long gone.

Such a selective awareness of the natural environment, such a stereotyped interpretation of man's place in the world, is not merely inclusive—by implication it also excludes possible alternatives. Because of the strain toward consistency in cultures such inclusions and exclusions are meaningful far beyond the specific activity which is overtly involved. Just as the "choice" of an individual at a crucial epoch commits him in certain directions for the rest of his life, likewise the original bents, trends, and interests, which become established in the life way of a newly formed society tend to channel a culture in some directions as opposed to others. Subsequent variations in the culture—both those which arise internally and those which are a response to contact with other cultures or to changes in the natural environment—are not random. Cumulative small changes tend to occur in the same direction.

This is inevitable because no human being, save a newborn child, can ever see the world freshly. What he sees and his interpretations of what he sees are filtered through the invisible screen of culture. As Ruth Benedict has written:

> The anthropologist's role is not to question the facts of nature but to insist upon the interposition of a middle term between "nature" and "human behavior"; his role is to analyze that term, to document man-made doctorings of nature and to insist that these doctorings should not be read off in any one culture as nature itself. Although it is a fact of nature that the child becomes a man, the way in which this transition is effected varies from one society to another, and no one of these particular bridges should be regarded as the "natural" path to maturity.

By the same principle the changes that occur in a people's culture when the people moves into a new physical environment are not simply the result of environmental pressures plus biological needs and limitations.

The use that is made of plants, animals, and minerals will be limited and directed by the existent or potential meanings that these have in the cultural lore. The adaptation to severe cold or extreme heat will depend upon the cultural skills available. Man's response is never to brute physical facts as such but always to such facts as defined in cultural terms. To people who do not know how to work iron the presence of iron ore in the natural habitat is in no significant sense a "natural resource." Hence cultures found in highly similiar physical environments are often far from identical, and cultures observed in different environments are sometimes very much alike.

The natural environments of the United States are very various, and yet the Americans of the arid Southwest and of rainy Oregon still behave in ways which are easily distinguishable from the ways of Australian desert dwellers on the one hand and inhabitants of verdant England on the other.

Tribes like the Pueblo and Navaho, living in substantially identical natural and biological environments, still manifest very different ways of life. The English who live in the Hudson Bay region and those who live in British Somaliland still share common designs for living. It is true, of course, that the different natural environments are responsible for observable alterations. But the striking fact is that, in spite of the tremendous differences in the physical environment, shared designs for living still persist.

The inhabitants of two not very distant villages in New Mexico, Ramah and Fence Lake, are both of the so-called "Old American" physical stock. A physical anthropologist would say they represented random samples from the same physical population. The rocky tablelands, the annual rainfall and its distribution, flora and fauna surrounding the two villages hardly show perceptible variations. The density of population and the distance from a main-traveled highway is almost the same in the two cases. Still, even the casual visitor immediately notices distinctions. There are characteristic differences in dress; the style of the houses is different; there is a saloon in one town and not in the other. A completion of this catalog would demonstrate conclusively that different patterns of life prevail in the two settlements. Why? Primarily because the two villages represent variants of the general Anglo-American social tradition. They have slightly different cultures: Mormon and transplanted Texan.

On the other hand, the differences between cultures that have long existed in the same physical environment do diminish, though differences never completely disappear. The Irish village of Adare was settled some two hundred and fifty years ago by German Protestants and still retains a distinct culture. The more marked the character of the environment, the more various cultures in it gradually come to resemble each other. Clothing and other aspects of material culture are especially likely to reflect the environmental situation, even if, as in the case of Europeans who continue to wear European style clothing in the tropics, there are instances where the cultural compulsive stubbornly resists the demand for environmental adaptation. Occasionally a particular physical setting makes the continuation of an imported cultural tradition quite impossible. More often, there are slow selective modifications under environmental influence. The gradual development of regional cultures in the United States is in part traceable to the differing characters of the populations who settled these sections, and in part to the general tendency for environmental areas to become culture areas. At the primitive level correlations between environment and economic or political life are generally much more marked. Rug techniques usually develop among nomadic peoples in arid regions. There is almost always an absence of strongly centralized government among desert folk. Under primitive conditions patrilineal bands of perhaps fifty members are the normal form of social organization in regions where the population is one per square mile or less. Steward has shown close resemblances between the social patterns of Bushmen, African and Malaysian Pygmies, Australians, Tasmanians, and Southern California Indians.

Nutrition is, of course, the joint product of environment and culture. The natural resources must be available, but a technology for exploiting them is equally necessary. The same climate and soil can support a vastly greater population if a new and more suitable crop is introduced by diffusion. A dense population, in turn, is the condition of certain types of cultural elaborations. Ralph Linton has suggested that a sudden spurt in the development of the prehistoric cultures of the American Southwest is connected with the introduction of the bean into this area. Human beings can do very well on a starchless diet, but a certain minimum of proteins and fats appears to be essential. In many parts of the world these are supplied by dairy products, in others by meat or fish, in still others by various types of bean. In aboriginal America dogs and turkeys were eaten in some places as occasional luxuries. Inland peoples for the most part had to depend on hunting and on nuts and a few wild plants for their proteins and fats. This meant that no large group could live permanently in one location. The development of a cultivated protein crop set a considerably higher population ceiling.

The physical environment both limits and facilitates. If we consider the geography of Greece, the slowness of political unification is not surprising. Conversely, since Egypt forms one compact strip of habitable land, early political union was easy. The physical environment may stimulate. To live at all in parts of the Arctic, the Eskimo had to become extraordinarily ingenious in developing mechanical techniques. The ruder a people the more obvious is the environmental warp in the fabric of the culture. But environment never in any literal sense creates. The harbors of Tasmania are as good as those of Crete or England, yet the Tasmanians never developed a maritime culture—partly to be sure, because Tasmania was so far from the main highways of developing civilization. A culture is always, of course, conditioned by its ways of making a living. An abundance of children is likely to be more valued by agriculturalists than by hunters. Small children are something of a nuisance to elders who must move about a good deal, and it is some years before a youngster makes much contribution to a hunting economy. A toddler, however, begins to be of use in weeding the garden and scaring off birds. Social stratification is not well developed in a group that lives by collecting and hunting in a region where the food supply is ample. Sophisticated arts and crafts do not arise except when the economy makes possible specialization and some leisure. But in each case note that the physical environment is a necessary but not a sufficient condition. Certain conditions make agriculture possible—given a certain technology (*i.e.*, culture). If agriculture is practiced, the social organization will probably differ from that of a group of hunters. However, the environmental foreground only invites agriculture: it does not compel it. The cultural background is the determining factor once the natural situation is permissive.

Yet both factors are of essential importance—as is also the biological. Under given circumstances some one of these factors may be of greater strategic significance than the others, but none must ever be lost to intellectual sight. Americans find it emotionally more satisfying to single out *the* key to the situation. This dangerous delusion is pleasantly satirized by W. J. Humphreys, a learned authority upon climate:

What is it moulds the life of man?
    The weather.
What makes some black and others tan?
    The weather.
What makes the Zulu live in trees,
And Congo natives dress in leaves
While others go in furs and freeze?
    The weather.
What makes some glad and others sad?
    The weather.
What makes the farmer hopping mad?
    The weather.
What puts a mortgage on your land,
That makes you sweat to beat the band,
Or takes it off before demand?
    The weather.

The riddle of the building of cultures may be solved only if we give three factors their just due: antecedent culture, situation, and biology. Situation includes the limitations and potentialities inherent in the physical environmental setting: soils and topography, plants and animals, climate, and location. Situation also includes facts, such as the density of population, which are the result of both cultural and biological factors. Biology takes in both the capacities and limits of human beings in general and those qualities that are specific to particular individuals and groups. These latter are peculiarly difficult to handle because it is so hard to disentangle the hereditary from the environmental. However, as Ellsworth Huntington says, "heredity runs like a scarlet thread through history." The role of individuals with exceptional hereditary endowments is beyond dispute. It is also probable that groups differ in the proportion of persons who are creative or who can adjust readily to changed conditions. The Polynesians learned to use firearms with incredible rapidity; the Bushmen after centuries of contact have not taken either to the gun or to the horse.

Some comparisons between cultural and biological development have already been made. It should be added that organic evolution, in spite of occasional sudden spurts, proceeds much more slowly. Some scholars believe indeed that cultural evolution has leaped so far beyond biological evolution in the last few thousand years that it is out of control, that man is now at the mercy of a superorganic machine that he created but can no longer direct.

At any rate that aspect of biological anthropology that is historically oriented has now traced much of the course of human evolution for at least half a million years. Certain crucial features are, as in the case of cultural evolution, still somewhat mysterious. Until not so long ago the picture seemed relatively simple in its main outlines and appeared to fit well with Darwinian notions of evolution. During the early part of the period geologists call the Pleistocene, there existed in Java a kind of ape man or man-ape known as *Pithecanthropus erectus*. By mid-Pleistocene times there were true men, though not of modern type, in China, Europe, and Africa. Many authorities felt that these biologically primitive, still somewhat apelike men represented the kind of evolution that might be expected from creatures similar to *Pithecanthropus*. From about 100,000 years ago to about 25,000 years ago the Neanderthal race, a variety evolving in the same direction but still crude, lived in Europe, North Africa, and Palestine. Then appeared types approaching the living species of man (which we modestly call *Homo sapiens*) who gradually exterminated the Neanderthals, possibly absorbing them to some degree.

The older interpretation was that the course of human evolution was steadily divergent, like a tree with many branches. The branches lower down the trunk, like the Neanderthals, withered away one by one, leaving *Homo sapiens* as the only surviving branch. The most recent development was the splitting of this branch into diverging twigs—the present human races. Present knowledge seems, however, to require a different view. The Java fossils are now generally regarded as a true species of man and closely related to China man (*Sinanthropus*) of the same period. *Homo sapiens*, instead of being a recent progressive branch, appears in Europe at least as early as the second interglacial period (*i.e.*, earlier than the more apelike Neanderthals). Some eminent scholars think that Piltdown man of England, who shows certain resemblances to modern man, must be dated in the first interglacial. A recent interpretation of these facts is that during the whole of the Pleistocene different strains of human beings were, in different regions and at different speeds, passing through parallel phases of the evolutionary process that led from apes to modern human types. According to this view, Java man may be considered a direct ancestor of the Australian aborigines, China man of the Mongoloid, Neanderthal man of the European races, and perhaps Rhodesian man or other African fossils of the Negroes.

Whence our ancestors came and when, what they were like, and how ancient are the distinctions between present varieties of men must still be regarded as undecided. We know that the process was long and complex. We know that biological evolution like cultural evolution tends to continue in the directions it begins. In the course of this "drift," selection is operative in both cases. But in the case of biological evolution the variations persist to the extent that they promote the survival of the human animal. Cultural selection centers increasingly around struggles over competing sets of values. Biological and cultural anthropology are a unity because both are necessary to answer the central question: how did each people come to be as it is?

Dixon has eloquently summarized the general principles that bear on this question:

. . . exotic traits brought by diffusion and local traits arising either out of their cultural heritage by adaptation or discovered and invented by their own genius and correlated in some degree often with their environment—of these two elements the fabric of a people's culture is woven. The foundation or warp comes from within, the exotic elements or weft, from without; the warp is static in that it is tied in some measure to the environment, the weft is dynamic, mobile, drifting along diffusion lines. The textile analogy may indeed be carried further with profit. For, if the environment of a people be strongly marked, the warp, the basic traits of their culture that are correlated in some degree with environment, will tend also to be sharply defined; and if the weft, the exotic traits which come to them, are few and weak, the warp will stand out in their culture, ribbed and strong as in a rep. So in the case of the Eskimo, the traits based on the very clearly defined environment stand out sharply, there being little in the way of exotic elements which have reached this isolated group. Where, on the other hand, the environment lacks strong individuality so that the basic traits are relatively undistinguished, whereas the exotic traits supplied by diffusion are many and striking, then the weft element may come to overlay the warp and largely conceal it, as in a satin. . . . The culture traits drawn by each people, then, from the opportunities and limitations of their habitat formed the basis of their culture, its warp, stretching between themselves and their environment. Across it the moving shuttles of diffusion spread the weft of exotic traits derived from far and near, combining warp and weft into a pattern which the genius and the history of each people determined for itself. . . . We live in a three dimensional world, and human culture is built in accordance with it. It is not linear and one-dimensional, as the extreme diffusionists would have it; it is not a mere two-dimensional surface of contrasted habitats, as the environmentalists might be said to describe it. It is rather a solid structure, set firmly on a base whose breadth lies in the variety of environment which the world affords, and whose length is the sum of all diffusion throughout the whole of human history. The height to which it rises is varied, and is measured by the elusive something, compounded of intelligence, temperament, and genius, possessed in differing degree by every tribe and nation and race.

Cultures are not constants but are always in the making. Biological evolution also is always going on. The events of both cultural and biological history are not isolated but patterned; history consists in patterns as well as in events. So long as the past and the present are outside one another, knowledge of the past is not of much use in the problems of the present. But if part of the past lives on in the present, even if hidden beneath the present's contradictory and more prominent features, then historical knowledge brings insight. The cultural fabric may be compared to a shot silk of contradictory colors. It is transparent, not opaque. To the trained eye the past gleams beneath the surface of the present. The business of the anthropological historians is to reveal the less obvious features hidden from a careless eye in the present situation.

CHAPTER IV

Skulls

An industrious Hungarian physical anthropologist, von Törok, used to take more than 5,000 measurements on each skull he studied. The great English anthropologist, Karl Pearson, devised an instrument called the cranial coordinotograph in order to be able to describe the skull in terms of certain modern geometries. He said that when he was in good practice he could deal with one skull in six hours.

Small wonder that physical anthropologists have seemed to the general public and even to their scientific colleagues to be obsessed with skulls. It is true that some of the measurements made by classical physical anthropology bore scant relation to what modern experimental embryology has taught us about the actual processes of growth of bones and tissues. It is also true that some of the thinking of physical anthropologists was not remodeled as quickly as it should have been to fit with the new knowledge of heredity first gained by Gregor Mendel's experiments with peas in a monastery garden. For a time physical anthropology was, on the whole, in the backwater of the sciences.

Nevertheless the preoccupation with measuring and with observation of small anatomical curiosities was part and parcel of anthropology's main task—the exploration of the range of human variation. The physical anthropologist was doing in human biology what was identical in principle with the work of the archaeologists and ethnologists on human culture. And the rigorous and standardized techniques of measurement developed by the physical anthropologists had immediate practical utility.

The first applications were in the field of military anthropology. It was possible to establish physical standards for recruits, saying accurately by how much a given man was above or below the average of a particular age and economic group in respect to stature, weight, and the like. This information facilitated scientific selection, rejection, and classification. A little later these types of classification were utilized by insurance companies and educational institutions. A further development in the military field was for problems of procurement. How many overcoats of size forty-two will be needed among a million men drafted from the Northeast Central States? Given certain ranges of distribution in a carefully selected sample measured by standardized techniques, it is possible to make predictions that are far better than guesses based on an unsystematic evaluation of previous experience.

The utility of physical anthropology in fitting clothing and gadgets to men progressed greatly during World War II. The problems presented were crucial. Gas masks aren't much help unless they fit properly, yet they can't be custom-built for each individual. Certain escape hatches in planes proved to be too small for safety, unless great care were taken to assign undersized men to particular posts. The numbers of men small enough to operate gun turrets were inadequate in many units. The paramount importance of space in aviation and in tank warfare required anthropological research on human factors in engineering design and in the assignment of personnel. In the operation of many war machines the limiting factor in accuracy became not the machine but the man who controlled it. The physical anthropologist helped greatly in ensuring that hand controls, foot controls, seating, and optical apparatus were geared to the natural positions and movements of the human body—assuming given distributions of limb measurements and the like within the groups selected for each task.

Applied physical anthropology is developing in the same directions in civilian life. Professor Hooton conducted extensive research for a railroad company to design seats that would accommodate the widest possible variety of shapes and dimensions of human bottoms. An English anthropologist is working on seating arrangements for school children. Manufacturers of clothing are realizing that they require knowledge of the needs of the consumer as well as of the retailer if they are to avoid dead inventories. Here the skills of the social anthropologist are being joined to those of the physical anthropologist, for account is being taken of regional, economic, and social-class groups. Systems are being worked out whereby accurate predictions may be made of the buying public's size distribution from year to year among, say, Arkansas farm women as contrasted with Pennsylvania factory women of the same age group. Designers can then size new garments to suit the particular populations for which these garments are intended.

As a result of all his measurings and minute observations, the physical anthropologist is also an expert on identifications. A skeleton is found. Is it a man or woman? Healthy or not? Young or old? Was the living person stocky or slender, tall or short? Is it the skeleton of an American Indian? If so, it doubtless represents a decent interment of a century or two ago. If, however, it is identified as of European stock, a question of murder may be involved. Physical anthropologists have settled many such questions for the FBI and for the state and local police. For example, Dr. Krogman, as a "bone detective," showed the Chicago police that two assortments of bones from separate addresses on North Halstead Street belonged to the same individual. In another case he proved that a skeleton was that of a boy of between eighteen and nineteen years of mixed Negro and Indian stock—not that of a white adult of thirty, as claimed by an anatomist testifying for an insurance company.

The main scientific questions to which biological anthropology has addressed itself have been these: what are the mechanisms of human evolution? through what processes do local physical types develop? what are the relationships between the structure and the functions of anatomical and physiological variations? what consequences do age and sex differences have? is there any connection between types of body build and susceptibility to particular diseases or propensity for certain kinds of behavior? what are the laws of human growth—by age level, by sex, and by race? what influence do environmental factors have on human physique? how can the form and function of the body during childhood and adolescence be so investigated as to develop standards for regulating demands upon the physical and mental performance of growing youngsters?

All of these questions are, in a way, specialized aspects of a single master problem: how do the variations in human physique and in human behavior relate, on the one hand, to the inherited stuff the organism is born with and, on the other hand, to the press exerted upon organisms by the environment? The hereditary potentials of human beings are carried upon twenty-four pairs of tiny threadlike bodies called chromosomes. Each one of these chromosomes contains a very large (though as yet not exactly determined) number of genes. Each gene (a submicroscopic package of chemicals) is independent in its action and retains its individual character more or less indefinitely, though occasionally there is a sudden change (mutation). Genes are inherited, yes. But the exact characteristics that an adult will show can only in a limited number of cases be predicted from a knowledge of the genetic equipment the child inherited at conception. What the genes will produce is influenced by the successive environments in which the organism matures. Take two simple examples from the plant world. There is a kind of reed which will grow either under water or in damp soil. Plants in the two locations have such an utterly different appearance that the layman can scarcely believe that their genes are identical. Some flowers produce red blossoms at one temperature, white at another. In the case of human beings the environment within the womb can vary considerably, and, after birth, variations in nutrition, care, temperature, and the like may have momentous consequences. The process is complex, not simple. As the distinguished geneticist Dobzhansky says:

> Genes produce not characters but physiological states which, through interactions with the physiological states induced by all other genes of the organism and with the environmental influences, cause the development to assume a definite course and the individual to display certain characters at a given stage of the developmental process.

An individual has the same genes throughout life. But he is a towhead as a child, blond as a boy, brown-haired as an adult, gray-haired as an old man. On the other hand, of course, no amount or kind of environmental pressure will produce a cactus from a rose plant or transform a fawn into a moose.

A vast complex of conditions external to man is covered by the term "environment." There is the cultural environment. There is the social environment—density of population, location of a community with respect to main avenues of communication, size of a particular family in so far as this is independent of cultural patterns. There is the physical environment: mineral content of the soil, plants, animals, and other natural resources; climate, solar and cosmic radiations; altitude and topography. Most of these environmental influences act on each other. In the total environmental matrix now one factor, now another bears on the organism with special intensity.

The human body is responsive to environmental pressures as well as to those arising from the inherited genes. Boas demonstrated that American-born descendants of immigrants differ in head measurements and stature from their foreign-born parents and that these changes increase with the length of time since migration. The children of Mexicans in the United States and Spaniards in Puerto Rico also vary from their parents in a patterned fashion. Shapiro found that Japanese boys born in Hawaii average 4.1 centimeters taller than their fathers and the girls 1.7 centimeters taller than their mothers. The body build of the Hawaiian generation also differed from that of the Japan-born parents.

Studying the children of an orphanage, Boas found that when diet was improved almost all of the children in the group attained the height normal for their age and biological stock. There is no doubt that quantity, quality, and variety of nutrition affect stature and other aspects of physique. However, it is equally certain that not all variations are traceable to this cause. Japanese remaining in Japan have tended to increase in height at least since 1878. This same trend has been going on in Switzerland since as far back as 1792 and may be documented for other European countries from the earliest time in the nineteenth century when adequate records become available. Of students entering Yale in 1941 those more than 6 feet tall formed 23 per cent of the class, whereas in 1891 they constituted only 5 per cent. Some sort of general evolutionary tendency is at work, for the change antedates the modern improvements in diet, hygiene, and exercise to which it has often been attributed. The only group of European stock as tall on the average as present-day American college students is the Cro-Magnon people of the Old Stone Age. Medieval Europeans and those of the late Stone Age were much shorter. Mills has argued that the increase in stature since medieval times has been primarily due to a gradual lowering of temperature. For the present this can be regarded only as a hypothesis that needs further testing. However, it is interesting that Thomas Gladwin has recently presented evidence for the view that men and other animals living in tropical climates have evolved in the general direction of reduction of size and robustness.

Selective migration is a complicating factor in interpreting comparisons between emigrants and the parental stocks. The Japanese men who came to Hawaii differed significantly from their close relatives in the home localities in 76 per cent of all indices calculated. Individuals of certain types of bodily constitution apparently respond more strongly than do others to an opportunity to migrate, and presumably bring to the new environment a special group of hereditary potentialities.

Difficulty in isolating environmental from hereditary factors and in segregating environmental factors from one another has prevented much progress beyond the generalizations that the human physique is unstable in some respects and that both long-time and astonishingly short-time developments may be detected when the same genes operate under different conditions. New work in experimental physical anthropology is testing the results of environmental stress in various ingenious ways. Recent statistical studies have also indicated some remarkable associations between bodily processes, weather conditions, and cycles.

This does not mean that "the weather is destiny" precisely. But, at least in the United States, persons conceived in May and June are more likely to be long-lived than those conceived in other months. A surprisingly large number of eminent persons were born in January and February. Europeans who move to warm climates that lack sharp contrasts in seasons tend to have a diminished life expectancy, and their reproductive rates alter. Huntington argues that the restlessness and incessant activity of Americans from the northern United States is stimulated by frequent storms and strong changes of weather. He has also produced evidence for seasonal fluctuations in crime, insanity, and suicide in the United States and European countries and for seasonal periodicity of riots in India. Finally, Huntington maintains that health and reproduction vary with the rhythms of an intricate series of long and short cycles.

Man is a domesticated animal. Domesticated animals show an especially great range of variation, and man appears to be one of the most variable of all the animals. Physical anthropologists have shown the importance of this variability for practical matters. Professor Boas, for example, was a pioneer in demonstrating that the chronological and physiological ages of school children often fail to coincide. Personality development can be warped if this range of variation is overlooked and expectations are based solely upon the stereotype for, say, twelve-year-olds. Boas also introduced a note of sanity into hysterical discussions of the increase of numbers in mental hospitals. In part, he said, this reflected merely a greater tendency to institutionalize such individuals rather than caring for them in the home. However, even if the proportion of the mentally ill were actually greater, this meant by the principles of statistical distribution that the proportion of superior individuals in the population had likewise increased on the same scale.

In many respects biological anthropology has constituted a valuable supplement to medicine. This has been true in even so apparently impractical a field as the study of human evolution. As Professor Hooton has written:

The specialty known as orthopedics deals, in some degree, with bodily difficulties due to man's imperfect adaptation to an erect posture and to a biped mode of progression. Man is a made-over animal. In the course of evolution, his ancestors have functioned as arboreal pronogrades and brachiators, or arm-progressing tree-dwellers—not to mention more remote stages involving other changes of habitat, posture and mode of locomotion. This protean history has necessitated repeated patching and reconstruction of a more or less pliable and long-suffering organism. The bony framework has been warped and cramped and stretched in one part or another, in accordance with variations in the stresses and strains put upon it by different postures and by changes in body bulk. Joints devised for mobility have been readapted for stability. Muscles have had violence done to their origins and insertions, and have suffered enormous inequalities in the distribution of labor. Viscera have been pushed about hither and yon, let down, reversed and inverted. In making a new machine out of an old one, plenty of obsolete spare parts have been left to rattle around inside. . . . That the specialty of orthopedics should be based upon the very broadest knowledge and understanding of these evolutionary changes seems to me so obvious that I need not labor the point.

In the same way physical anthropologists have aided dentists who specialize in troubles with the upper and lower jaws. They have also helped dentists by observing the effect of different kinds of diet upon the growth and decay of the teeth. A comparative study of the varying forms of the female pelvis as related to different infant and maternal mortality rates in a wide range of human groups has yielded information of practical benefit to obstetrics. Pediatrics is another medical specialty which has profited from the comparative researches of anthropology.

Anthropology has also had some little influence upon the general point of view of the medical profession. It has assisted in getting the idea of the whole man back into medicine. The success of Pasteur and Lister was so great that physicians tended to stop treating men and to treat only single symptoms or their assumed causes (*e.g.*, the germ held responsible for the disease). Physicians have, understandably, concentrated upon the individual patient and upon the sick as a group. Adequate standards of biological normality cannot be achieved on such bases. Anthropology has contributed to medicine valid methods of group analysis and a sense of the need for numerically adequate samples. It has shown that symptoms must often be interpreted only after allowance is made for the patient's position in an age, sex, body-build, and ethnic group. For certain symptoms tell much less about the patient as an individual than about him as the member of a group. Take an example from psychiatry. An old Sicilian, who spoke only a little English, came to a San Francisco hospital to be treated for a minor physical ailment. The intern who examined him noted that he kept muttering that he was being witched by a certain woman, that this was the real reason for his suffering. The intern promptly sent him to the psychiatric ward where he was kept for several years. Yet in the Italian colony from which he came everybody of his age group believed in witchcraft. It was "normal" in the sense of standard. If someone from the intern's own economic and educational group had complained of being persecuted by a witch, this would have been correctly interpreted as a sign of mental derangement.

The study of the special immunities and susceptibilities of various populations is still in its infancy. However, it is well known that groups in Africa and Asia are much more resistant to certain germs than are European immigrants to those areas. Cancer and liver disease are much more common in some populations than in others. Peculiarities of the blood, giving rise to the death of infants at birth (or while still in the womb), differ greatly in their incidence among Negroes, Chinese, American Indians, and whites. Metabolic processes are influenced by diet, environment, and other factors and are at most only partially determined by contrasting genes. The same must be said for many of the varying patterns of disease rates among different physical types, though some appear to be purely or mainly genetic. For example, the specialized character of the Negro skin seems, through its heavy pigmentation, to provide relative immunity to some diseases of the skin. The colored inhabitants of Java and South Africa are prone to cancer of the liver but develop less cancer of the breast and other organs than do Europeans. Some think, however, that this may be due to local infestation by parasites. Differing susceptibility to disease has probably been one of the chief agencies of natural selection in man. Whooping cough, goiter, and cretinism are especially frequent in Northern Europe; the peoples of Central Europe are also vulnerable to goiter and cretinism but have relatively few fatalities from pulmonary disease; American Negroes are resistant to malaria, yellow fever, measles, scarlet fever, and diphtheria, but fall prey to diseases of heart, lungs, and kidneys and to tuberculosis. Some of these variations are obviously traceable to physical environment and factors of isolation and exposure as well as to social and economic conditions.

Constitutional anthropology is also closely related to medical problems. As the comparative study of human groups, anthropology is interested in recognizing and describing every type of human physique, whether found within a cultural group or biological population or crosscutting these. Insurance companies discovered from experience that some bodily types among Americans were better risks than others. Medical clinicians long had the visual impressions that men and women of certain body builds were more susceptible to some diseases than were those of a different bodily structure. Physicians therefore sought from those who were skilled in measuring and observing the human body a scientific and workable scheme for describing and classifying those physical types that reflected individual constitution rather than the kind of physical heritage characteristics of whites as opposed to Negroes, Negroes as opposed to Eastern Asiatics, etc.

Various combinations of anthropological measurements and indices were shown to differentiate the majority of those afflicted with certain diseases from the general population. For instance, one investigator found that infants with eczema and tetany had relatively broader faces, shoulders, chests, and hips than a group of well infants from the same social environment. On the other hand, infants with acute intestinal intoxication and certain other ailments had relatively narrower faces and shoulders than the control groups. Another study aided in the rapid diagnosis and treatment of two kinds of arthritis by indicating that patients who were big-boned, big-muscled, and somewhat tapering in body build were much more likely to fall into the group with degenerative joint disease than into the rheumatic group.

Susceptibility to tuberculosis, ulcers of various types, certain kinds of heart disease, infantile paralysis, and diabetes has been plausibly linked to special classes of physique. A most torturing variety of headache, migraine, seems to go not only with particular psychological and personality tendencies but also with a pattern of anatomical features of the skull and face. Men who approximate the feminine type in a number of respects and women who have many masculine physical traits seem to be especially liable to various psychic disorders and also to a group of organic ailments. The most immediate practical utility of all of these correlations rests not so much in the aid given to rapid and correct diagnosis as in preventive medicine. If one is more likely than most people to develop an ulcer of the stomach one is well advised to pay more than ordinary attention to diet and to avoidance of emotional upsets.

Recent work points to at least rough correlations between body build and temperament or personality. Research by Dr. Carl Seltzer links a series of physical disproportions with a tendency to display a certain pattern of personality traits. Young men who are unusually tall in proportion to their weight, whose hips are broad in relation to their shoulders, who have large heads as compared to chest dimensions, and who exhibit all or most of other specified asymmetries, are, on the average, more sensitive, less stable, less capable of making easy social adjustments. Such an association does not, of course, hold in every individual case. However, such statistical analyses help not only by indicating high betting odds that a person of given bodily type will have certain personality trends but also by clarifying the relation of each individual to his group. The extent to which he approaches or departs from the group averages is an invaluable clue to understanding his particular problems.

One of the most famous studies in constitutional anthropology is that by Professor Hooton on the American criminal. His finding that criminals are, in general, biologically inferior has been disputed. Most reviewers have concluded that he took insufficient account of socioeconomic factors. Hooton makes it perfectly clear that criminals "do not bear the brand of Cain nor any specific physical stigmata whereby they can be identified at a glance." However, he presents good evidence for certain associations. For example, among criminals as a group, those convicted of burglary and larceny are likely to be short and slender; those convicted of sex crimes are likely to be short and fat.

For many of Hooton's major assertions the cautious reader must probably render the Scotch verdict of "not proven." On the other hand, a demonstration that some of Hooton's methods were unsatisfactory does not mean that a constitutional factor in criminality can be ruled out. In fact, a dispassionate critic must admit that the data strongly indicate that criminals in the United States do not constitute a random biological sample of the total population; nor is the distribution of physical types among those convicted of various classes of crimes that which would be expected from chance alone. To be sure, pressure of circumstances must fire the gun. But all that Hooton claims is that a constitutional predisposition makes some individuals more trigger-happy than others. Some individuals reared in slums and brought into close association with older criminals take to crime. Others do not. Why, if environmental factors are solely responsible for criminality, do not all individuals in the same situation make the same response? In certain cases it may be argued that a peculiar chain of events in a life history plus the general environment are enough to account for the fact that one brother becomes a thief and another a priest. It would be cheering to assume that the environment (which is potentially controllable) was always responsible. The hard facts, however, suggest that the biological factor deserves further study.

Enormous progress in the accurate description of various body builds has been made through the efforts of Dr. W. H. Sheldon and his collaborators. Before Sheldon developed the method called somatotyping, one could only give an over-all description of a given individual briefly by saying he was "stocky," "thin," or "medium." Otherwise one bogged down in an endless list of measurements, indices, and observations. Yet it was clear that actually observed individuals exhibited a vast number of gradations of fatness and leanness and of combinations of these. Sheldon's system takes care of this variation on a continuous scale. Each of five separate areas of the body is rated from one to seven with respect to the relative prominence of three factors: endomorphy (emphasis upon fat and viscera), mesomorphy (emphasis upon bone, muscle), and ectomorphy (emphasis upon surface area relative to bulk and of nervous system relative to mass). These ratings are combined to give a somatotype for the body as a whole. Thus the somatotype 226 means that the third component (ectomorphy) is most prominent. The individual is skinny and somewhat fragile in build but not at the extreme of this type, for the rating is 6 and not 7. He has slight muscular development, for the rating in mesomorphy is only 2. He has few fat or softly rounded areas in his body, for the endomorphy rating (2) is near the lowest possible point. Descriptively he would be called a "strong"—but not "extreme" ectomorph. About 25 out of every 1,000 college men studied received this rating.

The theoretical number of somatotypes is 343, but only 76 have been observed in the groups studied thus far. Out of 1,000 American males of college age the distribution of types was as follows: 136 endomorphs, 228 mesomorphs, 210 ectomorphs, 190 balanced, 236 sporadic rare types. In a series of 4,000 slightly more than three-fourths of the subjects fell into 29 somatotypes.

There is general agreement that Sheldon's descriptive classification marks a great advance, though further modifications and refinements may be necessary. But there is much controversy over the claimed association between somatotypes and certain patterns of sixty temperamental traits. It is asserted that mesomorphs are primarily interested in activity, ectomorphs in thinking, endomorphs in eating and enjoying life. Some evidence suggests that mental patients suffering from delusions of persecution and grandeur are likely to be mesomorphic and those suffering from exaggerated shifts in mood, either mesomorphic or endomorphic. Patients diagnosed as schizophrenic are commonly either ectomorphic or have an inharmonious physique. Prognosis for shock treatments seems to be best for those high in endomorphy and worst for those high in ectomorphy. Much work remains to be done on the correlations betweeen somatotype and personality and between somatotype and susceptibility to particular kinds of mental illness. However, there is already good reason to believe that some significant relationships exist.

Somatotyping must be regarded as a valuable technique still in the exploratory phase. Thus far most of the research has been done upon male college students. Few women have been studied. Few older and younger groups have been sampled. Little is known of age changes in the same individual or of the effects of diet or other environmental influences. However, Gabriel Lasker has shown that when thirty-four volunteers were subjected to a European type of famine diet for twenty-four weeks the somatotype of each individual was significantly altered. Most of the research has been done upon whites, and it is not known if the same tendencies would be found among Chinese or American Indians. The inheritance of somatotypes has not been worked out. The external physical characters may turn out to be the expression of varying genetic patterns influencing the activity of the ductless (endocrine) glands.

Thus far in this chapter we have been concerned primarily with certain applications of physical anthropology. Let us now turn to some implications. From all the careful work with the calipers, the minute study of small differences in bones, the more recent excursions into comparative physiology and constitution, physical anthropologists have been able to teach us four lessons of fundamental importance: man's animal nature and his close kinship to other animals, the fact that human evolution cannot be interpreted solely in terms of the survival of the fittest, the plasticity of biological man, the basic similarity of all types of men. These generalizations should be in the background of the thinking of all educated people.

The details of man's biological relationships to the apes and monkeys are still under dispute among the specialists. This much is agreed upon: no living primates are ancestral to humankind. The gorilla, the chimpanzee, the orangutan, the gibbon, the Old World monkeys, the New World monkeys, living and fossil *Homo*—all are descendants of common ancestors. At some vastly distant and as yet undetermined time their keels were laid down in the same port; but their voyages have been in different directions. The evolutionary history of the nonhuman primates has been toward specialization. Man has, on the other hand, continued comparatively undifferentiated; he has retained his plasticity. Possibly the living apes and monkeys escaped the pressures of severe environmental stimulation. They could eat well without developing further their potentialities for intelligence. One student of the chimpanzee in its native habitat has speculated that the abundance of fruit and other food has encouraged the species to divert its energies into emotional channels. The chimpanzee's life has not been hard enough to force the development of new skills and of culture for survival. Man has suffered little from such over-mechanization, from "trained incapacity."

Nevertheless we must recognize our brutish relatives as cousins in behavior as well as in a thousand minutiae of anatomy and physiology. An infant chimpanzee brought up in a human family in exactly the same fashion as its adopted "brother" learned everything, except toilet control and walking, more rapidly than did the human child. Some of this animal's achievements seemed to involve reasoning. In the curious standard pattern of broken somersaults which Hamadryas baboons perform around sexually maturing individuals one may be glimpsing the prototype of human rites of passage. The adult male baboon will permit one of his wives whose sexual skin is swelling to take his food without reprisal. Do we not see here one step in the evolution of altruism? Yerkes compares the mutual grooming of primates to the affectionate mutual delousing practiced by primitive people; he sees in such acts the evolutionary prototype of all social-service activities from the barber's to the physician's.

The difference between human and primate behavior is quantitative, not qualitative, save for speech and the use of symbols. Even in this respect, one must be cautious in speaking of a clear-cut qualitative distinction. Chimpanzees learned to manipulate a machine called the chimpomat. They learned that tokens of different colors would bring them varying numbers of grapes or bananas. They learned to reject brass or other worthless tokens. They learned to work for tokens and to keep them until they were next brought to the room where the chimpomats were. There was the same kind of variation range in speed of learning as among human subjects. The rudiments of speech—or at least differentiated cries—have been identified among monkeys as well as among chimpanzees and gibbons.

Just as the differences among the primates, including man, are gradations or steplike differences, so the kinship of all the primates to certain insignificant insect-eating little animals is also clear. All living things are part of a natural order, and men will do well to recognize their nature as animals. Man's history as an organism is incredibly ancient, and only to some extent can the limitations of this history be escaped or transcended through religion or other creations of the human mind.

However, that plasticity which is the distinctive feature of man as an animal does permit an amazing variety of adaptations. Few other animals live equally in the tropics, in the Arctic wastes, on high mountains, and in deserts. When a white man moves to the tropics there is an average lowering of 10 to 20 per cent in basal metabolism, but the individual variability is great. Various peoples eat putrefied wood, clay, snakes, vermin, and rotten meat or fish. Some tribes live almost exclusively on meat and fish, others mainly on vegetables. This flexibility has enabled man to survive in regions where animals more specialized in their food habits would have starved.

No other organism so manipulates its own body. The skull of infants is deformed into weird shapes without more damage than an occasional headache in the case of the more severe types of deformation. Noses, ears, waists, and even the sexual organs are subjected to cruel distortions. The fact that no culture has patterns that implement the full potential muscular repertory of the human body is shown by the exercise of the yoga cult. Yogis learn to vomit at will, to cleanse the stomach by swallowing and expelling a cloth, to practice colonic irrigation—which involves voluntary control over the relaxation of the anal sphincter muscles. On the other hand, certain limits to biological plasticity are attested by the fact that yogis have not been able to learn to open the urethral sphincters at will. The bladder is washed only after inserting a tube. The variety of sitting and walking postures and various uses of the great toe also show that no single culture employs all muscles in all possible ways. In fact, it is estimated that human beings in general perform muscular work to only about 20 per cent efficiency.

It is in large part because of this plasticity and because of what men can do with their minds and their hands that man has remained a single species. All men are symbol-using animals. All men use tools that are almost physiological objects or extensions of the bodily mechanism. Monkeys and apes have adapted by organic differentiations to the different environments in which they live and to environmental changes. The result is that there are many different species and genera and families that can no longer interbreed and have fertile offspring. Male and female of every human type can have children. Their adaptations have been made primarily in terms of their ways of life, their cultures.

This is not to say that man has remained uninfluenced by the evolutionary process. Human types, readily distinguishable in terms of a few features, have evolved. Natural selection and sexual selection have played their part. Human evolution has also been complicated by the factor of social institutions. In some societies one must marry the children of one's maternal uncles or one's paternal aunts. In other societies marriage with the children of one's paternal uncles is preferred. In still others marriage to cousins or other relatives is specifically forbidden. These and other kinds of social selection will, after some generations, result in the development of distinct physical types because of the differing selection and recombination of heredity materials involved.

During the earlier phases of human history, small bands lived for long periods in isolation. This had a double effect upon the evolutionary process. First, through the normal operation of the genetic mechanism some hereditary materials disappear. Second, if the isolation occurred in regions where the environmental pressures were somewhat special, those individuals who happened to vary in a direction helpful to survival under the special conditions would be more likely to perpetuate their stock. Of particular interest in this connection is the presence or absence of minerals that stimulate the ductless (endocrine) glands. It has, for example, been speculated that the ancestors of the Chinese and other Mongoloid types were isolated in a region of iodine deficiency during the period between the last two great glaciations.

In addition to the factors of natural, sexual, and social

selection and isolation, evolution is influenced by irregularities in the process by which the new organism gets chromosomes from its parents and by mutations (sudden alterations in the genetic materials). How and why mutations occur under normal conditions we do not know. Environmental stimulation may have a part in the process. We do know that mutations constantly occur. Perhaps in the long run Queen Victoria's greatest claim to fame will rest in the fact that a mutation for hemophilia took place in her body. Of all the countless mutations that occur only those finally survive that are either dominant or that give the individual greater chance for survival. Finally, evolution has been affected by the new combinations of genetic materials produced when race mixture occurs.

Thus, though natural selection has played its part in human evolution, chance variations, geographical isolation, and recombinations of hereditary materials have probably been more important. There also seem to be broad trends in the evolution of species and of whole groups of animals that go on more or less independently of environmental pressures and of isolation. Some variations, in other words, appear to be not random but rather the completion of a pattern predetermined by obscure forces in the biological inheritance of the species or family. Hooton views with alarm certain apparent tendencies in human evolution at present: "Man appears to be an animal that has entered upon a terminal and decidedly retrogressive course as respects not only his teeth, jaws, and face, but also his brain case, its contents, and many other body parts." Yet the extent to which human beings might consciously control the direction of the evolution of their kind is highly doubtful.

Certainly the processes involved in evolution are infinitely more complex than Darwin and Huxley imagined. Hence the social Darwinism that has pictured "advancement" as due solely to bitter competition, to "the war of all against all" is a gross oversimplification of the truth. As Morris Opler has eloquently written:

> Primates did not survive to become men because they were particularly strong, because they tended to match their bodies against other living forms, or because of special physical attributes which favored them in bloody competition. They survived because they were particularly sensitive and adaptable in their total reactions to each other, to other animals, and to their environment. Fitness has acquired a meaning in biology more subtle than that of victory in physical combat. We are coming to see that aggression, organic competition, and appeal to physical force apparently counted for little in the development of man and his precursors in the past. Even if we did not know this, we could be certain that they challenge his stability and his very existence today. It is time that political science and social science in general draw from these pertinent biological facts instead of from the organicism which has been so popular and so pernicious.

Some evolutionary variations have survival value in specialized environments. One may instance adaptations to extreme cold and heat. Eskimos and Tibetans are stocky, with a layer of fat; the peoples of Indonesia are slender with relatively large surface areas for evaporation of sweat; African Negroes have developed many sweat glands and deep pigment. A narrow nose is best adapted to the slow intake and warming of air in a cold climate. Yet narrow-nosed northern Europeans survive and reproduce in the tropics. Though other variations that evolution has brought to different human types are interesting curiosities and of some scientific importance, their significance as inevitably conditioning human life is slight.

The Japanese have an unusual muscle in their chests. Certain hereditary diseases such as hereditary optic atrophy and Oguchi's disease of the retina are more frequent in Japan. The

Bushmen of South Africa have a queer protuberance of the buttocks which scientists call by the delicious word, "steatopygia." The external genital organs of both male and female Bushmen also have an unusual conformation. The arteries around the ankle show a different incidence of various forms among certain healthy African Negroes and among whites of the same region. Ruptures of the navel at birth are markedly more frequent among East African Negroes than among East African whites. White men get bald much more frequently than men of other races. However, almost none of these differences—and the list could be considerably extended—are all-or-none differences. They reflect differing proportions of certain genes in varous populations. Probably more than 95 per cent of the biological equipment of any human being in the world is shared with all other human beings, including members of races popularly considered to be most distinct from his own. As a well-known physical anthropologist, W. W. Howells, has written:

> Our brains and theirs have the same structure, are fed by the same amount and kind of blood, are conditioned by the same hormones and titillated by the same senses; that is all well known, and nothing in their performance has ever been discovered to point the contrary.*

There is, of course, tremendous individual variability—based upon physical inheritance—in the appearance, strength, and capabilities of men. But these variations crosscut local, regional, and continental physical types. Nor do "race," language, and culture vary together. Occasionally an intermarrying group of people with a common language and culture—which Ellsworth Huntington has called a "kith"—may for

* From *The Heathens,* by William Howells. Copyright 1948 by William Howells. Reprinted by permission of Doubleday & Company, Inc.

some time be a distinctive and potent force, in part because of its special biological inheritance. The Puritans provide one of Huntington's good examples. They represented a selection from the total British population; they remained in relative biologic isolation in the New World for some generations so that their distinctive inheritance tended to be maintained by inbreeding. Note, however, that such a biological group does not correspond to the popular conception of a "race."

CHAPTER V

Race: A Modern Myth

UNTIL RECENTLY physical anthropologists were, more than anything else, describers and classifiers of the physical varieties of man. All living types of man belong to the same species. No populations have been completely isolated reproductively since their differentiation. Throughout human history there has been exchange of genes between different varieties of man. Some authorities are convinced that even the most ancient fossil men of Java, China, and Europe represented only geographical varieties or races of the same species.

In general biology the term "race" or "variety" is used to designate a group of organisms that physically resemble one another by virtue of their descent from common ancestors. Most living species of animals are more or less clearly differentiated into geographic races. When races are separated by migration barriers, the distinctions between them are definite and consistent. If two or more races come to inhabit the same territory over a long period of time, the differences are gradually erased, and the races are fused into a single population that is more variable than any of the original constituent elements.

There are undoubtedly human races. However, the make-up of breeding populations has shifted so frequently in the course of migrations that sharp demarcations are few. Moreover, human inheritance is so complex and so imperfectly known as yet that differences in visible physical features are not always sure guides to differences in ancestry. The extent of present confusion is indicated by the fact that the numbers of races distinguished by competent students range from two to two hundred. Hence, though the concept of race is genuine enough, there is perhaps no field of science in which the misunderstandings among educated people are so frequent and so serious. Racial classifications still published by certain physical anthropologists are in some respects meaningless or actually misleading in the light of contemporary knowledge about human inheritance. The significance of a sound genetic classification, if we had one, is not yet clear. The one thing certain is that in the modern world many peoples react suspiciously, defensively, or hostilely toward individuals who differ in obvious physical characteristics such as skin color, hair form, and nose shape.

Throughout human history, societies and individuals have been conscious of the differences that set them off from other societies and other individuals. Group spokesmen have been concerned to assert that their way of dressing, or marrying, or believing was intrinsically superior. Sometimes the existence of other customs has been treated as an insupportable affront to the pride of the group or the laws of its gods. This threat to the dominance of the one true way of life has stimulated wars or has, at least, provided handy rationalizations for them. Seldom, prior to the nineteenth century, however, were such differences in group habits explained as due to variations in the biological heredity of human societies.

Although ties of "blood" were certainly much invoked to support community loyalty, differences in custom were usually linked to divine gifts or instructions, to the inventions of bygone human leaders, or to other historical experiences of the group rather than to physical inheritance. In the ancient and medieval religions the idea of race had little or no place. Most of the great world religions have been deeply committed to the concept of universal brotherhood. Often this concept has included the explicit or implicit premise that brotherhood was a feasible goal because all human beings were the physical descendants of a single pair of original ancestors. The messianic religions have necessarily held the view that heathens were in error not because they were inherently inferior, but because they had known no opportunity to learn the true way.

In the past it has usually been the culturally alien rather than the biologically alien that has borne the brunt of religious as well as political antagonisms. The Bible describes vividly the drastic disillusionment resulting from marriages to non-Jews in the time of Ezra, but "blood" is treated as the secondary and accidental factor, culture as the essential. The self-isolation of the Jew in Christian Europe during the Middle Ages was more a matter of culture than of biology. Jewish motivations arose from the fervent desire to preserve intact a way of life, and especially a religion, and not from the wish to keep a line of blood unsullied—even though there were occasional references to "the seed of Abraham."

Only in the small primitive or folk society where almost everyone is in fact biologically related to almost everyone else have the primary loyalties been frequently anchored to blood kinship. In the cosmopolitan societies of the ancient world, in the nations that gradually emerged toward the close of the Middle Ages in Europe, the major shiftings of individuals and whole peoples were too numerous and too recent for any national or regional population to be victimized by the illusion of descent from common ancestors distinct from the ancestors of its neighbors.

It is true that, before the dawn of history, the Bushmen and other groups depicted the physical types of foreign peoples and that the Egyptians, three thousand years ago, pictured "the four races of man." Probably there has never been a time when any people was completely indifferent to the physical differences between itself and other peoples. But it is a historical fact that in the last hundred and fifty years awareness of these variations and emotional reactions to them have heightened enormously. The first Negroes in modern Europe were received in aristocratic households as equals; nor was intermarriage frowned upon. Certain European racial classifications of the seventeenth and eighteenth centuries lumped American Indians with Europeans. Until the beginning of the nineteenth century all inhabitants of Europe, except the Lapps, were considered a single race.

Why, then, in the late nineteenth and early twentieth centuries has a naïve biologism become rampant? An underlying condition to the flowering of this new mythology was undoubtedly the tremendous advance made by biological science. Men's minds were intoxicated by the revolutionary theories of Darwin, and by the immediately practical discoveries of Mendel, Pasteur, Lister, and a host of others. Most men, and especially Americans, want simple answers. In a world where living, however joyous at times, is always precarious and happiness is always threatened by present problems and unforseen contingencies, men lust after certainty. The absolutes of religion were weakened by the schisms within the Christian Church, on the one hand, and by historical criticism of the Bible and scientific findings, on the other. The movement was by no means complete, of course, but Western humanity tended to seek in science the security formerly supplied by religious faith. Physical science was to bring about a millennium of ease and comfort; biological science was to abolish all the ills to which flesh had been heir. The twain would rapidly answer all the riddles of the universe. What was more natural than to assume that the puzzling question of differences in the behavior of individuals and whole groups had been solved?

Prior to the mid-nineteenth century Europeans and Americans had theories that satisfied them as explanations of observed facts. The story of the sons of Noah helped to explain the presence of humans of different skin colors and general physical appearance. Other variations were dismissed as the will of God. There were no authoritative descriptions of biological mechanisms. In the seventeenth and eighteenth centuries there were a number of widely current speculations about the influence of climate on physique. The American Indians, for instance, were held by some to be the descendants of Phoenicians or of Welsh adventurers or of the lost tribes of Israel, with their distinctive appearance explained as having been produced by the physical environment of the New World.

The discoveries of Darwin, Mendel, and others put everything on a new footing. From the popular point of view, laws had been evolved that stated immutable and watertight connections between biological processes and all sorts of other phenomena. A magic key had been created which unlocked all previous perplexities about human behavior. Unfortunately, the step from science to mythology is short and all too attractive.

An investigation by A. M. Tozzer of a large number of contemporary biographies showed very dramatically the hold biological mythology has upon our thinking. In every case the biographer seized upon physical heredity as the explanation of the personality traits of his subject. Where no plausible ancestors were available, legends were used or invented. Perhaps the most farfetched of these was the fantasy that the true father of Abraham Lincoln was Chief Justice John Marshall.

The fact that human beings usually acquire their physical and most of their culture heritage from their parents has helped perpetuate these beliefs. It is part of common experience that peculiar traits do "run in families," but this does not necessarily prove that these traits are inherited in the genetic sense. Parents train their children by the same standards that were invoked when they were children; happy children take their parents as models. In homogeneous and relatively stable cultures, family traits may be perpetuated for generations, even though "the blood line" is broken again and again—as is evidenced by Japanese and Roman lineages where remarkable continuity of character was preserved in spite of frequent adoptions to keep the family line intact.

Misconception is also generated by the circumstance that personality development ordinarily goes on at the same time that the child is growing up physically; both types of development usually stop or at least slow up at about the same time. In general, the status of adulthood implies both physical and social maturity. Since the two forms of development occur side by side, there is a tendency to assume that both are the expression of the same process, that is, biological maturation. A human animal, however, can easily come to physical maturity without learning to speak, use table utensils, or keep himself clean. Children do not stop crying over frustration because of progressive atrophy of the tear ducts or change in the vocal cords, but because they are taught to respond in other ways. In the process of getting food, shelter, and other prerequisites for normal physical growth, most individuals encounter conditions, both social and physical, which force them to accept those responsibilities and restraints which are considered the hallmarks of socialized adults. If children become responsible adults through the operation of biological processes, home and school training is a waste of energy. Every parent and teacher knows that children do not automatically become socially mature as they mature physically.

The same exaggeration of the role of biological forces may be noted in popular notions about different peoples. Here also, the fact that "race" and life habits vary together has fostered the impression that both are due to the common cause of biological heredity. However, a closer inspection of the facts shows that this inference is untenable. Not only do Canadians, Australians, and New Zealanders show different typical personality structures from each other and from their relatives in Britain, but the British stock in the same environment has had a different character at various historical periods. Between the sixteenth and nineteenth centuries there were no successful invasions of Britain, no substantial introduction of new materials of physical heredity. And yet Franz Boas rightly contrasts "the boisterous joy of life of Elizabethan England and the prudery of the Victorian age; the transition from the rationalism of the eighteenth century to the romanticism of the beginning of the nineteenth century." In American Indian tribes where the percentage of mixed bloods is still trifling, the personality types most frequently encountered today are not at all those described by writers at the time of the original contact with white men. Furthermore, it has been demonstrated again and again that a child brought up in a foreign society acquires the life ways and the characteristic personality traits of the foreign "race." If pigmentation or other physical differences are obvious, these may create special problems for him in his new social group, but where these are not conspicuous he fits in as well as the native-born.

However, this argument must not be made to explain too much. Overemphasis upon social conditioning is just as harmful and one-sided as making a magic key of biology. Nothing can be more certain than that any individual's physical characteristics resemble those of his relatives more than those of a random sample of the population at large—and obviously this resemblance cannot be due to training or to imitation. Good predictions can be made as to what proportion of the descendants of an original couple will manifest a certain physical peculiarity of the parents—provided the number involved is large. Anyone's temperamental and intellectual traits are partially determined by the genes supplied by his ancestors, but it is definitely established that these are not the only influences of importance.

As usual, however, the generalization of a scientific theory is too simply conceived and explains too much. The fact that simple questions can be put does not mean that there are simple answers. To say that physical heredity is enormously important in understanding the appearance and behavior of human beings is one thing. But it is quite another to jump from this correct statement to the implications: *(a)* that biological inheritance is the only important factor and *(b)* that one may pass easily from talking about the hereditary equipment of individuals to that of groups.

Superficially, biology might seem to give scientific support to racist theories. If physical heredity admittedly sets limits to the potentialities of individuals, "isn't it just common sense to believe that the pecularities of various groups of individuals are the consequence of their genetic equipment?" The thinking, often completely sincere, of those who follow this line of reasoning is weakened by a number of major errors. They forget that race is strictly a biological concept; they erroneously transfer what is known about individual inheritance to group inheritance; they greatly underestimate biological complexities and their interactions with nonbiological processes; they overestimate present knowledge of the mechanisms of inheritance.

To classify human beings as a race on other than a purely biological basis destroys the proper meaning of the term and removes even the support provided by the one-sided biological argument. "Aryan" is a linguistic designation. Hence "the Aryan race" is a contradiction in terms. As Max Müller remarked long ago it makes about as much sense as a "brachycephalic dictionary" or a "dolicocephalic grammar." Unless there were grounds for believing—which there most certainly are not—that all individuals who speak "Aryan" (Indo-

European) languages are descendants of the same ancestors, there could be no justification for confusing linguistic and biological classifications. Similarly, nationality and "race" must not be confused. To speak of "the Italian race" is nonsense, for there is every reason to assume that the Italians of Piedmont share more ancestors with persons who are French or Swiss than they do with their fellow Italians of Sicily. "The Jewish race" is equally a misnomer because there is great diversity in physical type among those who practice or whose parents or grandparents have practiced the Jewish religion and because the physical stereotype which is popularly considered Jewish is actually common among all sorts of Levantine and Near Eastern peoples who are not and have never been Jewish in religion or in other aspects of culture.

Jews have mixed so much with the varying physical types of the different countries in which they have lived that by no single physical or physiological feature nor by any group of such features can they be distinguished as a race. Huntington regards them as a kith, like the Icelanders, the Parsis, and the Puritans. That some Jews can be identified on sight is due less to physically inherited traits, than, as Jacobs says, to "those emotional and other reactions and conditionings which take the form of distinctive facial behavior, bodily posturings and mannerisms, sentence tone, and temperamental and character peculiarity" which can be traced to Jewish customs and to the treatment of Jews at the hands of non-Jews.

In the light of the biological preoccupation of our recent thinking, the naïve view that there *must* be a connection between physical type and character type is understandable. The "personality" of the poodle *is* different from that of the police dog. The temperament of the Percheron *is* different from that of the Arabian race horse.

Men are animals. But *man* is a very special kind of animal, and the transfer of observations from nonhumans to humans dare not be made so glibly. In the first place, nonhuman animals derive their character and personality mainly from their physical heredity, though domestic animals are also influenced by training. While animals learn from experience, they learn hardly more than crude survival techniques from each other. The factor of social heredity is unimportant. A diving bird brought up in complete isolation from all other birds of its species will still dive like its ancestors when released near a body of water. A Chinese boy, however, brought up in an English-speaking American household, will speak English and be as awkward at using chopsticks as any other American.

And so, though the fact that nonhuman animals of similar physical appearance behave in about the same way is correctly interpreted as due mainly to their genetic relationship, the matter is not so simple when it comes to the human animal. The existence of physical stereotypes for human groups that live in the same area or speak the same language or practice the same religion is probably to be traced to the preconception that organisms that resemble each other in action ought to resemble each other in physique. In any such group there *are* large numbers of individuals who are closely related biologically and who approximate a certain physical norm. The lay observer focuses his attention on these similar persons and either fails even to notice the others or dismisses them as exceptions. We thus get the persistent stereotype of the Swede as blond and blue-eyed. Dark Swedes are commented upon with surprise, though, in fact, blond individuals are distinctly in a minority in a number of districts in Sweden.

Among nonhuman animals resemblance in physical appearance is a fair basis for assuming close relationship. If two dogs who look like pure Dachshunds breed, we are amazed if any of the puppies look like fox terriers, police dogs, or Airedales.

But if a man and a woman whom ten competent physical anthropologists classify as "pure Mediterranean" marry, their ten children may approach in varying degrees the Mediterranean, Alpine, and Atlanto-Mediterranean types.

Wild animals ordinarily breed only with others of the same type. The lines of most domestic animals are kept pure by human control of breeding. There are exceptions, such as mongrel dogs. But virtually all human beings are mongrels! For countless thousand of years human beings have been wandering over the surface of the globe, mating with whomever opportunity afforded or fancy dictated.

The significance of physical heredity in family lines is not to be minimized. But heredity acts only in lines of direct descent, and there is no full unity of descent in any of the existing races. The observable physical types, just as the varieties of nonhuman animals, arose mainly as a consequence of geographic isolation. Physical differences which characterize all animal races are in large measure the product of chance samplings which took place at the time ancestral groups separated, plus accumulated variations that have occurred since the groups became isolated, plus certain inherent trends.

It should not be forgotten, furthermore, that we know much less about the details of human heredity than about animal heredity. This is due partly to the greater complexities involved, and partly to the fact that we do not experiment with human beings. Also, men mature so slowly that the statistics of ordinary matings do not accumulate as rapidly as those of laboratory animals. Since the beginnings of recorded history in Egypt there have been only 200 human generations, while the mouse has had 24,000.

One difference between humans and nonhumans is the fact of preferential mating. In some societies one is expected to marry one's maternal first cousin; in others one may not marry so close a relative. But the important difference is that animal races tended to remain in geographical isolation, and did not interbreed with other races of the same species. With humans, however, continual intermixture, often among the most diverse types, has been the rule in history's broad perspective. Looking at particular societies within the framework of a narrower time span, one can indeed point to populations isolated on islands, in inaccessible valleys, or infertile deserts where inbreeding in a relatively small group has prevailed over some hundreds of years. The same has been true for royal families and other special groups. Lorenz has shown that in 12 generations the last German emperor had only 533 actual ancestors as compared with a theoretical 4,096.

Undoubtedly there are local physical types. This is true not only of populations of small islands and of peasant groups. Hooton's studies of American criminals have revealed the existence of fairly well-differentiated regional types in the United States. In such instances relative genetic homogeneity and stability have been attained. This, however, is recent. A longer time perspective shows that such homogeneity is based upon an underlying heterogeneity. If one compared the number of different ancestors such groups had during the past ten thousand years with the number of different ancestors of a horde of South American monkeys or of African zebras during the same period, the human population would prove to have drawn from a significantly larger number of genetic lines. In any case the total of such recently isolated and inbreeding populations is small. Throughout Europe, the Americas, Africa, and Asia, constant formation of new and largely unstable blends has been the keynote of the past thousand years. This means that the diversity of genetic strains in even a superficially similar population is great. It means also that outward resemblance in two or more individuals is not necessarily indicative of common descent, for the similarities may be the product of chance combinations of characters derived from an altogether different set of ancestors. Practically no one can even name all of his ancestors for seven generations. If we except connection through the dynastic line of Charlemagne, there is probably not a single European family, save the Byzantine Palaeologues and Spanish Jews such as the de Solas, that has a bona fide pedigree going back before A.D. 800 even in the name line.

Europeans or Americans who can place those ancestors from whom they take their family names are all too likely to underestimate ludicrously the mixed nature of their ancestry. They feel that the statement, "Oh, we come of English stock," is an adequate description of "racial affiliation." If pressed, they will admit that the recent population of England represents an amalgam of physical strains brought in by Stone Age, Bronze Age, Saxon, Dane, Norman, and other invaders. But few of us can even imagine the tremendous diversity that would be represented by the total assemblage of our ancestors, during even the past thousand years. Charles Darwin was a member of a middle-class family:

> . . . we think of his mind as a typical English mind, working in a typical English manner, yet when we come to study his pedigree we seek in vain for 'purity of race'. He is descended in four different lines from Irish kinglets; he is descended in as many lines from Scottish and Pictish Kings. He had Manx blood. He claims descent in at least three lines from Alfred the Great, and so links up with Anglo-Saxon blood, but he links up also in several lines with Charlemagne and the Carlovingians. He sprang also from the Saxon Emperors of Germany, as well as from Barbarossa and the Hohenstaufens. He had Norwegian blood and much Norman blood. He had descent from the Dukes of Bavaria, of Saxony, of Flanders, the Princes of Savoy, and the Kings of Italy. He had the blood in his veins of Franks, Alamans, Merovingians, Burgundians, and Longobards. He sprang in direct descent from the Hun rulers of Hungary and the Greek Emperors of Constantinople. If I recollect rightly,

Ivan the Terrible provided a Russian link. There is probaly not one of the races of Europe concerned in the folk wanderings which has not a share in the ancestry of Charles Darwin. If it has been possible in the case of one Englishman of this kind to show in a considerable number of lines how impure is his race, can we venture to assert that if the like knowledge were possible of attainment, we could expect greater purity of blood in any of his countrymen? What we are able to show may occur by tracing an individual in historic times, have we any valid reason for supposing did not occur in prehistoric times, wherever physical barriers did not isolate a limited section of mankind?

—KARL PEARSON

When I was a student in England, I used to be annoyed at advertisements in British newspapers: "Americans! Descent traced to Edward III, £100!" I felt this was another evidence of the European playing upon the gullibility of my fellow countrymen. But, if the American could name a single ancestor in an English parish registry, the chances were good that his ancestry could be traced to Edward III, or to any other Englishman living at that period who left a number of adult children in a place where records were preserved.

By the laws of chance, essentially every person whose ancestry is at least half European can include Charlemagne in his "family tree." But he is equally descended from the bandit hanged on the hill, from the half-witted serf, and from every other person living in A.D. 800 who left as many descendants as did Charlemagne. The principal difference between the family of the snob and the "lower-class" citizen is that the former has the money to pay a genealogist to trace or to fake a lineage. The amusing thing about those who maintain that "blood will tell" (over the distance of eleven centuries) is that they are usually too ignorant to realize that a man of 1948 may be able truly to claim Charlemagne as a forefather without having any trace of Charlemagne's "blood." The child gets not all but only a random assortment of the genes of the father and mother. A person could have Charlemagne as his own great-grandfather and still not have inherited a single one of Charlemagne's genes. Over more than thirty generations the betting odds are excellent that few of that fabled emperor's genes exist at all in certain localities where he has many descendants, whereas some of them may well constitute part of the genetic equipment of practically all peasants in isolated Swiss valleys.

In Darwin's time heredity was thought to be a matter of continuous aggregates of materials. A new organism's inheritance was the result of blending the total hereditary potential of the father with that of the mother. In these terms it made a little sense to believe that any descendant of Charlemagne had a portion (albeit diluted) of what had made the emperor great.

But the studies of the famous monk, Gregor Mendel, led to the discovery that every child got part and only part of the germ plasm of each parent. This meant that the children of the same parents (except multiple births formed from a single egg) had a different heredity. In fact, geneticists estimate that if a man and his wife had thousands of children no two would look exactly alike. This is because the particular heredity which a new organism gets from the two genetic lines that are crossing depends upon the accidental way in which the two germ cells exchange parts of chromosomes.

From the standpoint of the modern science of heredity (genetics), all snobbism that is supposed to be founded upon biological heredity from one or a few distant ancestors is essentially absurd. We have at present no techniques for determining all the genes an individual actually possesses. Human beings reproduce too slowly and have too few offspring to make it possible to use the methods that have been successfully applied to establishing genetic charts for other animals. With men we must go almost entirely by the appearance of the organism, if we wish to assign the individual to a race. In nonhuman animals this gives good results in practice. But the human beings of the great peoples and nations of the contemporary world have had ancestors of too diverse physical strains to make it likely that classifications on the basis of similarities in appearance correspond to the true genetic picture. Groups of different appearance may have drawn from the same pool of ancestors; groups of the same appearance perhaps from different pools of ancestors.

Human populations are too mongrel and too variable to be grouped into races as meaningful as animal varieties. A classification on the basis of their genes is not yet possible. The classifications by appearance are not consistent. There are almost as many different groupings as there are physical anthropologists. The difficulties physical anthropologists have in reaching agreement on race classification is testimony that the data do not fall neatly and nicely into line as they ought to do if they truly represent an order in nature. Of course in all biological classifications there are some borderline instances and some disagreements among specialists as to what the standards for a separate variety, species, or genus should be. Among anthropologists one too often gets the impression that almost every case is a borderline case; and, even when there is agreement as to standards, there is dispute as to whether a given individual or group of individuals meet them. With some qualifications and exceptions, one may say that, if all living people were ranged in a single sequence according to degree of resemblance, there would be no sharp breaks in the line but rather a continuum where each specimen differed from the next by almost imperceptible variation.

Classifications made according to different sets of criteria either badly overlap or hardly meet at all. A map of world distribution of head form does not fit at all well with one for stature or one for skin color. In some instances relatively consistent divisions can be made on the basis of particular combinations of a few such characteristics. The researches of Boas, Shapiro, and others have cast doubt on the fixity of these characteristics. German and Russian children who suffered from the famines following World War I differed markedly from their parents both in stature and in head form. Over longer time spans the changes are still more startling. For example, one group of "Nordics" appears to have become twelve points more round-headed between 1200 B.C. and A.D. 1935.

If the physical characteristics chosen as a basis for racial classification are susceptible of rapid modification under environmental pressure, how can the classification be presumed to represent ancient genetic divisions? As W. M. Krogman, one of the leading American physical anthropologists, has recently written: "A race at best is not a clearly defined biogenetic entity; it is now seen to have a transitory definition as well. It is plastic, malleable, varying with time, with place, and with circumstances."

Even if one were willing to waive this problem of the adaptiveness or stability of the standards, the stubborn and irreducible fact is that no world-wide system encompassing a multiplicity of physical characteristics and taking account both of similarities and of differences has ever stood the test of criticism in the light of historically known movements of peoples and intermixture between them. The results given by one set of measurements fail to fit the picture obtained from another set. This discrepancy might be explained on the ground that the traditional measurements made by orthodox physical anthropology are hardly chosen in accord with the knowledge of growth that recent experimental biology has provided. The same thing applies to divisions on the basis of blood-group frequencies (the only criterion widely used where the actual genetic mechanisms are well worked out), skin color, hair form, and the like. Racial researches founded upon blood-group data were unpopular in Germany, largely, one may suspect, because such studies showed that some parts of Germany had frequency distributions almost identical with parts of Negro Africa.

It is the large number of genes and the fact that they are for the most part transmitted independently which explains the inconsistency of the subgroupings of mankind. Such a superficial characteristic as the difference in skin color between Europeans seems to be due to rather few genes, but R. A. Fisher's statistical analysis of data collected by Karl Pearson indicates that skeletal differences are due to a large number of genes. If the various genes responsible for a particular set of observable characteristics stuck together, popular theories about race would be more nearly true. If human genes behaved like the genes of the common snail whose offspring usually get all or none of the different genes that determine a particular shell pattern, there would be a solid measure of stability and predictability in human physical types. But even where linkage of genes does occur this endures for only a few generations in a human population. After a number of generations of breeding at random the linked genes have a chance distribution within the group.

One objection may be raised to the argument thus far, and it must be met. Some critics will say, "There is something to your point of view in so far as European races and other small racial subdivisions are concerned. But your criticisms are entirely inapplicable to the major racial stocks: Negro, white, and Mongoloid." It is true that the term "race" has been used in scientific discourse to apply to entities that are not strictly comparable. When applied to a small population, long isolated (the aboriginal Tasmanians, for example), the word may have a meaning almost comparable to that which it has when applied to nonhuman animals. If a small group has inbred long enough to attain genetic stability and homogeneity, one can speak of group as well as individual heredity. If one knows the hereditary characters of the group as a whole, useful predictions can be made about the genetic equipment of any individual in the group. However, such groups are better called "breeds" to avoid confusion. In any case their existence has little relevance to the problems of race in the contemporary world.

The second type of entity is that represented by the Nordic, Alpine, East Baltic, Mediterranean, and other "races" of Europe and by comparable subdivisions of the other two great stocks. These may be described correctly and briefly, in scientific jargon, as "phenotypic statistical abstractions." That is, they are classifications based wholly on similarities in appearance where such similarity is by no means proof of underlying genetic equivalence. As Boas and others have demonstrated, the curves of variation for two family lines within the same "race" may fail to overlap at all for certain features, whereas one of them may closely approximate that of another family line in a completely different race.

No one has ever seen a "Nordic" who conformed in every detail to the type description of Nordics given by various physical anthropologists, unless one means the very simple popular formula occasionally also given by anthropologists defining a Nordic as a blond, blue-eyed, long-headed, narrow-nosed individual. "Nordic"—as precisely defined by a long list of measurements and observable characteristics—is an abstraction in the minds of the scientists. The "Nordic race" is made up, according to one view, of populations that, considered statistically, show average or modal distributions which tend to fit this ideal picture. According to another current view, the "Nordic race" is made up of individuals who show more Nordic than non-Nordic traits or who have an assemblage of physical traits each of which, though no one of them may fit the type description perfectly, approaches the standards set. That is, individuals are selected from a population, and the selected group is called "Nordic," even though few individuals come close to identity with the imaginary type of the "pure Nordic."

Now of course physical anthropologists may pick out all the individuals in the world who look more or less alike, though there will be plenty of disagreements among the anthropologists when it comes down to cases. One might also group together all persons whose left leg is slightly shorter than their right, who have at least one mole on the chest, etc. This at least could be done reliably and validly. But the tough-minded will ask: what good does it do other than keeping some people rather harmlessly employed? At most, one may grant a descriptive convenience for some purposes and the satisfaction of a perhaps not very scientific curiosity. As Whitehead has long pointed out, classification is never more than a halfway house in science. The classifiers who have dealt with such "races" have continued to go their way, serenely unaware of the results of experimental biology and Mendelian genetics. Geneticists today agree that it is the geographical distribution of the genes which needs to be studied.

Turning to the "stocks" it must be freely granted that here one cannot dismiss racism so easily. While the best physical anthropologist in the world can't look at a hundred white individuals and say with 70 per cent correctness, "the parents of *A* were Nordic and Alpine, of *B* both Mediterranean, etc.," almost everyone one can look at the child of a pure white or a pure Negro and correctly guess the racial stocks of the two parents. This is a fact, and there must be no attempt to explain it away. On the other hand, the significance of this fact must not be exaggerated. That skin color, hair form, shape of the eye, shape of the lips, and other physical features persist in unmistakable form for many generations does not prove that the carriers of these variations also share mental and emotional capacities that distinguish them equally sharply. The number of hereditary trait–potentialities *known* to differ (between groups, not individuals) is very small. Indeed one anthropologist, M. F. Ashley Montagu, has estimated that less than 1 per cent of the total number of genes is involved in the differentiation between any two existent races. Another, S. L. Washburn, expresses that same idea in terms of human evolution by saying, "If the time from the divergence of human and ape stems to the present be represented by an ordinary pack of fifty-two playing cards placed end to end, all racial differentiation would be on less than one-half of the last card."

The variations within the three major racial stocks must not be minimized. In the popular mind "a Negro is a Negro." To the scientist the matter is not so simple. A prominent geneticist, in fact, sees evidence that the differences between two groups of African Negroes are greater than the differences between one of them and various "white" races. Certainly it is true that for many measurements and characters the differences between "whites" and "Negroes" are less than the range of variation found in either stock considered by itself. It is likewise true that in crosses between whites and the Negroes of South Africa, skin color is often inherited separately from head shape and a "white" type turns up in the hybrids, whereas in the second generation of West African–European crosses the European type rarely, if ever, is observed.

The traditional notion of race is essentially a scholastic one: that is, races are regarded as fixed entities that can be sharply distinguished on the basis of simple physical variation in hair, eye, skin, bodily dimensions, and proportions. But the physical types of human groups are not unchanging. Even the genetic constitution has been demonstrated to have an orbit of plasticity. The dividing lines are far from sharp. Rather, there is a gradual merging of all populations of the present day. The biological oneness of mankind is far more significant than the relatively superficial differences.

The crucial flaw in the older view of "race" is that it does not square with present knowledge of the process of physical heredity. If "bloods" mixed as alcohol and water mix, there would be many pure "races," and populations could be correctly described by statistical averages. But with separate and independent genes, a child is, in the genetic sense, the child of his parents but hardly of his "race." "A race defined as a system of averages or modal points," says Dobzhansky, "is a concept that belongs to the pre-Mendelian era, when the hereditary materials were pictured as a continuum subject to a diffuse and gradual modification. . . . The idea of a pure race is not even a legitimate abstraction; it is a subterfuge used to cloak one's ignorance of the phenomenon of racial variation."

Local variations undoubtedly exist. In colonies of flies living only about one hundred meters apart statistically significant racial differences have been observed. It is probable that the incidence of particular genes is appreciably different in human villages of the same population. Broader geographical variations are also likely, but until the distribution of human genes has been mapped—a task that has barely begun—we must not jump to sweeping conclusions on the basis of a few superficial characteristics that happen to have high social-stimulus value. Our present knowledge of the genetics of human populations has been obtained by traveling in a rowboat over a vast sea of ignorance and dropping a sounding lead here and there.

It is one thing to say that subgroupings of mankind thus far proposed are not to be taken too seriously. It would be quite another to suggest that no meaningful subgroupings are discoverable. It is one thing to insist that the evidence we now have indicates that the differences between human societies are not primarily traceable to different biological inheritance. It would be quite another to imply that varying physical heredity played no role of importance.

Because race prejudice leads to social and international sickness there is the temptation to deny without sufficient evidence all validity and significance to the concept of race even in the sense of "breed" or "stock." The fact that current popular notions of "race" are largely mythological and without acceptable scientific underpinning should not lead us to throw the baby out with the bath. Without question, certain external physical characteristics are more frequent among some peoples than among others. If this were all, we might let the matter rest by remarking that—so far as present scientific knowledge goes—the principal importance of the several physical types of mankind is that they do possess features which have a high degree of social visibility. The fact that human beings react negatively to other human beings must not be overlooked.

However, it is now known that there are at least some differences in physiological processes among the major racial stocks. Most of these differences are, to be sure, only differences in frequency of occurence of the characteristic in question and do not represent all-or-none variations. For example, the Rh blood factor which is connected with a fatal condition at or before birth is far more frequent among American whites than among American Negroes and hardly occurs at all among the Chinese and Japanese. Nevertheless it must be emphasized that no "blood" is diagnostic of all individuals in any "race" or stock. All of the four main blood groups turn up in all "races" and stocks.

Mental, temperamental, and character traits are almost impossible to isolate in pure form because from the very day of birth the influence of social tradition modifies the biologically inherited trends. It is, however, more than possible that the potentialities for such traits are present in different proportions among the various human stocks. The distribution of musical and other special capacities does not appear to be equal in all peoples. Biological causes are probably involved; and, even though these account for only a small fraction of cultural differences, they are still true causes. Here also, unhappily, it is easier to say what anthropology has found *not* to be the case than to present substantiated positive findings.

To some degree physical traits and mental qualities are found associated in ordinary experience. This coexistence is probably due much more to similarities in life experience and training among peoples who share the same color or other physical traits, than to biological heredity. There is no evidence whatever that the genes which determine skin color or hair form are correlated with genes influencing temperament or mental capacity. The idea of deducing character from color is intrinsically absurd. The English setter and the Irish setter have the same temperament, though the latter is red-haired and the former white with spots. No one thinks of determining the temperament of a horse by using a color chart. In a well-mixed population that is more or less homogeneous biologically there is no correlation between traits due to different genes. As Haldane has pointed out:

> For example, if we consider Central and Northern Europe, we find a considerable correlation between hair color and cranial index. As we go north the hair becomes, on the whole, fairer, and the skull longer. We find the same correlations in England as a whole. But if we take a well-mixed population—say, from an English rural area, a population whose members have been intermarrying for many centuries—we find that this correlation disappears. A long-headed man is no more likely to have blue eyes than a short-headed. It also follows that a man with blue eyes is no more likely to have a specially large proportion of Anglo-Saxon or Scandinavian ancestors than a brown-eyed man in the same village.

The fragility of popular impressions about "racial" temperament is attested by the fluctuation in stereotypes. In 1935 most Americans characterized the Japanese as "progressive," "intelligent," and "industrious." Seven years later these adjectives had given place to "sly" and "treacherous." When the Chinese were wanted as laborers in California they were "thrifty," "sober," and "law-abiding"; whereas, when the Exclusion Act was being advocated, they had become "filthy," "loathsome," "unassimilable," "clannish," and "dangerous."

A scientific evaluation of the historical achievements of different peoples is next to impossible because of lack of agreement on standards. To many American soldiers the natives of India appeared "dirty" and "uncivilized." But to Hindu intellectuals Americans seemed incredibly "boorish," "materialistic," "unintellectual," and equally "uncivilized." While the not inconsiderable cultural creations of Negro Africa are too little known to Westerners, it is true that the total richness of Negro civilizations is at least quantitatively less impressive than that of Western or Chinese civilization. However, some facts should not be forgotten. The twelfth-century Negro university at Timbuktu compared favorably with contemporary European universities—as did the general level of civilization in the three great Negro kingdoms of that time. The iron working which is so important a base of our technology may be a Negro creation. In any case, the anthropologist thinks it more valid to attribute this quantitative difference to the geographical isolation of Africa, and to historical accidents. Environmental factors always make it hard to estimate the innate capacities of peoples. For example, English writers often speak of the Bengalis of India as "naturally intellectual" and of the Marathas as "natively warlike." But the Bengali plains are chronically infested with malaria and hookworm, the hills of Maratha comparatively free of these diseases debilitating to aggressive energy. It is fortunate for us that the Romans did not decide that our unpromising forefathers, crude barbarians of the British and German forests, were incapable of absorbing or creating a high civilization.

Whether intelligence tests measure "intelligence" is an arguable question, yet they are the only bases for comparison we have that are standardized and possess any pretensions to objectivity. They indicate that highly gifted children turn up among all peoples. One American Negro, apparently "pure-blooded," was found to have an I.Q. of 200. As for groups, Negro children in Tennessee averaged 58, those in Los Angeles 105. This range shows that Intelligence Quotient is not determined mainly by "racial" capacity. In World War I, Negroes from certain Northern states who could read and write obtained higher averages on Army Alpha tests than did literate whites from certain Southern states. Negroes from Ohio and Indiana proved superior to whites from Kentucky and Mississippi in both Alpha and Beta tests. These and similar figures parallel too closely the relative amounts spent on education in various states and with other environmental conditions for the correlation to be mere coincidence. In 1935–1936 California expended more than $115 per year per child. Mississippi spent less than $30 per white child and about $9 per Negro child. And it has been proved that Negro children who move from the South into the North are not superior in "intelligence," as measured by these tests, when they first come North.

The tendency to rate biological groups as inferior or superior to one another is due in part to a holdover from Darwinian thinking. Just as the conceptions of heredity among educated people have not yet caught up with the facts and theories of today's genetics, so also most of us tend to cling to vague notions about straight-line evolution. We have a propensity for ranking everything in a "scale of evolution," usually being careful to put our own group at the top of this "scale." Such thinking lags far behind scientific knowledge.

There is no evidence from the biological point of view that "race" mixture is harmful. Some anthropologists assert that crosses between "races" are harmless or even beneficial but that crosses between the three major stocks are deleterious. However, few data support this assertion. Fleming, an English anthropologist, discovered dentofacial disharmonies in the progeny of Negro-white hybrids crossed with Negro-Chinese and Chinese-European hybrids. Even here it is possible that dietary deficiencies modified the strictly genetic influence.

This whole problem is enormously complicated by social conditions and attitudes. Almost everywhere matings between persons of different stocks are so disapproved that most of them occur in the lower economic strata; the parents and their children are forced to live as social outcasts. In those few instances (the Pitcairn Islanders, for example) where mixed bloods have had a fair chance, they seem by universal judgment to be superior in most particulars to either of the parent groups. Even under conditions of discrimination but where malnourishment has not been characteristic, the hybrids have been better specimens physically: taller, longer-lived, more fecund, healthier.

The phenomenon of "hybrid vigor" appears to be as important among humans as among other animals. The record of history likewise indicates that mongrel peoples are more creative than the more inbred groups. Almost all of the civilizations that humanity agrees were most significant (Egypt, Mesopotamia, Greece, India, China) arose where divergent peoples met. Not only was there cross-fertilization from varying ways of life, but there was also interchange of genes between contrasting physical strains. It does not seem implausible that this also had its part in those great bursts of creative energy.

Nowhere in the "race" field is mythology more blatant or more absurd than in the beliefs and practices relating to "miscegenation." The people who are the most convinced that Negroes have a special innate psychology are the very ones who will explain the abilities of a light-colored "Negro" by his "white blood." Yet Mendelian genetics tells us that there is no reason to believe that such an individual has appreciably fewer genes for "Negro temperament" than the darker brothers and sisters in the same family. Of course the utter illogicality of popular belief is reflected by the fact that anyone with a small proportion of "Negro blood" is always called Negro, whereas it would be just as reasonable to call everyone with a small amount of "white blood" white.

While anthropological outlook and anthropological researches must be kept open to the possibility that there exist differences between human populations that are significant in terms of capacities and limitations, the only scientific conclusion tenable at present is "not proven." Since we are accustomed to associate appearance (including costume) with distinct ways of behaving, we fall into the error of assuming that the qualities of temperament and of intelligence of "Negroes," for example, must necessarily, *on a biological basis*, be different from those of "whites." Our tendency is to exaggerate whatever biologically determined differences there may be, because of the fact that whites and Negroes, for example, have had very different cultural histories and, today, different opportunities. The general point is well made by Boas:

> The same individual does not behave in the same way under different cultural conditions and the uniformity of cultural behavior

observed in every well integrated society cannot be attributed to a genetic uniformity of the constituent individuals. It is imposed upon them by their social environment notwithstanding their great genetic differences. The uniformity of pronunciation in a community develops notwithstanding the great anatomical differences in the formation of the articulating organs. The appreciation of definite forms of graphic and plastic arts, of style of music are historically developed and shared by all those who participate in the cultural life of the group. The claim that there is a definite relation between the distribution of bodily build in a group and cultural behavior has never been proved. The mere fact that in a group a certain type prevails and that the group has a certain culture does not prove that these are causally connected. There are superior and inferior individuals, there are individuals of different mental characteristics, but nobody has ever proved that their cultural behavior is stable, independent of social history, and that similar behavior may not be found in every one of the large divisions of mankind.

There are tall individuals and short individuals, and this difference is undoubtedly conditioned by heredity. The average differences in physical characteristics between various human populations are, however, small compared to the overlap in the range of single features and the duplications of types in different races. Study of the variability of measurable characteristics in existent races and analysis of the few established genetic facts suggest that the same biological strains are represented in all large "racial" groups, though in varying fashion. There are no unchanging pure races, but rather populations whose physical characteristics have altered through time under the influence of domestication; natural, social, and sexual selection; environmental influences; spontaneous variations; inbreeding and outbreeding.

Gunther (who received the Goethe medal for art and science in 1941) tells us that the soul in the Dinaric race appears to be dark green. It is easy to recognize absurdities of this extravagance. But the subtle distortions of our thinking which arise from Darwinian (pre-Mendelian) conceptions are hard to eradicate. If we will think carefully through the implications of this statement by the distinguished Swedish biologist, Dahlberg, we will see clearly why—given the facts of human migrations and casual crossbreeding, "pure races" are strictly mythological:

> Before Mendel it was assumed that the inheritable matter is a substance and that, in the process of crossing the hereditary substances are mixed as when fruit juices and water are mixed. If a Negro is crossed with a white man, a simple dilution takes place, and the result is a mulatto. Half-bloods are then spoken of. If mulattoes are crossed, the result according to the older substance doctrine ought to be solely mulattoes, in the same way as, when two glasses of fruit juice of the same concentration are mixed one does not expect to get any difference in color. As a matter of fact, the crossing of mulattoes gives offspring ranging from more or less white to more or less black. The result agrees with Mendel's doctrine, according to which every individual possesses a mosaic of genes, all of which appear in pairs containing one gene from the father and one from the mother. In passing on, these genes are reshuffled. Half is discarded, and when the sperm cell fuses with the egg, a new mosaic is set up, which may have varying characters.

In summing up the discussion of race in the proper biological sense, the following points stand out. Popular thinking and some scientific work need to be brought up to date with Mendelian genetics and experimental biology generally. In an atmosphere where biological explanations were popular the tendency has been to neglect cultural and environmental factors and to jump to oversimple biological conclusions. There is no evidence that race mixture is harmful. There is no scientific basis for an over-all rating of races on a superiority-inferiority scale. Certain genes are present in different numbers in different human groups; however, the variability of all large human populations needs to be stressed.

Elementary geography books still list the white, black, yellow, brown, and red races. It is easy—and correct—to point out that five pigments and an optical effect (arising from the fact that the overlying layers of the skin are not transparent) are responsible for the skin color in all humans and that these pigments are present in the skins of all normal men and women (albinos lack a dark pigment called melanin). Hence differences in skin color are due only to the relative amounts of each pigment present, and there is continuous range of variation among living human beings. It is equally easy—and correct—to point out the difficulties inherent in the attempt to classify races on other than an arbitrary and inconsistent basis if one uses such criteria as head form, stature, or skeletal features.

Nevertheless, in conclusion, it must be emphasized that valid objections to all existent methods of classification do not constitute proof of the insignificance of racial differences. Let us not overlook the depths of our present ignorance on some relevant matters. For example, it is commonly said that most of the visible external characters used in racial classification are too trifling to assist or hinder the perpetuation of races in any way. Yet the survival of such differences seems unlikely unless selective factors are somehow involved. Weidenreich has recently concluded that an increase in brain size entails certain modifications of the skeleton. In other words, if he is right, bone changes not in themselves adaptive still reflect a change that has survival value. Further investigation may show that the older physical anthropologists used some of the right criteria but gave the wrong reasons for so doing and employed objectionable methods. On the other hand, it may turn out that the only significant classification must be based not on a somewhat random assortment of externals but on the relative numbers of somatotypes which represent the conformation of the whole body and presumably reflect organic differences and physiological functions. Although the similarities in human biology among all peoples are enormously important for the understanding of human life, there are also strong presumptive grounds for believing that the differences are likewise of some significance.

Is there an inborn tendency to withdraw from or be hostile toward people of different physical appearance? The evidence on this point is somewhat puzzling. On the one hand, one of the more remarkable findings of general biology is that of species cohesion. In the wild state, organisms which we know, from observation of specimens in captivity, can interbreed and have fertile offspring commonly do not do so. In nature, more often than not, animals avoid or are actively hostile to similar animals of different odor or appearance. On the other hand, the vast numbers of mulattoes in the United States can hardly be said to support this theory. In various lands there appears to have developed little repugnance to intermixture of groups of markedly different physical appearance. The absorption of substantial numbers of Negroes in eighteenth-century England, the attitude toward Negroes in France, the notable tendency of Portuguese and Dutch colonials to intermarry, or the virtually complete absorption of the Negro in Mexico (where at one time Negroes markedly outnumbered the whites) are all cases in point. In fact, as Huxley and Haddon have shown in *We Europeans*, a good case can be made for actual physical attraction between members of different human races where marked social bars have not existed. Even should an inherent tendency toward hostility be proved, this does not mean that such hostility should be accepted as unchangeable. Among the Mohammedans, in Brazil, and perhaps in Soviet Russia, the socially coherent groups are not "racially" uniform.

Present arbitrary racial classifications have exceedingly limited scientific utility, and their popular implications make them socially dangerous. A hundred years ago such terms were a convenience, for in many cases they indicated not only physical type but also geographical origin, language, and culture with a fair degree of probability. Today with the shiftings of population and social changes that have taken place these "brand names" lead more often than not to distorted or mistaken predictions. A "Negro" may be anything from very black to quite white in color; he may speak French, Arabic, English, American, Spanish, or Ashanti; he may be a chain-gang laborer or a world-famous chemist; he may be illiterate or may write polished Arabic or be an American college president. Even in strictly biological terms almost every "brand" is a "blend."

The physical anthropologist finds no basis for ranking "races" in relative order of superiority and inferiority. Even though the scientist finds evaluation untrustworthy, Western society has shown itself more than ready to pass unequivocal and harsh judgments. "Racial" discrimination is, to be sure, only one part of the more general problem of social discrimination. But modern man of Western Europe and the United States says, in effect, "If races do not exist, we must invent them." As someone has said, "In racial categories it is not nature but society that acts as judge." The really important factor in the contemporary scene is not the existence of biological "races" but of what Robert Redfield has called "socially supposed races." It is the association of a label with real or imagined biological differences and real cultural differences that brings about a "socially supposed" race. That the biological differences are not always apparent to the naked eye is proved by such facts as the Nazis' finding it necessary to compel "Jews" to wear the star of David so that good "Aryans" would always know a "Jew" when they saw one. Other biological variations presumed to distinguish "races" are in the realm of pure mythology. For instance, it is said that even octoroons will reveal their Negro "blood" through a one-piece nasal cartilage, whereas the fact of the matter is that not only all humans but even all monkeys and apes have a split cartilage. On the other hand, the general public pays no attention whatever to some differences that are real enough (*e.g.*, the relative flatness of the shin bone of some populations) because no one but a few anthropologists know that they exist.

During the nineteenth and early twentieth centuries in Europe a number of popularizers (notably Gobineau and Chamberlain) plucked the zoological idea of race from the tree of learning. By grafting it into a highly selective and lurid interpretation of history and by vivid writing, they won a wide audience for their glorifications of "Nordics," "Aryans," and "Teutons." Before the Civil War, various American apologists for slavery attempted by studies of skulls and living types to show that Negroes and whites were entirely different sorts of human beings, that Negroes indeed were much more closely related to the apes. These American writings were widely quoted in England, France, and Germany.

None of these men was a scientist, but they managed to convey that their fantasies had scientific warrant. Somehow a mixture of historical, economic, and intellectual circumstances had created an atmosphere favorable to the acceptance of these speculations, even in academic circles. The nineteenth century was the classic age of "race" making. Darwinian biology supported the assumption that there were some original races entirely blond and blue-eyed, others entirely dark-haired and dark-eyed. It is curious that a myth of an original red-haired "race" was not created, although there are large numbers of red-haired individuals among such peoples as the Irish, Scots, Jews, and Malays.

After the end of World War I, pseudo-scientific racism was systematically used for political demagoguery. Madison Grant's *The Passing of the Great Race* and Lothrop Stoddard's *Rising Tide of Color* were much invoked in connection with exclusionist legislation on immigration into the United States. These works were later quoted at length in Nazi writings. The data from "intelligence tests" given to American soldiers were distorted and misinterpreted to give the semblance of documentation to prejudice against Negro and foreign-born Americans.

In the recent twentieth century, as political and economic pressures became more intense in various parts of the world, the basic psychological workings of "race hatred" became clearer. Race prejudice is, fundamentally, merely one form of scapegoatism. When the security of individuals or the cohesion of a group is threatened, scapegoats are almost always sought and found. They may be either other individuals within the group or they may be an outside group. The first phenomenon may be observed alike in the chicken yard and in any human society. The second phenomenon seems to be the principal psychological basis for modern wars. This question of "what to do about hate satisfaction" faces every social order. This is the basic psychological process. Whether victims are defined as "witches" or as "unbelievers" or as "members of inferior races" depends upon circumstances and upon the types of rationalization that are fashionable at a given moment.

People who look different make easily identifiable objects of aggression. Moreover, if a speciously plausible "scientific" theory is at hand to show that this group is inherently inferior or evil, then one can have all the fun of venting one's spite against them without feeling guilty about it. Usually, however, a "safe-goat" and not a "scape-lion" is chosen. The weak seem to invite attack from some people, perhaps from most people who are themselves discontented. A minority group or a powerless, subdued majority are the usual mass victims of social aggression. If conflict between different "races" is presumed to be in the nature of things, then the good citizen who otherwise pays considerable deference to the sentiment of fair play need not have a troubled conscience. As Goethe said, we never feel so free from blame as when we expatiate on our own faults in other people.

In simple societies hostility is ordinarily directed against individuals who play specific roles: one's wife's relatives, medicine men, sorcerers, chiefs. In complex societies like ours many types of group conflict are observed. People acquire patterned dislikes of persons they have never seen, and these hates are not justified on the ground that all doctors are bad or all political leaders are untrustworthy but on the basis of membership in a group apart. Such stereotyped prejudices, of which race prejudice is only one, tend to be more intense in areas—such as recently industrialized sections—where social integration is low.

Economic conditions are stimulants to rather than causes of race prejudice. Aversion is not very active unless there is a real or imagined conflict of interests. "Race" relations may begin as economic problems but become social and cultural problems as soon as the minority attains awareness of the values of the dominant group and develops articulate leaders. In American society where great emphasis is placed upon success, but where many individuals fail to achieve it, the temptation to blame an "out-group" for one's own failure "to measure up" is especially strong. One survey showed that 38 per cent of those dissatisfied with their economic position also manifested anti-Semitism, whereas only 16 per cent of these in the same group who were content with their economic status expressed such views.

Americans like to personalize. It is psychologically more satisfying to blame "Wall Street operators" than "the laws of supply and demand," "Stalin's clique" than "communist ideology." Americans feel that they understand labor problems much better when a John L. Lewis can be singled out. This widespread tendency helps us to understand the persecution of scapegoats selected along the lines of supposed biological descent. American society is highly competitive, and many individuals lose out in the struggle. Economic security is very precarious, quite apart from individualized competition. Actually in a highly organized world economic structure most of us are more or less at the mercy of impersonal forces or at least of the decisions of individuals we never see and whom we cannot reach. Given a personalizing psychology, we feel better if we can identify definite persons as our enemies. A "racial" group can all too easily be identified as our opponents. There is almost always a grain of truth in the vicious stereotypes that are created, and this helps us swallow the major portion of untruth —because we must in order to find a partial escape from confusion.

The frustrations of modern life are sufficient to breed any number of latent and unconscious prejudices. In the larger sense these are even more threatening than any open manifestations that have yet occurred. For "race" prejudice is not isolated—it is part of a chain of tendencies. Many studies have shown that those individuals who have the most pronounced hatreds against Negroes and Jews are ordinarily those who are also strongest in their antipathies against labor, against "foreigners," against all types of social change, however needful. A *Fortune* poll in 1945 showed that "the percentage of anti-Semites is substantially above or below 8.8 in only three groups:

the extremely anti-British (20.8 per cent), the rich (13.5 per cent), and Negroes (2.3 per cent)." These facts are intuitively realized and exploited to the fullest by politicians, many of whom have a vested interest in the perpetuation of cleavages.

Bigotry directed against any segment of the population may set off a powder chain leading to suppression of the traditional liberties of the English-speaking peoples or to utter social disorganization. This is the internal threat. The external one is at least as serious. We must never forget that four-fifths of the population of the earth consists of colored peoples. In a world in which the barriers imposed by distance have almost disappeared we cannot ignore the colored peoples. Nor, assuredly, can we expect to continue to treat them as subordinate. We must learn to get along with them. This demands mutual respect. It does not mean pretending that differences do not exist. It does mean recognizing differences without fearing, hating, or despising them. It means not exaggerating differences at the expense of similarities. It means understanding the true causes of the differences. It means valuing these differences as adding to the richness and variety of the world. Mere acquaintance does not, unfortunately, always bring friendship. Antagonism was of merely academic interest as long as differing peoples did not need to have relations with one another, but under contemporary conditions the issue is vitally practical.

This is a social disease for which there is no panacea. As Ronald Lippit says: "It is now easier to smash an atom than to break prejudice." Not very much can be accomplished through new legislation or even through better enforcement of existing laws, for laws are only as effective as the conviction of the majority of citizens that they are right and necessary. More can be done by changing the conditions which create race prejudice than by a frontal attack.

All types of conflict feed on fear. Freedom from fear is the best way to cure race prejudice. This means freedom from the fear of war, from the fear of economic insecurity, from the fear of personal loneliness, from the fear of loss of individual prestige. Until there is world order, until there is a greater measure of personal security, until, perhaps, the texture of American life is less tensely competitive, the race question will be with us. As Rosenzweig has written:

> Just as the body in its resistance to infectious disease adopts non-disruptive protective reactions as long as possible but eventually resorts to defense reactions which, as symptoms of the illness, seriously interfere with the patient's normal behavior; so when psychological constancy cannot be achieved in more adequate ways, less adequate ones are inevitably adopted.

But this does not mean that nothing useful can be done in the meantime. We should first of all remember that in so far as we aid in the solution of these larger problems, we are also helping to liquidate the "race" issue. Secondly, to the extent that individual citizens will take full responsibility for their public and private acts, many small improvements can be achieved in many different situations bearing directly on "race" problems. Such improvements can have a tremendous cumulative effect. Within the United States some genuine gains have been achieved within the last fifteen years. Even five years ago there were only four Negroes on the faculties of northern non-Negro colleges; today there are forty-seven.

We can treat people as people rather than as representatives of "racial" groups. We can show our friends how absurd it is to think of whole groups as "all bad" or "all good." We can discredit the sadists in our own circle of acquaintances. We can ridicule and deflate demagogues and rabble-rousers. We can circulate jokes which bring out the virtues of fair play and tolerance at the expense of Jew-baiters, for example. We can do our part to see to it that newspapers and radios represent minority groups as enjoying public support rather than as weak and isolated. In our own talk we can emphasize the facts of assimilation and adjustment to American life of minority groups as much as the facts of difference. We can insist that our leaders express their disapproval of attempts of the unscrupulous, whether in government, industry, or labor, to turn the hatred of the citizenry from their real enemies to innocent scapegoats. We can raise children who are more secure and free so that they do not have an inner need to hurt and to attack. We can increase our own self-understanding, winning greater freedom and a higher degree of responsible behavior as we gain deeper insight into our own motives. We can demand a calm and peaceful working out of the conflicts between groups. We can rouse our fellow citizens of good will from complacency and apathy. We can play upon American pride in diversity and strengthen loyalty to the totality of our heterogeneous society. Almost all Americans are, after all, descended from minority groups abroad.

We can likewise act against hasty and ill-considered emotional action which is likely to worsen a situation. While insisting that there are moral issues which are the concern of all American citizens, we can remind our too impassioned friends of the important variations in local conditions and of the need to speak and act in terms that are locally relevant. Every community tends to resent outside interference, and change will be less disturbing and more permanent if it grows from within and is promoted by natural leaders of the community.

Minorities also have their prejudices, of course, so it is no simple matter of the majority adopting the "right attitude." Members of less privileged groups tend to use their disadvantaged status as a cover for inferiority feelings arising out of their experience as individuals. They will themselves behave unfairly toward groups still lower in the power structure. Behavior within a minority must always be related also to the wall of prejudice which surrounds them. The frequency of crime and bloodshed among Negro Americans, for example, must be understood in part as a result of frustration at being unable to express hostility toward whites and as a consequence of white tolerance toward crimes that do not infringe on white privileges. This fits beautifully with the white stereotype that attributes "animal passions" to the Negro—even though in the same breath insisting that Negroes are "happy-go-lucky" and like to be submissive to whites. Group prejudice is complex in many other ways. The same individuals will act without prejudice in one situation and with great antagonism in another. Attitudes are not the same toward all minority groups. Jews, in general, are punished because they refuse to be assimilated, Negroes because they want to be. Many Americans do not like Jews at all, but they like Negroes "in their place." Tolerance and sympathy flow and recoil with local and national economic conditions and with the international situation. Americans have had to face a more serious problem during the past thirty years because, as has been remarked, "The safety valve of the frontier is no longer an appreciable protection against the mounting pressure within the turbulent melting pot."

The anthropologist in his professional capacity can and has helped in many ways. Working for Mayors' Committees and similar organizations in American cities where tensions have been acute, anthropologists have made surveys of potential trouble spots and predicted where flare-ups were likely, so that social-service agencies and law-and-order organizations were more adequately prepared. As specialists in the customs of different peoples, the anthropologists have also been able to make practical suggestions for soothing out temporary situations by pointing out symbols of discontent that are not immediately obvious and by suggesting the right words to use in reconciliation. As students of social organization, they have discovered who were the real leaders of conflicting groups. In industry they have performed similar services and have given practical advice on which minorities will, and which will not, work together peaceably.

In addition to acting as "trouble shooters," anthropologists have acted as advisers to many projects for the long-term improvement of "race" relations. Besides assisting in the application of knowledge now available about these problems, they have likewise called attention to dangers in carrying out these projects not apparent at the common-sense level. For example, talking too loudly about the sufferings of disadvantaged groups is a two-edged sword. The sympathies of the kindhearted may be aroused, but the antagonisms of the aggressors may also be activated the more strongly—the "boomerang effect." Also, a program in behalf of one group may simply have the effect of deflecting the hostility toward another group. One outlet is blocked but a substitute that is socially as bad or worse is found.

As part of the long-term job, anthropologists have been active in education in the broadest sense: nursery-school programs; public meetings; adult education; preparation of radio programs and newspaper articles; writing, checking, and revision of public-school textbooks; planning cartoons and other graphic materials; preparing museum exhibits and books for children and adults. The University of Chicago Department of Anthropology directed a vigorous program of lectures and discussions in the high schools of Kansas City, Chicago, Milwaukee, and other cities.

The anthropologist realizes that erroneous theories of "race" and racism are both cause and effect of "racial" discrimination. Just as political expediency led the Nazis to proclaim the doctrine that the Japanese were, after all, "yellow Aryans," so in the heat of the war amazing popular theories of the "racial" origins of the Japanese were developed in this country. Though the loyal and valiant deeds of countless Japanese-American soldiers were even then giving the lie to such ridiculous extravagances, no amount of scientific evidence would in 1942 have convinced many Americans that a United States Senator was not speaking sober truth when he declaimed, "I do not believe that there stands upon the free soil of the United States of America one single solitary Jap, one single solitary person with Japanese blood in his veins, but what there stands a man who will stab you in the back. Show me a Jap, and I will show you a person full of treachery and deception."

Nevertheless the anthropologist, while laboring under no delusions as to the power of the purely rational, believes that the dissemination of the icy facts about "race" can play a useful and important part in resolving the problem. As the physical anthropologist, Harry Shapiro, has written:

> Science has another duty beyond the impassioned and objective *search* for truth. It has also the responsibility of *keeping* the truth inviolate and uncorrupted. On some occasions this assumes the form of revealing the underlying insecurity of popular as well as scientific speculation.

CHAPTER VI

The Gift of Tongues

> Our misapprehension of the nature of language has occasioned a greater waste of time, and effort, and genius, than all the other mistakes and delusions with which humanity has been afflicted. It has retarded immeasurably our physical knowledge of every kind, and vitiated what it could not retard.
>
> —A. B. Johnson, *Treatise on Language*

It's a pity that so few of us have lived down our childhood struggles with grammar. We have been made to suffer so much from memorizing rules by rote and from approaching language in a mechanical, unimaginative way that we tend to think of grammar as the most inhuman of studies. Probably Americans, who dramatize themselves and their independence, have a kind of unconscious resentment against all patterns that are so set as to constitute a gratuitous insult to the principle of free will. For whatever reasons, Americans have been characteristically inept at foreign languages. Like the British, we have expected everybody else to learn English.

Yet nothing is more human than the speech of an individual or of a folk. Human speech, unlike the cry of an animal, does not occur as a mere element in a larger response. Only the human animal can communicate abstract ideas and converse about conditions that are contrary to fact. Indeed the purely conventional element in speech is so large that language can be regarded as pure culture. A Burmese weaver, moved to Mexico, would know at once what a fellow craftsman in Mexico was doing, but would not understand one word of the Nahuatl tongue. No clues are so helpful as those of language in pointing to ultimate, unconscious psychological attitudes. Moreover, much of the friction between groups and between nations arises because in both the literal and the slangy senses they don't speak the same language.

We live in an environment which is largely verbal in the sense that we spend the most of our waking hours uttering words or responding actively or passively to the words of others. We talk to ourselves. We talk to our families and friends—partly to communicate to them and to persuade them, partly just to express ourselves. We read newspapers, magazines, books, and other written matter. We listen to the radio, to sermons, lectures, and movies. As Edward Sapir says:

> Language completely interpenetrates direct experience. For most persons every experience, real or potential, is saturated with verbalism. This perhaps explains why so many nature lovers do not feel that they are truly in touch with nature until they have mastered the names of a great many flowers and trees, as though the primary world of reality were a verbal one, and as though one could not get close to nature unless one first mastered the terminology that somehow magically expresses it. It is this constant interplay between language and experience which removes language from the cold status of such purely and simply symbolic systems as mathematical symbolism or flag signalling.*

The dictionaries still say that "language is a device for communicating ideas." The semanticists and the anthropologists agree that this is a tiny, specialized function of speech. Mainly, language is an instrument for action. The meaning of a word or phrase is not its dictionary equivalent but the difference its

* From "Language," by Edward Sapir, *Encyclopedia of the Social Sciences*, vol. ix. Copyright 1933 by The Macmillan Company and used with their permission.

utterance brings about in a situation. We use words to comfort and cajole ourselves in fantasy and daydream, to let off steam, to goad ourselves into one type of activity and to deny ourselves another. We use words to promote our own purposes in dealing with others. We build up verbal pictures of ourselves and our motives. We coax, wheedle, protest, invite, and threaten. Even the most intellectual of intellectuals employs only a minute fraction of his total utterance in symbolizing and communicating ideas that are divorced from emotion and action. The primary social value of speech lies in getting individuals to work more effectively together and in easing social tensions. Very often what is said matters much less than that something is said.

To the manipulation of this verbal environment, the anthropological linguist has made some immediately practical contributions. Forced by the absence of written materials and by other circumstances attendant upon work with primitives, he has become an expert on "the direct method." He knows how to learn a language by using it. Though sensitive to the broader implications of a subtler, rarer forms of a language, he is skilled in the socially practical. He knows how to dodge the subjunctive when the immediate objective is to get a conversation going. The training of the conventional teacher of languages tempts him to his besetting sin of preoccupation with the niceties. He loves complicated rules and even more the exceptions to those rules. This is one of the principal reasons that after eight years of instruction in French an American can read a French novel with pleasure but is terrified to ask street directions in Paris. The anthropologist can't look up the rules in the book. He is hardened to making small and large mistakes. His tradition is to break through, to concentrate on the essential, to get on with the talk at all costs.

Since many odd languages were of military significance during World War II, the anthropological linguist had a chance to introduce his method of working directly with the native informant. He prepared educational materials that highlighted anthropological short cuts in learning how to speak languages. The results have influenced the traditional methods of language instruction in the United States. The anthropological linguist has also worked out ways of teaching adults who have no written language and ways of teaching illiterates to write and read their own tongue.

Because anthropological linguists have usually been trained as ethnologists and have often done general field work, they have tended less than other students of language to isolate speech from the total life of the people. To the anthropologist, language is just one kind of cultural behavior with many interesting connections to other aspects of action and thought. Analysis of a vocabulary shows the principal emphases of a culture and reflects culture history. In Arabic, for example, there are more than six thousand different words for camel, its parts, and equipment. The crudity and the special local words of the vocabulary of Spanish-speaking villages in New Mexico reflect the long isolation of these groups from the main stream of Latin culture. The particular archaisms used show that the break with the main continuity of the Spanish language occurred during the eighteenth century. The fact that the Boorabbee Indians of Panama use words like *gadsoot* (gadzooks), *forsoo'* (forsooth), *chee-ah* (cheer), and *mai-api* (mayhap) suggests a possible connection with Elizabethan buccaneers.

A great deal is now known about the history of languages, especially those languages that have been the great carriers of culture: Greek, Latin, Sanskrit, Arabic, Chinese, and English. Certain regularities have been discovered. In contrast to the general course of cultural evolution, languages move from the complex to the simple. Chinese and English have today lost almost all inflections. The uniformities of phonetic change are most encouraging to those who believe that there is a discoverable order in human events. As Bloomfield has said:

> These correspondences are a matter of historical detail, but their significance was overwhelming, since they showed that human action, in the mass, is not altogether haphazard, but may proceed with regularity even in so unimportant a matter as the manner of pronouncing the individual sounds within the flow of speech.

The phonetic side of language beautifully illustrates both the selective nature of culture and the omnipresence of patterning. The sound of the p in pin is uttered with a slight puff of breath that is lacking when we sound the p in spin. Yet the speakers of English have entered into an unconscious agreement to treat them as the same signals, though they are not acoustically identical. It is like the motorist trained to stop at a light that is any shade of red. If I am investigating an unknown language and discover two sounds that are somewhat similar to those represented by English "b" and "d" but differ in being softly whispered, I can immediately predict that sounds in the new language of "g" type will conform to the same pattern.

Language is as consistently nonrational as any aspect of culture. We cling stubbornly to functionless capital letters. One may also instance our absurd English spelling. "Ghiti" ought to spell fish—gh as in laugh, ti as in ambition. In hiccough, gh has a p sound. "Ghoughteighteau" could be read as potato—figure it out yourself. We say "five houses" when "five house" would be simpler and convey the meaning equally well.

Small pecularities of linguistic usage are very revealing. It is no accident that French Catholics address the deity with the familiar form of the personal pronoun *(tu)* and Protestants with the formal (*vous*). In all sectors of French society save the old aristocracy spouses use *tu* to each other. But in the *Faubourg St. Germain* the duke calls his duchess *vous*—it being well understood between them that he reserves *tu* for his mistress.

A whole monograph could well be written on differences in the social structure of European nations as exposed by linguistic habits relating to the second personal pronoun. In France one comes to *tutoyer* few people after adolesence. This familiarity is restricted to immediate relatives and to a few intimate friends of childhood. In the German-speaking world, however, a student who did not soon come to use the familiar *Du* with those whom he saw frequently would be regarded as stuffy. In the army of imperial Austria all officers in the same regiment called each other *Du* regardless of rank. Failure to use the familiar form was equivalent to a challenge to the duel. In Austria and in other European countries the initiation of the familiar usage between adults is formalized in a ceremony. There is an embrace and a drink from each other's glasses. In Spain and Italy the introduction of the *tu* relationship in later life is considerably easier than in France but less frequent than in southern Germany and Austria. In Italy there is the further complication of a special form of respectful address (*Lei*). Choice of *Lei* or the more common formal pronoun became a political issue. The Fascist Party forbade the use of *Lei*. In Sweden also, passions have been aroused over the pronoun *ni* which is used toward those of lower social status—and, in accord with the familiar principle of inverted snobbery,* toward royal personages. Clubs were formed to abolish this word. Indi-

* Another illustration of the "principle of inverted snobbery": In an American college that is small or struggling for prestige, faculty members who are members of Phi Beta Kappa would as soon appear on the campus without their pants as without their keys. In old well-established universities, ΦBK keys are worn only by a few older professors.

viduals wore buttons saying, "I don't use *ni* and I hope you don't either." Persons were brought into court for using *ni* toward people who considered themselves the equals or superiors of those who derogated them by using *ni* in address. "You are *ni* to me; I am not *ni* to you."

These are also instances of the intensely emotional symbolism of language. During the course of the development of nationalism and the romantic movement, every tongue was seized upon as the tangible manifestation of each culture's uniqueness. In the earlier part of the nineteenth century Magyar nobles spoke Latin in the Hungarian Parliament because they could not speak Magyar and would not speak German. Magyar, Irish, Lithuanian, and other tongues have been revived within the last hundred years from the category of practically dead languages. This tendency is about as old as written history. In the Bible we learn that the Gileadites slew everyone at the passages of Jordan who said *sibboleth* instead of *shibboleth.*

Groups within a culture emphasize their unity by a special language. Criminals have their own argot. So, indeed, do all the professions. One school in England (Winchester) has a language, compounded of medieval Latin and the accretions of the slang of many generations, that is utterly unintelligible to the uninitiated. "The linguistic community" is no meaningless phrase. The use of speech forms in common implies other things in common. The hunting or "county" set in England affects the dropping of final g's as a badge of their being set apart. Understatement is the mark of unshakable psychological security. If a member of the English upper classes is a member of the Davis Cup team he says, "Yes, I play a little tennis." Individuals of many countries pronounce words in certain ways in order to associate themselves with particular social classes. The extent to which an elderly or middle-aged Englishman is still identifiable as Harrow or Rubgy—and not as a

Yorkshireman nor even as an Oxonian nor as an army man—proves the identification of distinctive language with social status. You can pretty well place an Englishman by his tie and his accent. Idiomatic turns of speech identify to society at large the special positions and roles of its various members. Cliques and classes unconsciously use this device to prevent absorption into the larger group. "He talks like one of us" is a declaration of acceptance. Euphemisms, special terms of endearment, and slang are class labels.

The essential aroma of each culture or subculture may be caught as a fragrance of language. In the Berlin of 1930, when one met an acquaintance on the street one bowed and stiffly said, "Good day." In Vienna one called out, "I have the honor," to a superior; "May God greet thee (you)," to an intimate; or, "Your servant," to a fellow student or fellow aristocrat. That *gewisse Liebenswürdigkeit* (a certain graciousness) which was the hallmark of Viennese culture came out most clearly and immediately in certain phrases that were not unknown in northern and Protestant Germany but were much less frequent in the stuff of daily conversation: "Live well," "the lady mother," "I kiss the hand, noble lady," and many others. In Austria when the delivery boy brought the groceries to the kitchen he said, "May God greet thee," if the maid received them; "Kiss the hand, noble lady," if the mistress were there.

Although one could press this point of view too far, there is *something* significant in the lists of words from each European language that have become widely current in other languages. From English: gentleman, fair play, week end, sport. From French: *liaison, maitresse, cuisine.* From Italian: *diva, bravo, bel canto.* From German: *Weltschmerz, Sehnsucht, Weltanschuauung, Gemutlichkeit.* In *Englishmen, Frenchmen, and Spaniards,* de Madariaga has suggested that the words, fair play, *le droit,* and *el honor* are the keys to the respective cultures. Here is a sample of his discussion of English:

> There is deep satisfaction in the thought that English—the language of the man of action—is a monosyllabic language. For the man of action, as we know, lives in the present, and the present is an instant with room for no more than one syllable. Words of more than one syllable are sometimes called in English "dictionary" words, *i.e.*, words for the intellectual, for the bookworm, for the crank, almost for the un-English. They are marvellous, those English monosyllables, particularly, of course, those which represent acts. Their fidelity to the act which they represent is so perfect that one is tempted to think English words are the right and proper names which those acts are meant to have, and all other words but pitiable failures. How could one improve on splash, smash, ooze, shriek, slush, glide, squeak, coo. Who could find anything better than hum or buzz or howl or whir. Who could think of anything more sloppy than slop? Is not the word sweet a kiss in itself and what could suggest a more peremptory obstacle than stop?

Certainly the recurrent turns of phrase, the bromides, of each culture and of different time periods in the same culture are illuminating. They embody in capsule form the central strains and stresses of the society, major cultural interests, the characteristic definitions of the situation, the prime motivations. You can't swear effectively in British to an American audience and vice versa. The Navaho greeting is "All is well"; the Japanese, "There is respectful earliness"; the American, "How do you do?" or "How are you getting on?" Each epoch has its stock phrases. As Carl Becker has written:

> If we would discover the little backstairs door that for any age serves as the secret entranceway to knowledge, we will do well to look for certain unobtrusive words with uncertain meanings that are permitted to slip off the tongue or pen without fear and without research; words which, having from constant repetition lost their metaphorical significance are unconsciously mistaken for objec-

tive realities. . . . In each age these magic words have their entrances and their exits.

In a way there is nothing very new about semantics. The Roman grammarian, Varro, pointed out in a learned treatise that he had discovered 228 distinct meanings for the word "good." His basic point was the same as Aldous Huxley's: "There ought to be some way of dry-cleaning and disinfecting words. Love, purity, goodness, spirit—a pile of dirty linen waiting for the laundress." We are always bringing together by words things that are different and separating verbally things that are, in fact, the same. A Christian Scientist refused to take vitamin tablets on the ground that they were "medicine"; he willingly accepted them when it was explained that they were "food." An insurance company discovered that behavior toward "gasoline drums" was ordinarily circumspect, that toward "empty gasoline drums" habitually careless. Actually, the "empty" drums are the more dangerous because they contain explosive vapor.

The semantic problem is almost insoluble because, as John Locke said, "So difficult is it to show the various meaning and imperfections of words when we have nothing else but words to do it by." This is one of the reasons that a cross-cultural approach is imperative. Anyone who has struggled with translation is made to realize that there is more to a language than its dictionary. The Italian proverb "*traduttore, tradittore*" (the translator is a betrayer) is all too correct. I asked a Japanese with a fair knowledge of English to translate back from the Japanese that phrase in the new Japanese constitution that represents our "life, liberty, and the pursuit of happiness." He rendered, "license to commit lustful pleasure." English to Russian and Russian back to English transmuted a cablegram

"Genevieve suspended for prank" into "Genevieve hanged for juvenile delinquency."

These are obvious crudities. But look at translations into half-a-dozen languages of the same passage in the Old Testament. The sheer difference in length will show that translation is not just a matter of finding a word in the second language that exactly matches a word in the original. Renderings of poetry are especially misleading. The best metrical translation of Homer is probably the fragment done by Hawtrey. The final two lines of the famous "Helen on the wall" passage of the third book in the *Iliad* goes as follows:

> So said she; but they long since in earth's soft arms were reposing
> There in their own dear land, their fatherland, Lacedaemon

Hawtrey has caught the musical effect of Greek hexameter about as well as it is possible to do in English. But the Greek says literally, "but them, on the other hand, the life-giving earth held fast." The original is realistic—Helen's brothers were dead and that was that. The English is sentimental.

Once in Paris I saw a play called "The Weak Sex." I found it charmingly risqué. A year later in Vienna I took a girl to see a German translation of the same play. Though she was no prude, I was embarrassed because the play was vulgar if not obscene in German.

I think I got my first genuine insight into the nature of language when my tutor at Oxford asked me to translate into Greek a few pages from an eighteenth-century British rhetorician which contained the following phrase, "she heaped the utmost virulence of her invective upon him." I struggled with this and finally committed the unforgivable sin of looking up each word in an English-Greek dictionary. My tutor glanced at the resultant monstrosity and looked up at me with mingled disgust, pity, and amazement. "My dear boy," he said, "don't you know that the only possible way you can render that is *deinos aedeitai*, she blamed very strongly?"

Really, there are three kinds of translation. There is the literal or word-for-word variety which is always distorted except perhaps between languages that are very similar in structure and vocabulary. Second, there is the official type where certain conventions as to idiomatic equivalents are respected. The third, or psychological type of translation, where the words produce approximately the same effects in the speakers of the second language as they did in those of the original, is next to impossible. At best, the rendering must be extremely free, with elaborate circumlocutions and explanations. I once heard Einstein make a slip of the tongue that stated the deeper truth. He said, "I shall speak in English this evening, but if I get excited during the discussion I shall break into German and Professor Lindeman will traduce me."

If words referred only to things, translation would be relatively simple. But they refer also to relations between things and the subjective as well as the objective aspects of these relationships. In different tongues relationships are variously conceived. The Balinese word *tis* means not to be cold when it is cold. The Balinese word *paling* designates the state of a trance or drunkenness or a condition of not knowing where you are, what day it is, where the center of the island is, the caste of the person to whom you are talking. The subjective aspects arise from the fact that we use words not only to express things and relationships but to express ourselves; words refer not only to events but to the attitudes of the speakers toward those events.

The words prostitute and whore have exactly the same denotation. The connotation, however, is very different. And a word's connotation is at least as important as the denotation in rousing feeling and producing action. Examine carefully the richest field of modern verbal magic—advertisements.

The same words often don't mean the same thing to different generations within the same culture, Margaret Mead writes:

> Take the word *job*. To the parents a job was something you got when you finished school—the next step, a little grim, a little exciting, the end of carefree school days. A job was something you were going to get, bound to get, something that waited for you at the end of school, just as certainly as autumn follows summer. But job—to those born in 1914, 1915? Something that you might never get, something to be longed for and prayed for, to starve for and steal for, almost—a job. There weren't any. When these two generations talk together and the word *job* is used, how will they understand each other? Suppose the issue is the draft— "A shame a fellow has to give up his job." To the elders this is arrant unpatriotic selfishness. To the young it is obvious sense. They find it strange that older people can see the sacrifice involved when married men with children must leave their families to go away in the defense service. Yet these same people don't see that any one should mind leaving a job. "Don't they know what a *job* means now, in the thinking of those born in 1915, 1916, 1917? Don't they know that just as among the ancients one was not a man until one had begotten a male child, so today one can't think of one's self as a full human being, without a job? We didn't say a guy wouldn't go because he had a job. We just said it was tough on him. We weren't saying anything they wouldn't say themselves about a man with kids. But gee—how they blew up!"

The British and the Americans are still under the delusion that they speak the same language. With some qualifications this is true as far as denotations are concerned, though there are concepts like "sissy" in American for which there are no precise English equivalents. Connotations, however, are often importantly different, and this makes for the more misunderstanding because both languages are still called "English" (treating alike by words things that are different). An excellent illustration is again supplied by Margaret Mead:

> . . . in Britain, the word "compromise" is a good word, and one may speak approvingly of any arrangement which has been a compromise, including, very often, one in which the other side has gained more than fifty per cent of the points at issue. On the other hand, in the United States, the minority position is still the position from which everyone speaks: the President *versus* Congress, Congress *versus* the President, the State government *versus* the metropolis and the metropolis *versus* the State government. This is congruent with the American doctrine of checks and balances, but it does not permit the word "compromise" to gain the same ethical halo which it has in Britain. Where, in Britain, to compromise means to work out a good solution, in America it usually means to work out a bad one, a solution in which all the points of importance (to both sides) are lost. Thus, in negotiations between the United States and Britain, all of which had, in the nature of the case, to be compromises, as two sovereignties were involved, the British could always speak approvingly and proudly of the result, while the Americans had to emphasize their losses.

The words, then, that pass so readily from mouth to mouth are not entirely trustworthy substitutes for the facts of the physical world. The smooth-worn standard coins are slippery steppingstones from mind to mind. Nor is thinking simply a matter of choosing words to express thoughts. The selected words always mirror social situation as well as objective fact. Two men go into a bar in New York and are overcharged for bad liquor: "This is a gyp joint." The same thing happens in Paris: "The French are a bunch of chiselers."

Perhaps the most important contribution of anthropological linguistics has come from the difficulties the anthropologist goes through in trying to express the meanings contained in speech structures completely foreign to the pattern of all European tongues. This study and this experience has forced upon the anthropologist a rather startling discovery which is fraught with meaning for a world where peoples speaking many different idioms are trying to communicate without distortion. Every language is something more than a vehicle for exchanging ideas and information—more even than a tool for self-expression and for letting off emotional steam or for getting other people to do what we want.

Every language is also a special way of looking at the world and interpreting experience. Concealed in the structure of each different language are a whole set of unconscious assumptions about the world and life in it. The anthropological linguist has come to realize that the general ideas one has about what happens in the world outside oneself are not altogether "given" by external events. Rather, up to a point, one sees and hears what the grammatical system of one's language has made one sensitive to, has trained one to look for in experience. This bias is the more insidious because everyone is so unconscious of his native language as a system. To one brought up to speak a certain language it is part of the very nature of things, remaining always in the class of background phenomena. It is as natural that experience should be organized and interpreted in these language-defined classes as it is that the seasons change. In fact the naïve view is that anyone who thinks in any other way is unnatural or stupid, or even vicious—and most certainly illogical.

In point of fact, traditional or Aristotelian logic has been mainly the analysis of consistencies in the structures of languages like Greek and Latin. The subject-predicate form of speech has implied a changeless world of fixed relations between "substances" and their "qualities." This view, as Korzybski has insisted, is quite inadequate to modern physical knowledge which shows that the properties of an atom alter from instant to instant in accord with the shifting relationships of its component elements. The little word "is" has brought us much confusion because sometimes it signifies that the subject exists, sometimes that it is a member of a designated class, sometimes that subject and predicate are identical. Aristotelian logic teaches us that something is or isn't. Such a statement is often false to reality, for both-and is more often true than either-or. "Evil" ranges all the way from black through an infinite number of shades of gray. Actual experience does not present clear-cut entities like "good" and "bad," "mind" and "body"; the sharp split remains verbal. Modern physics has shown that even in the inanimate world there are many questions that cannot be answered by an unrestricted "yes" or an unqualified "no."

From the anthropological point of view there are as many different worlds upon the earth as there are languages. Each language is an instrument which guides people in observing, in reacting, in expressing themselves in a special way. The pie of experience can be sliced in many different ways, and language is the principal directive force in the background. You can't say in Chinese, "answer me yes or no," for there aren't words for yes and no. Chinese gives priority to "how?" and nonexclusive categories; European languages to "what?" and exclusive categories. In English we have both real plurals and imaginary plurals, "ten men" and "ten days"; in Hopi plurals and cardinal numbers may be used only for things that can be seen together as an objective group. The fundamental categories of the French verb are before and after (tense) and potentiality vs. actuality (mood); the fundamental categories of one American Indian language (Wintu) are subjectivity vs. objectivity, knowledge vs. belief, freedom vs. actual necessity.

In the Haida language of British Columbia there are more

than twenty verbal prefixes that indicate whether an action was performed by carrying, shooting, hammering, pushing, pulling, floating, stamping, picking, chopping, or the like. Some languages have different verbs, adjectives, and pronouns for animate and inanimate things. In Melanesia there are as many as four variant forms for each possessive pronoun. One may be used for the speaker's body and mind, another for illegitimate relatives and his loincloth, a third his possessions and gifts. The underlying conceptual images of each language tend to constitute a coherent though unconscious philosophy.

Where in English one word, "rough," may equally well be used to describe a road, a rock, or the business surface of a file, the Navaho language finds a need for three different words which may not be used interchangeably. While the general tendency is for Navaho to make finer and more concrete distinctions, this is not inevitably the case. The same stem is used for rip, light beam, and echo, ideas which seem diverse to speakers of European languages. One word is used to designate a medicine bundle with all its contents, the skin quiver in which the contents are wrapped, the contents as a whole, and some of the distinct items. Sometimes the point is not that the images of Navahos are less fluid and more delimited but rather just that the external world is dissected along different lines. For example, the same Navaho word is used to describe both a pimply face and a nodule-covered rock. In English a complexion might be termed "rough" or "coarse," but a rock would never, except facetiously, be described as pimply. Navaho differentiates two types of rough rock: the kind which is rough in the manner in which a file is rough and the kind which is nodule-encrusted. In these cases the differences between the Navaho and the English ways of seeing the world cannot be disposed of merely by saying that the Navaho language is more precise. The variations rest in the features which the two languages see as essential. Cases can indeed be given where the Navaho is notably less precise. Navaho gets along with a single word for flint, metal, knife, and certain other objects of metal. This, to be sure, is due to the historical accident that, after European contact, metal in general and knives in particular took the place of flint.

Navahos are perfectly satisfied with what seem to Europeans rather imprecise discriminations in the realm of time sequences. On the other hand, they are the fussiest people in the world about always making explicit in the forms of the language many distinctions which English makes only occasionally and vaguely. In English one says, "I eat," meaning, "I eat something." The Navaho point of view is different. If the object thought of is actually indefinite, then "something" must be tacked on to the verb.

The nature of their language forces the Navaho to notice and report many other distinctions in physical events which the nature of the English language allows speakers to neglect in most cases, even though their senses are just as capable as those of the Navaho to register the smaller details of what goes on in the external world. For example, suppose a Navaho range rider and a white supervisor see that a wire fence needs repair. The supervisor will probably write in his notebook, "Fence at such and such a place must be fixed." If the Navaho reports the break, he must choose between forms that indicate whether the damage was caused by some person or by a nonhuman agency, whether the fence was of one or several strands of wire.

In general, the difference between Navaho thought and English thought—both as manifested in the language and as forced by the very nature of the linguistic forms into such patterns—is that Navaho thought is ordinarily much more specific. The ideas expressed by the English verb to go provide a nice example. When a Navaho says that he went somewhere he never fails to specify whether it was afoot, astride, by wagon, auto, train, airplane, or boat. If it be a boat, it must be specified whether the boat floats off with the current, is propelled by the speaker, or is made to move by an indefinite or unstated agency. The speed of a horse (walk, trot, gallop, run) is expressed by the verb form chosen. He differentiates between starting to go, going along, arriving at, returning from a point. It is not, of course, that these distinctions *cannot* be made in English, but that they *are not* made consistently. They seem of importance to English speakers only under special circumstances.

A cross-cultural view of the category of time is highly instructive. Beginners in the study of classical Greek are often troubled by the fact that the word *opiso* sometimes means "behind," sometimes "in the future." Speakers of English find this baffling because they are accustomed to think of themselves as moving through time. The Greeks, however, conceived of themselves as stationary, of time as coming up behind them, overtaking them, and then, still moving on, becoming the "past" that lay before their eyes.

Present European languages emphasize time distinctions. The tense systems are usually thought of as the most basic of verbal inflections. However, this was not always so. Streitberg says that in primitive Indo-European a special indicator for the present was usually lacking. In many languages, certainly, time distinctions are only irregularly present or are of distinctly secondary importance. In Hopi the first question answered by the verb form is that of the type of information conveyed by the assertion. Is a situation reported as actuality, as anticipated, or as a general truth? In the anticipatory form there is no necessary distinction between past, present, and future. The English translation must choose from context between "was about to run," "is about to run," and "will run." The Wintu language of California carries this stress upon implications of validity much further. The sentence "Harry is chopping wood" must be translated in five different ways, depending upon whether the speaker knows this by hearsay, by direct observation, or by inference of three degrees of plausibility.

In no language are the whole of a sense experience and all possible interpretations of it expressed. What people think and feel and how they report what they think and feel are determined, to be sure, by their personal history, and by what actually happens in the outside world. But they are also determined by a factor which is often overlooked; namely, the pattern of linguistic habits which people acquire as members of a particular society. It makes a difference whether or not a language is rich in metaphors and conventional imagery.

Our imaginations are restricted in some directions, free in others. The linguistic particularization of detail along one line will mean the neglect of other aspects of the situation. Our thoughts are directed in one way if we speak a language where all objects are classified according to sex, in another if the classification is by social position or the form of the object. Grammars are devices for expressing relations. It makes a difference what is treated as object, as attribute, as state, as act. In Hopi, ideas referring to the seasons are not grouped with what we call nouns but rather with what we call adverbs. Because of our grammar it is easy to personify summer, to think of it as a thing or a state.

Even as between closely related tongues, the conceptual picture may be different. Let us take one final example from Margaret Mead:

> Americans tend to arrange objects on a single scale of value, from best to worst, biggest to smallest, cheapest to most expensive, etc., and are able to express a preference among very complex objects on such a single scale. The question, "What is your favorite color?" so intelligible to an American, is meaningless in Britain, and such a

question is countered by: "Favorite color for what? A flower? A necktie?" Each object is thought of as having a most complex set of qualities, and color is merely a quality of an object, not something from a color chart on which one can make a choice which is transferable to a large number of different sorts of objects. The American reduction of complexities to single scales is entirely comprehensible in terms of the great diversity of value systems which different immigrant groups brought to the American scene. Some common denominator among the incommensurables was very much needed, and over-simplification was almost inevitable. But, as a result, Americans think in terms of qualities which have uni-dimensional scales, while the British, when they think of a complex object or event, even if they reduce it to parts, think of each part as retaining all of the complexities of the whole. Americans subdivide the scale; the British subdivide the object.

Language and its changes cannot be understood unless linguistic behavior is related to other behavioral facts. Conversely, one can gain many subtle insights into those national habits and thought ways of which one is ordinarily unconscious by looking closely at special idioms and turns of speech in one's own and other languages. What a Russian says to an American doesn't really get across just from shuffling words—much is twisted or blunted or lost unless the American knows something about Russia and Russian life, a good deal more than the sheer linguistic skill needed for a formally correct translation. The American must indeed have gained some entrance to that foreign world of values and significances which are pointed up by the emphases of the Russian vocabulary, crystallized in the forms of Russian grammar, implicit in the little distinctions of meaning in the Russian language.

Any language is more than an instrument for conveying ideas, more even than an instrument for working upon the feelings of others and for self-expression. Every language is also a means of categorizing experience. The events of the "real" world are never felt or reported as a machine would do it. There is a selection process and an interpretation in the very act of response. Some features of the external situation are highlighted; others are ignored or not fully discriminated.

Every people has its own characteristic classes in which individuals pigeonhole their experiences. These classes are established primarily by the language through the types of objects, processes, or qualities which receive special emphasis in the vocabulary and equally, though more subtly, through the types of differentiation or activity which are distinguished in grammatical forms. The language says, as it were, "notice this," "always consider this separate from that," "such and such things belong together." Since persons are trained from infancy to respond in these ways, they take such discriminations for granted as part of the inescapable stuff of life. When we see two peoples with different social traditions respond in different ways to what appear to the outsider to be identical stimulus situations, we realize that experience is much less an objective absolute than we thought. Every language has an effect upon what the people who use it see, what they feel, how they think, what they can talk about.

"Common sense" holds that different languages are parallel methods for expressing the same "thoughts." "Common sense," however, itself implies talking so as to be readily understood by one's fellows—in the same culture. Anglo-American "common sense" is actually very sophisticated, deriving from Aristotle and the speculations of scholastic and modern philosophers. The fact that all sorts of basic philosophic questions are begged in the most cavalier fashion is obscured by the conspiracy of silent acceptance which always attends the system of conventional understandings that we call culture.

The lack of true equivalences between any two languages is merely the outward expression of inward differences between two peoples in premises, in basic categories, in the training of fundamental sensitivities, and in general view of the world. The way the Russians put their thoughts together shows the impress of linguistic habits, of characteristic ways of organizing experience, for

> Human beings do not live in the objective world alone, nor alone in the world of social activity as ordinarily understood, but are very much at the mercy of the particular language which has become the medium of expression for their society. It is quite an illusion to imagine that one adjusts to reality essentially without the use of language and that language is merely an incidental means of solving specific problems of communication or reflection. The fact of the matter is that the 'real world' is to a large extent unconsciously built up on the language habits of the group. . . . We see and hear and otherwise experience very largely as we do because the language habits of our community predispose certain choices of interpretation. —EDWARD SAPIR

A language is, in a sense, a philosophy.

CHAPTER VII

Anthropologists at Work

IT IS OBVIOUS that anthropologists have special knowledge and special skills for assisting governments in administering primitive tribes and dependent peoples. They have been so employed by the British, Portugese, Spanish, Dutch, Mexican, French, and other governments. An understanding of native institutions is a prerequisite for successful colonial government, though, thus far, anthropologists have been used more to implement policies than to formulate them. From colonial government to working upon problems of minority groups in a complex modern state is an easy step. Anthropologists served on the staff of the War Relocation Authority in dealing with evacuated Japanese Americans and assisted the War Labor Board and the Office of War Information in handling other minority problems within the United States.

During the war anthropological knowledge was put to use in handling native workers, in growing food in native areas, and in securing native cooperation for the Allied cause. Many anthropologists helped to train 4,000 Army officers and 2,000 Navy officers for military government in occupied territories. Anthropologists played an important part in working out the series of booklets issued to men in the armed forces which ran the instructional gamut from the use of Australian slang to the correct behavior toward women in the Moslem world. They helped to discover the best way of inducing Japanese, Italian, and German prisoners to surrender and promoted continued resistance in countries occupied by our enemies.

Since the peace, anthropologists have been called upon by

teachers, doctors, administrators in government and industry. Because we can experiment upon human beings only to a very limited extent, the nearest we can come to the experimental method that has been so successful in chemistry and physics is to note and analyze the results of the many different experiments that have been carried out by nature in the course of human history. This means in education, for example, that if some new practice is being considered, one useful thing to do would be to analyze all the different human groups in which children have been trained somewhat along these lines. By finding out how this has worked in other societies, some idea can be obtained as to whether or not the introduction of this kind of training will be a good bet. By concentrating upon the conspicuous differences between our educational practices and those of other peoples, we get a better understanding of our own conception of education. We might see, for instance, that primitives emphasize the stable and sacred, whereas our notions have been shaped by our will to assimilate immigrants, to improve, to be "up to date." Thus we have come to believe in education as an instrument for creating something new, not merely for perpetuating the traditional. Study of contrasting educational systems could likewise make the efforts of Government and missionary teachers among colonial and dependent peoples more efficient. Without this perspective, these teachers are all too likely to assume that the incentives which work best with children of their own group will work equally well with youngsters of another tradition. In fact, such incentives may not only fail to motivate children of another culture but may have the opposite effect. Anthropology is also significant in college education today because of its role in the organization and teaching of rounded programs on various major regions of the world.

The uses of physical anthropology to some medical specialties have already been discussed, and the implications for pediatrics and psychiatry of the study of personality in culture will be considered in the next chapter. The broadest utility of cultural anthropology to medicine consists in the anthropological faculty for swiftly apperceiving the principal currents of a culture as they impinge on individuals. Carefully designed quantitative studies to give a cross-cultural testing of theories on mental health are just beginning to emerge. Donald Horton has shown that the higher the level of anxiety in a society the greater is the frequency of alcoholism. He has also correlated the intensity of drinking with certain cultural patterns for aggression release and for sexuality. The essentials of this method of discovering what types of custom tend to be consistently found together could be applied to many other problems. It has been speculated that adolescent suicide occurs more often where marriage is late and where premarital sexual expression is severely punished. This theory would be vindicated only if examination of the facts proved a higher rate in the more repressive societies and a lower one in the more permissive.

Though the individual range of variation is wide in every society, the anthropologist knows that in any given culture the majority of individuals will respond much more readily to some appeals than to others. This is important not only in administration but also in the work of the State Department in influencing public attitudes abroad in such a way as to secure understanding and acceptance of our short-term and long-range policies. It is not sufficient to inform the governments of other states in the conventional legal and rational documents of statecraft. For there are now few nations in which policy is not influenced by public opinion. The background of United States policies must be kept in the foreground of peoples' minds. This can be done only if we present our basic goals and the reasons for them in terms that take account of the situation and the sentiment patterns of the various peoples we wish to influence.

Baffled by the strange behavior of peoples they were trying to administer in the newly occupied islands of the Pacific and elsewhere, governments:

> Just as they have looked to geology, entomology, and the other physical and biological sciences in handling the resources of the territories concerned, and to tropical medicine in meeting health problems, so they have drawn on anthropology to throw light on the exceedingly difficult problems of human relations, especially the adjustment of the so-called native or indigenous peoples to modern civilization. —Felix Keesing

Applied anthropology, however, is a relatively new term. *Applied Anthropology*, the journal, dates only from 1941. Apart from the contributions of physical anthropology to the identification of criminals and the selection of army recruits, the first evidence that anthropology could be put to immediate practical use was perhaps the Golden Stool incident. In 1896 and once in this century Britain was involved in costly wars with the Ashanti, a people of the West Coast of Africa. The reasons for the disturbances were obscure to the colonial officials. In 1921 a similar outbreak was narrowly averted when an anthropologist pointed out the tremendous symbolic significance to the Ashanti of what to the British appeared to be merely a king's seat—the Golden Stool.

Shortly after this affair, anthropology became a required course of study for candidates for the British colonial services. In 1933 Commissioner John Collier added an anthropological staff to the United States Office of Indian Affairs. Mexico and other Latin-American countries soon recognized the contributions anthropology could make to creating literacy in native Indian languages and to easing the adjustments of aboriginal cultures to the modern world. Anthropologists began to be employed by the Soil Conversation Service and the Bureau of Agricultural Economics of the Department of Agriculture.

In these early efforts the role of the anthropologist was primarily that of the trouble shooter. He was sent out when killings or the rise of an aggressive cult created an immediate problem. A poverty-stricken Indian tribe engaged in the wasteful practice of destroying every house in which death occurred. An anthropologist suggested that the people's own religious culture provided for nullifying threats from the supernatural world by practices analogous to fumigation. The Indian service introduced fumigation, and the houses and property of the dead were no longer destroyed. In Papua anthropologists utilized the principle of cultural substitution by introducing a pig instead of a human body in a fertility rite, a football to replace a spear in discharging hostilities between factions in a tribe.

Applied anthropology, however, has the function of instructing the general public as well as that of advising the administrator. Ignorance of the way of life in other countries breeds an indifference and callousness among nations, a misinterpretation and misunderstanding which becomes ever more threatening as the world shrinks. Sophisticated exhibits in anthropological museums can greatly aid in breaking down deep-seated irrational attitudes toward alien cultures. By utilizing other appealing methods of voluntary education—films, lectures, popular publications—anthropologists are little by little informing public opinion that the customs of others are as necessary to them as ours are to us, that each culture has its special needs.

During the recent war applied anthropology blossomed. British anthropologists held important posts in the Foreign

Office, the Admiralty, the British Information Service, the Wartime Social Survey, and in the field. One man was political adviser for the whole Middle East, another carried the main administrative burden for the vast Anglo-Egyptian Sudan, still another handled liaison problems with native peoples in Kenya and Abyssinia. A woman anthropologist, Ursula Graham Bower, became popularly known as "the T. E. Lawrence of World War II." Because she was able to win and hold the confidence of the Zemi, a strategically placed tribe on the Assam-Burma frontier, the Japanese invasion of India had a different history than might otherwise have been the case.

In the United States anthropologists operated in their professional capacities in Military Intelligence, the Department of State, the Office of Strategic Services, the Board of Economic Warfare, the Strategic Bombing Survey, Military Government, the Selective Service Organization, the Office of Naval Intelligence, the Office of War Information, the Quartermaster Corps, the Federal Bureau of Investigation, the War Relocation Authority, the Alcan Highway Project, the Hydrographic Office of the Chief of Naval Operations, the Foreign Economic Administration, the Federal Security Administration, the medical branch of the Army Air Forces, and the Chemical Warfare Division. In part, they worked on "spot" research. A soldier's handbook on Eritrea had to be prepared. A military phrase book on pidgin English needed checking. A man who could deal properly with savage Indians of Ecuador was the spearhead of an expedition seeking new sources of quinine. What were the distinctive forms of tatooing in the Casa Blanca region? Who had been in Bora Bora in the Society Islands? A manual on "Jungle and desert emergencies" was prepared to assist stranded aviators in recognizing and preparing edible foods. Advice was given on designing clothing and equipment for the arctic and the tropics. Assignments ranged from screening Indian draftees of uncertain knowledge of English to preparing a memorandum on "how to identify stale fish" (which was promptly classified by the Army as "confidential"). Visual education materials were prepared to help in the training of personnel detailed to secret work abroad, and anthropologists lectured in many orientation courses.

However, as the war progressed, anthropologists were in demand as something more than experts on the customs and languages of critical areas. Their skills were applied in diagnosing and correcting morale problems in our armed services and in various sectors of the home front, notably that of race relations in industry. They also helped to close up the gap between nutritional knowledge and nutritional practice. It became increasingly clear to many top administrators that effective prosecution of the war involved people as well as machines and materials. Hence anthropologists—and many other kinds of social scientists—had their opportunity. In the following discussion the focus will be upon the specifically anthropological contribution, but it should be stated explicitly that many of these projects were collaborative.

In analyzing enemy propaganda and in advising on the construction of our own psychological warfare, in predicting how the enemy would react under given circumstances, in making plans for building morale in our own nation, anthropologists had an opportunity for drawing upon the widest informational and theoretical stores of their science. For instance, anthropologists were asked these sort of questions by policy makers: in reporting the early events of the war, ought we to minimize the disasters? will this course give greater confidence? will greater confidence give greater efficiency? In anthropological terms, the policy makers were asking: which types of motivation are preponderantly standardized in American culture? The greatest services of the anthropologist were in preventing his colleagues from casting both enemies and allies in the American image and in forever reminding intellectuals of the significance of the nonrational. Certain professors and literary men wanted to use our broadcasts to discuss democracy with the Japanese on a high intellectual plane. But you can't reason men out of irrationality.

In a school for training officers for military government in Italy an anthropologist was severely criticized by some of the "liberal" faculty of the school for making contacts between the officers and local Italian-Americans. It was complained that some of the latter had shown Fascist sympathies and also that they did not all speak standard Italian. It was maintained that distinguished Italians like Salvemini could teach the officers all they needed to know about Italy. The rejoinder of the anthropologist was that, after all, the officers were going to have to deal with Italians who had had Fascist sympathies, who were imperfectly educated—and not with Salveminis. Contact implied not complete moral acceptance but an opportunity to gain understanding and information of a sort not ordinarily provided by Ph.D's.

Two illustrations will show the contrast between the anthropological point of view and the culture-bound point of view in dealing with our enemies. Controversy raged in Washington over our propaganda treatment of the imperial institution in Japan. The liberal intellectuals in general urged that we should attack this as the prop of a fascist state. They maintained that it was dishonest and a betrayal of the deepest American ideals to allow the Japanese to assume from our silence that we would tolerate the monarchy after our victory. The anthropologists opposed this policy. They had the general objection that the solution to conflicts between the United States and other peoples can never rest on a cultural imperialism that insists upon the substitution of our institutions for theirs. But they had more immediately practical objectives. They pointed out, first, that if one examined historically the place of the imperial institution in Japanese culture it was clear that there was no inevitable linkage with the contemporary political attitudes and practices that we were bound to destroy. Second, since the imperial institution was the nucleus of the Japanese sentiment system, to attack it openly was to intensify and prolong enormously Japanese resistance, to give freely to the Japanese militarists the best possible rallying cry for morale. Third, the only hope for a unified Japanese surrender of all the forces scattered over Pacific Islands and on the continent of Asia was through this sole symbol that was universally respected.

Anthropologists showed that it is almost always more effective in the long run to preserve some continuity in the existing social organization and to work at reorganization from the established base. This had been demonstrated by the British anthropologists when they created the principle of "indirect rule." If the United States and its allies wished to abolish the monarchy it could be abolished eventually by the Japanese themselves if we handled the situation adroitly and adopted an astute educational program. When an institution is destroyed by force from without, there usually follows a compensatory and often destructive reaction from within. If a culture pattern collapses as a result of internal developments, the change is more likely to last.

The second illustration is that of the attitude toward psychological warfare directed at the Japanese armed forces. Most of our top military men reasoned this way: We know that the Nazis are fanatics, but the Japanese have proved themselves still more fanatical. How can leaflets and broadcasts possibly affect soldiers who will go readily into a *Banzai* charge or fight under hopeless conditions in a cave, finally blowing themselves to pieces with a hand grenade? Why should the lives of our men be risked in attempting to secure more prisoners when it is obvious that Japanese prisoners will not provide us with intelligence information?

The generals and admirals who argued in this fashion were highly intelligent men. In common-sense terms their picture was perfectly sound. Common sense was not enough, for it assumed that all human beings would picture the same situation to themselves in identical terms. An American prisoner of war still felt himself to be an American and looked forward to resuming his normal place in American society after the war. A Japanese prisoner, however, conceived of himself as socially dead. He regarded his relations with his family, his friends, and his country as finished. But since he was physically alive he wished to affiliate himself with a new society. To the astonishment of their American captors, many Japanese prisoners wished to join the American Army and were, in their turn, astonished when they were told this was impossible. They willingly wrote propaganda for us, spoke over loud speakers urging their own troops to surrender, gave detailed information on artillery emplacements and the military situation in general. In the last six months of the war some Japanese prisoners flew in American planes within forty-eight hours after their capture, spotting Japanese positions. Some were allowed to return within the Japanese lines and brought back indispensable information.

From the American point of view there was something fantastic about all this. The behavior before and after capture was utterly incongruous. The incongruity, however, rests on a cultural point. The Judaic-Christian tradition is that of absolute morality—the same code is, at least in theory, demanded in all situations. To anthropologists who had steeped themselves in Japanese literature it was clear that Japanese morality was a situational one. As long as one was in situation A, one publicly observed the rules of the game with a fervor that impressed Americans as "fanaticism." Yet the minute one was in situation B, the rules for situation A no longer applied.

The majority of American policy makers were taken in by a cultural stereotype of the Japanese which was interpreted in terms of motives and images projected from the American scene. The anthropologist was useful in making a cultural translation. Moreover, he had grounds in established principles of social science for challenging the assumption that the morale of any people was or could be absolutely impregnable. Morale might be relatively high under certain conditions but it could not be a constant under all conditions. The problem was to find the right means for widening the cracks and fissures that would inevitably open up with local and general defeats, the pressures of starvation and of isolation. The official Japanese line was that no Japanese was taken prisoner unless he were unconscious or so badly wounded he could not move. We swallowed this for a long time. Days or weeks after capture an interrogator behind the lines would ask a prisoner how he happened to be taken. He would give the standard reply, "I was unconscious." This would be entered in the tabulations. Eventually, however, skeptics began to check the reports made at the time of the incident. It was found that Private Watanabe who had been listed as taken while unconscious was actually captured while swimming. The difference between behavior and cultural stereotype is important.

Just as knowledge of the nature of ourselves and of our enemies was a powerful weapon in the armory of psychological warfare, in political manipulation, and even in the timing and character of our actual military operations, so knowledge of the cultures of our allies helped in getting us over the rough spots of combined action and in maintaining effective unity during the war. Here the problem was, for example, that of convincing the British and the Americans that each people was working toward the same goals by somewhat different techniques. It was necessary to show one nation that forms of words frequently used in the newspapers of the other had a different meaning to that audience from the meaning the same words would have in the press of the ally. It was useful to point out to the British that the sexual behavior of American GI's in Britain rested in part on their interpreting the behavior of British girls as signifying what the same behavior of American girls would indeed have indicated. Conversely, ill feeling toward the British was lessened by conveying to the GI's a picture of what their conduct meant in British as opposed to American terms. Leo Rosten's *112 Gripes about the French* was a clever and helpful translation of French culture into American.

No claim is made that these anthropological efforts of various sorts were uniformly successful. On the contrary, the war clearly demonstrated certain immaturities of anthropology as a science and especially as an applied science. What remained solid were certain values in the anthropological approach. The utility of detailed information about certain areas was a somewhat accidental by-product of anthropological research. As an area expert, the anthropologist supplies less specialized knowledge than the geographer, the economist, the biologist, the public health worker. The unique contribution of the anthropologist to regional studies rests on the fact that he alone studies all aspects of a given area—human biology, language, technology, social organization, adaptation to the physical environment. His training equips him to learn the essential facts about an area quickly and organize them into a well-rounded scheme. Because he has under one skull knowledge about the relation both of man to man and of man to nature, he is in a position to help the specialists understand the relation of their specialty to the total life of a community.

Not because of their superior intelligence but because of the conditions under which they have had to do their work, anthropologists have developed ways of studying human groups which have been found to have certain advantages over the methods characteristic of the workers in other fields. The anthropologist is trained to see regularities. He views a society and culture as a rounded whole. This outlook must be contrasted with the more specialized but inevitably one-sided study of some isolated aspect. The anthropologist maintains that when one separates public schools or methods of taxation or recreation out of the total culture and deals with them like distinct layers in the face of a cliff there is some distortion of reality. The anthropologist is accustomed, whatever he may be concentrating upon in detail, to get the general social organization, the general economic pattern, etc. He may be working especially upon the myths of a people, but, even though he does not study the maize argiculture in detail, he never quite loses sight of the fact that maize is the basis of the economic system. This perspective is one of the keys to the anthropological approach. To see the parts in relation to the whole is more important than to know all the details. The facts are the scaffolding, while perspective is the structure itself. The structure may persist when most of the facts have been forgotten, and continue to provide a framework into which a new fact may be fitted when acquired.

A second important hallmark of anthropological method is, of course, the cultural point of view. On the one hand, the anthropologist adapts to the cultural habits and values of policy makers and administrators whom he is advising. On the other hand, to the administrators he says, in effect:

> If you are used to a steam engine but suddenly confronted with a machine that is obviously different, what would you do? Wouldn't you try to learn about it before trying to get work from it? Instead

of cursing the engine for lying down on the job, you would try to find out how it operated. Even if you think a steam engine is more efficient, you wouldn't treat an internal combustion engine like a steam engine—if only an internal combustion engine was available.

The applied anthropologist continually draws attention to the fact that what may to the foreigner appear to be simple and trivial habits that may be ignored are often so related to the deepest feelings as to invite serious conflict if they should be scorned. The anthropologist always asks: how does this look from *their* point of view? Otherwise policies will be formulated in terms of unconscious assumptions that are appropriate to administrator's culture but by no means shared by all men.

Some natives uninfluenced by Western culture can hardly conceive of the salability of land. One must forever beware of the influence of the sentiments that have been so thoroughly absorbed from one's culture as to remain unexamined "background phenomena." Thus to a member of the Anglo-Saxon tradition, a "fair trial" in a criminal case is taken for granted as trial by jury. However, large groups, even in the European pattern, are accustomed to Roman law which has as great a claim to being a great tradition of justice as has the Anglo-Saxon common law. The American judge must always justify his ruling on a particular case by referring to some established general principle; the Chinese judge must never do so. An American whose car injured a Turk in Istanbul expected a lawsuit. When he visited his victim in the hospital the latter disposed of the incident by remarking, "What is written is written."

The specific goals of endeavor in one's own society (for example, the striving for money) cannot be taken for granted as psychologically natural. That incentives are not identical for all groups explains the partial failure of educational undertakings carried on by missionaries and by colonial governments. Social institutions cannot be understood apart from the people who participate in them. Nor can the behavior of an individual be understood without reference to the systems of sentiments possessed by social groups of which he is a member.

In the third place, anthropological method consists in applying to a particular situation what is known about societies and cultures in general. The anthropologist's contribution to the study of rural problems in the United States does not rest in an initial familiarity with a given rural area but in his training for discovering the pattern of customs and sentiments and for analyzing how these operate as a total system. At best, the applied anthropologist is a social doctor, and, like the successful physician, he has good judgment in applying general knowledge to one case.

Problems in industry, in soil conservation and agricultural extension work, in persuading people to change their food habits appear at first glance to be within the realm of technology. In soil conservation, for example, the problem appears to be one for engineers and agricultural experts. These technologists, however, can only discover the rational, scientific answer to a situation. Much experience shows that people who live on the land will not necessarily follow the advice of experts when it is just presented to them as a scientific conclusion. Unless they are "sold" on a program of soil conservation by men who understand their customs, their ways of thought, and their deeply rooted feelings, a valuable and even essential project is likely to fail through human resistance and quiet sabotage. In other words, there is an essential human element in the successful carrying out of all technological operations. Social anthropologists, in studying whole societies from a detached point of view, have learned ways of watching and listening that enable them to be rather shrewd in determining where pressure should be applied and where it should be relaxed.

Industrialists, engineers, and nutritionists are highly trained, but their training is not along these lines. They can tell why a machine doesn't work or how many acres of topsoil are washed away in a year or what foods are good for us, but they can seldom figure out why one group of people work well together and another don't, or discover the quickest and most effective way of persuading a whole community to start eating an unfamiliar food. Food habits may be as important as food supply in determining whether a particular group is adequately nourished. Men do not treat food as mere nourishment; they endow it with symbolic value and place different foods in a prestige ranking. The subsistence value of food cannot be altered; the prestige or ritual value of food can be manipulated in various ways. Habitual behavior patterns in food folkways are usually automatic responses to stimuli based on childhood impressions. Fixed notions as to which foods are attractive in appearance, what foods can suitably or healthfully be eaten together, the proper utensils for each food are included in such patterns. Because of their automatic character they are the most difficult to change.

Conditioned emotional responses to diets play an important part in food habits. National folkways, traditional family customs, religious scruples, aesthetic values, motor reactions, concepts of personal privileges, and individual health wishes are among such emotional responses. They are usually strongly established in the individual, and resistance inevitably develops to rational and logical arguments advocating their change. Hence adequate nourishment or proper distribution of food during wartime are not merely physiological or financial problems but also problems in human relations. The same sum can buy an inadequate diet in one case and an adequate diet based upon wise choice in another. Nor is the problem, as welfare agencies can testify, solely that of the distribution of surplus commodities, for certain available foods may not be eaten if the local culture rejects them as low in prestige or (on irrational grounds) as unhealthful. After World War I starving Belgians refused to eat maize—they were accustomed to feeding it to their cattle.

There is a necessary intermediate step between the discovery of socially useful technical knowledge and the utilization of that knowledge by the citizenry. The application of any set of skills is determined not only by the skills themselves and by the physical environment in which they are used but also by the sentiments, traditions, and ideals of the people for whom they are intended. Anthropological methods are well adapted to handling this intermediate step of getting people to want or accept what natural science shows they need. The technical task of anthropology is discovering the factors in a culture or subculture that make for acceptance or nonacceptance, and pointing out the type of mental climate that must be created if living habits are to be changed. From this point of view the anthropologist's study of culture change may be compared to the physician's work in public health. In what sort of total environment does a disease spread? In what sort is it checked? What are the susceptibilities and immunities of various populations? What are the carriers of infection?

The anthropologist's experience with exotic cultures makes him cautious about interpreting in terms of familiar patterns; he is alert to the possibility of unfamiliar or unobvious explanations. Because much of "primitive" behavior seems so nonsensical or irrational from the point of view of Western culture, anthropologists have become accustomed to take everything they see and hear seriously. This does not mean that they think everything they hear is "true." It means only that they recognize the possible significance of the "untrue" and the "irrational" in understanding and predicting how individuals or groups react.

The more technical aspects of anthropological methods are also interesting. These involve ways of drawing people out and of evaluating what is said, gathering personal documents, using various tests. Anthropologists have learned to their cost that it may make a great deal of difference whether one is introduced into a new group by a trader or by a missionary or by a government employee, by a liked or by a disliked individual. They have also found out how important it is whether one's first friends in the society being investigated are placed toward the top or toward the bottom of that society. The habit of being wary on these and similar points pays good dividends in complex modern societies which are composed of a number of more or less separate local, occupational, and prestige groups.

Anthropologists are being more and more drawn into the planning and administering of various types of programs. Sometimes their role is merely that of advising or of doing background research, but an increasing number are themselves becoming administrators. Whatever the precise field of activity, there are certain general characteristics of practical anthropology. Emphasis is always placed upon the importance of symbolic as well as utilitarian considerations in human relations. Communication from the administrator to his superiors and subordinates as well as to the administered group must take account of both the rational and nonrational aspects of communication. Applied anthropology has now moved beyond the phase where the primary task was that of inculcating respect for and understanding of native customs. The problem is now seen as two-sided. The content and structure of the culture of the administered group must still be analyzed. The practical anthropologist must also have a systematic understanding of the special subcultures of the policy makers, the supervisory administrators, and the field operators.

Hence the anthropologist tends often to be a middleman whose indispensable function is that of making one group see the point of view of another. This position has its difficulties, as anthropologists in the War Relocation camps and in industry have discovered. To the Japanese in the camps the anthropologist seemed strange, for he was the one staff member who gave no orders. To other staff members the anthropologist appeared equally queer, for he appeared at least in part to identify himself with the Japanese evacuees—to be in the administration but not of it. The Japanese suspected the anthropologist to be a spy of the administration; the administration frequently feared the anthropologist as a spy of the Washington office. Only by scrupulously protecting the confidences of both sets of clients could the anthropologist establish trust in himself as a go-between. The top administrators were convinced of the need for attorneys and doctors, but only gradually were they convinced that specialists in human relations were useful in maintaining social health. In most cases the anthropologist won the confidence of his project director by proving that he could be a reliable forecaster of the social weather, by pointing a finger at trouble spots ahead so that the administration might adopt preventive measures or at least be prepared to deal with trouble when it came.

The same kind of approach has been applied in community settlement, regional rehabilitation, and in laying the groundwork for future peace in occupied areas. The job of the anthropologist has been to discover sources of irritation and conflict among the groups being aided that were not obvious to officials and technicians from the outside. The tendency used to be to consider man only as a physical animal and land as a physical resource. Anthropologists have drawn attention to the fact that a whole set of values and customary patterns of social life intervene between men and natural resources and that this total network must be investigated. As Redfield and Warner say:

> The problems of the American farmer have been attacked chiefly on the side of agricultural technology, credit, and marketing and to some extent in terms of the varied and special efforts at rural betterment, sometimes called social welfare. From the viewpoint of social anthropology, the agricultural techniques, farm credits, land tenure, social organizations and morale of a farming community are all more or less interdependent parts of a whole. This whole, as such, can be studied objectively.

Identical principles apply in the realms of military government and colonial administration. The morale of every society depends upon the security which individuals feel that in acting with others their own needs will be fulfilled. The administrator must never forget that this security may rest upon premises and upon emotional response sequences which are quite different from those to which he is accustomed. Americans are a highly practical people. They commonly assume, without reflection or analysis, that the ultimate criterion of any act is its utility, conceived in material terms. A given course of action may make sense to an American and yet seem arbitrary, unreasonable, or oppressive to a people of a different cultural tradition. An apparently innocent and technologically helpful improvement may bring confusion into social relations. When the western-style house was introduced into Samoa the lack of posts abolished the fixed cues to seating positions for persons of different ranks. These positions had symbolized the whole structure of Samoan society. Their sudden disappearance disrupted the normal way of life.

Military government and colonial administration are inevitably attempts at directed culture change. Change is always going on in all societies—though at varying rates. The country of Yeman is at the moment stepping suddenly from the thirteenth century into the twentieth. Directed change is often necessary and can bring much more gain than loss to a preindustrial group. But if it be forced too rapidly and if new motivations for carrying on socially valuable aspects of the culture are not introduced, change can be disruptive to the extent that whole groups become perennial reservoirs of delinquency and criminality. Or, as has been the case with certain Pacific Islanders, they completely lose a zest for life and commit race suicide. The measures taken by missionaries, administrators, and educators have all too frequently produced not an acceptable imitation of a Christian European but a chaotic individual not rooted in any definite way of life. Both culture change that is forced with destructive rapidity and willful holding back on the part of a governing power create maladjustment and hostility.

If we understand that even the most casual culture traits may be intimately linked to the aspirations of a people, we realize that needful changes will be made slowly if they are to be constructive. The blocking of familiar channels of action and expression can be at least as disturbing as the problems created by innovations. And innovations do not necessarily create motivations corresponding to those in Western culture. Rather, as Frederick Hulse says, they may have "a depressive effect upon such incentives as previously existed." Hulse draws an excellent illustration from Japan:

> Those incentives to productive activity which are taken for granted by most western economists are lacking among the laboring class in Japan, and such social incentives as the hope for admiration of their skill and ingenuity, which were adequate and proper under the feudal system, could not be effective among the great majority, who had never attained a craftman's skill. All that

remains is the necessity of somehow getting food, clothing, and shelter for oneself and one's family. Consequently the early collapse of the rationing system, the booming of the black market, the overcrowding of trains by people visiting their farmer relatives, became inevitably a greater and greater drain upon the war potential of Japan.

When culture contact is haphazard and shortsighted, the effects can boomerang back to the exploiting nations. Had the European countries who so brashly pried open the doors of Japan and China truly understood cultural relativity, there might today be no Pearl Harbor to remember and no threat from the vast disorganization of China. It is, to be sure, equally true that it was a misunderstanding of the less superficial aspects of American life that led the Japanese to their blunder of Pearl Harbor.

During the past century many peoples have been jostled about and abused by the dominant nations of Europe and America. The more this occurs the more such peoples are likely to cling together in aggregates—Pan-Asiatic, Pan-Islamic, or similar potentially military groupings. This can happen even if we treat them by what *we* consider just standards, for the critical question must always be: do *they* feel themselves to be justly treated? Bernard Shaw's quip is to the point: "The Golden Rule is really: 'don't do unto others as you would have them do unto you—their tastes may be different.'" Nor is it any use to say: let other cultures alone. Contacts between peoples must inevitably increase and mere contact is itself a form of action. A people is altered by the mere knowledge that others are different from themselves. The important thing is that whatever is done shall be appropriate, shall bear some meaningful relation to the cultural values and expectations of both sides.

If the values of the minority group are destroyed, the major power has not only obliterated potential enrichment to general human nature but has also created problems for itself. In Fiji, for instance, prestige used to depend on how big a feast and how much goods a man could give away to his clan. A man was not refused that for which he asked, but was expected to give if he could, and social approbation went to the giver. Thus a strong competitive motive, both for production and for an equitable distribution of food, was ordinarily assured. Seeking to replace this pattern by encouraging thrift and by other well-meaning gestures, British officials and missionaries succeeded only in undermining the whole economic system. With great numbers of the population dying in epidemics introduced from Europe, a sharply falling birth rate, and the pauperized survivors barely existing on handouts of rice, it seemed for a time that the Fijians were doomed to extinction.

The tempo with which changes are introduced is always a difficult problem, with complications incident to each specific case. Decisions will necessarily represent compromises between practical requirements and theoretically desirable time intervals. Ideally, changes should increasingly be initiated by the administered people themselves. The goal of the anthropological administrator is not attained when some understanding of the alien culture has been attained by representatives of the governing power. The anthropologist ought also to help the administered group to understand themselves in comparative terms, to grasp the alternatives, and to choose the directions in which they wish to move:

> Social Engineers in that case would come to help the weak and the devastated, not like a road engineer who arrives with his own blueprints for a road to a distant and alien city of his own choosing, but as one who says "In what direction, friends, have you always travelled? Let us study that road and see if we can rebuild it so that you can safely arrive." —LYMAN BRYSON

During the last twenty years there has been created at the Harvard Business School, the Massachusetts Institute of Technology, and the University of Chicago a new specialty which is sometimes known as industrial anthropology. In the now famous studies of the Western Electric Plant at Cicero, Illinois, it was decided to approach the human problems of industry in the manner that the anthropologist had been forced to employ in studying primitive tribes. That is, observers were to banish their preconceptions as to why people worked hard, why they did or didn't get along. The observers were to proceed as if they were entering a completely alien world: to note and to analyze without introducing assumptions that did not arise from the data.

Industrial anthropology consists in applying to one sector of our own society the techniques and types of reasoning developed in anthropological field work and in anthropology as used in colonial administration. Previous personnel work had been directed toward the development of greater efficiency rather than toward the maintenance of cooperation. But it was discovered that physical improvements in working conditions did not increase output unless the workers interpreted them as a favorable social change. New routines that actually resulted in lessened physiological fatigue brought about decreased production because they disturbed customary social relations. Engineers tended to think, act, and communicate in rational terms. Workers reacted in nonrational fashion according to the logic of the sentiments current in their particular subculture. Because strikes occurred even when workers' demands for hours, wages, and physical facilities were fully met, management was finally led to social as well as technological engineering. Anthropologists helped management to realize that, whereas an engineer's drawing will accurately indicate the workings of a machine, the chart in the president's office showing the chain of command in the formal organization of an industry is not a fully correct representation of the lines of significant communication. Every culture has behavioral as well as ideal patterns. Informal systems of behavior, involving clique structures and the consequences of a foreman's individuality as well as his status, can effectively short-circuit the neat and rational flow of energy indicated on the chart.

This is, of course, not limited to industrial organizations. Plans carefully thought through in the United States Indian Office in Washington failed of fruition because of informal patterns of relationships in a field office which were not taken into account by the planners. A program can be thoroughly sabotaged at the operating level by overliteral compliance, by strategic delays, by action that is verbally correct but emotionally hostile. American popular imagination pictures a "big executive" as "running" an organization. However, it is pure fiction to suppose that an executive can attain his objectives by sitting in an office and giving orders. As they say in the State Department, "policy is made on the cables." That is, an incident occurs in a foreign country, and instructions must immediately be sent to our representatives there. This particular contingency has not been foreseen by the top men who are supposed to formulate policy. A decision is made in a hurry by a subordinate and, in nine cases out of ten, the Department is committed to a policy by the action taken. In most organizations these decisions determine policy. The ideal pattern is blocked by the power of informal behavior patterns that are left out of consideration in administrative planning.

Nevertheless there are discoverable regularities in the human just as much as in the technological problems of industry and of all organizations. The informal organization, just exactly where and how the formal and informal charts mesh, the semantic aspects of communication, the sentiment systems and symbols of each subculture can be mapped out with enough accuracy to be useful. As Eliot Chapple has written:

On questions of a technological nature, the anthropologist is not trained to give judgment; he is not primarily concerned with the comparative efficiency of two methods of farming, nor with the value of a new system of cost accounting. What he can do is to predict what will happen to the relations of people when such methods are introduced. It is the administrator's business to make the decision, weighing the evidence furnished by the anthropologist and the technical expert.

By using anthropological methods, the administrator can attain a control in the field of human relations comparable to that which he already has in the field of costs and production. He can understand and estimate the effects of change, and see what steps have to be taken to modify his organization or to restore it to a state of balance. He can do this both through acquiring a knowledge of anthropological principles, and by using anthropologists to make analyses of existing situations.

The earlier anthropological work in industry was largely confined to human relations within the factory. The interdependence of industry and community also needs to be investigated. The special form of labor problems in the Piedmont industrial area of the South is seen as patterned by the persistence of cultural habits governing landlord-tenant relationships. The plastics industry in New England is found to be dependent upon continuation of one type of family structure found among some immigrant groups where the younger generation continues to submit to parental authority even after marriage and to maintain an economic unit with the parents. Conrad Arensberg has pointed out how some of the special features of behavior in automobile unions are related to the fact that so many of these workers were drawn from the hill regions of the South.

Technological changes inevitably bring about changes in

social organization both outside and within the factory. It is the anthropologist's task so to map social space and to chart the main flows of cultural currents that the unexpected consequences of the rational acts of the engineer and the efficiency expert can be minimized. Otherwise the nonrational aspects of social life will become irrational. Just as a too rapid pace of culture change brings about apathy or hostility or self-destruction, so sudden technical innovations lead to vast social erosion within our society. It is not just that job opportunities are destroyed. If the worker is rushed without warning into a new job where he cannot use the skills upon which his self-confidence was based, a job that has no name that brings social recognition outside the workroom, free-floating anxiety and potential aggression may burst into civil strife.

The applied anthropologist has useful ways of getting and conveying all sorts of information on human relations. Because he considers any one group's behavior as an exemplification of general social and cultural processes, he can often make a swift diagnosis on the basis of a few clues, like a palaeontologist who reconstructs a whole animal from a few bones on the basis of his general knowledge of the structure of similar animals. Because he knows what happens when a few threads in the pattern are pulled, he can warn of the unexpected consequences of planned social action. By reconnoitering the cultures of administrators and administered, he perceives the natural rivalry lines in each group. He discriminates between the characteristics of decision-making personnel, those of the public they represent, and those of the people toward whom action is directed. Hence he is an effective liaison man between all groups. He knows that sometimes it is necessary to direct the boat upstream to get to the opposite shore.

All in all, the practical anthropologist will do well to conceive his role as that of the social doctor rather than as that of the social engineer. In some quarters applied anthropology is decried as "the manipulation of people." Epithets ranging from "scientific prostitute" to "the hired hands of empire" are freely used. (The other side replies, of course, with "ivory-tower escapist.") Granted that no profession should be composed of a set of technicians who sell their services to the highest bidder without regard for other considerations, some of the excitement seems a little foolish. The industrial anthropologist is equally available to labor unions and to management. His knowledge is published—not the jealously guarded trade secret of a capitalist Gestapo. People are manipulated in advertising, in the movies, on the radio, and indeed in teaching. If an anthropologist is permitted to discuss cultural change with sophomores, it is probably safe to let him advise the Indian service. There is need for the development of a more explicit and generally accepted professional code, and the Society for Applied Anthropology has been working to this end for several years. Most anthropologists, however, would already subscribe to John Embree's statement:

> Just as the medical doctor has a basic doctrine that he should prevent disease and save life, so the applied anthropologist tends to operate on a basic doctrine that he should prevent friction and violence in human relations, preserve the rights and dignity of administered groups, and that he should save lives . . . aid in establishing peaceful and self-respecting relations between peoples and cultures.

CHAPTER VIII

Personality in Culture

THE ANTHROPOLOGIST, like the psychologist and the psychiatrist, is trying to find out what makes people tick. The question of the flexibility of "human nature" is no mere academic quibble. A sound answer is essential to realistic educational schemes and to practical social planning. The Nazis assumed they could fashion people into almost any shape they wanted if they started early enough and applied sufficient pressures. The Communists tend in some ways to assume that "human nature" is everywhere and always the same—as, for instance, in their assumption that the primary motivations are inevitably economic ones. Within what limits can human beings be molded? The only scientific way of obtaining at least the minimum range is to look at the record of all known peoples, past and present. How do different groups train their children in such a way that the personalities of adults, though varying among themselves, nevertheless exhibit many traits that are less characteristic of other groups? The statistical prediction can safely be made that 100 Americans will display some features of personal organization and behavior more frequently than will 100 Englishmen of comparable age, social class, and vocational assortment. In so far as it can be discovered precisely how this is brought about, much progress will have been made toward being able to revamp childhood training in the home and formal education so as to create the traits thought most desirable. A tremendous step forward in the understanding of international differences and frictions will also have been taken.

Which of the many courses of behavior within an individual's physical and mental capacities he characteristically takes is determined in part by culture. Human material has a tendency toward shapes of its own, but a definition of socialization in any culture is the predictability of an individual's daily behavior in various defined situations. When a person has surrendered much of his physiological autonomy to cultural control, when he behaves most of the time as others do in following cultural routines, he is then socialized. Those who retain too great a measure of independence are necessarily confined in the asylum or the jail.

Children are brought up in different ways in different societies. Sometimes they are weaned early and abruptly. Sometimes they are allowed to nurse as long as they like, gradually weaning themselves at the age of three or more. In certain cultures the child is harshly dominated from the beginning by mother or father or both. In others affectionate warmth prevails in the family to the extent that parents refuse to take the responsibility for disciplining their children themselves. In one group the youngster grows up in the isolated biological family. Until he goes to school he must adjust only to his mother, his father, a brother or sister or two, and, in some cases, one or more servants. In other societies the baby is handled and even nursed by several different women, all of whom he presently learns to call "mother." He grows up in an extended family where many adults of both sexes play approximately equivalent roles toward him and where his maternal cousins are scarcely distinguished from his own brothers and sisters.

Some of each child's wants are those common to all human animals. But each culture has its own scheme for the most desirable and the most approved ways of satisfying these needs. Every distinct society communicates to the new generation very early in life a standard picture of valued ends and sanctioned means, of behavior appropriate for men and women, young and old, priests and farmers. In one culture the prized type is the sophisticated matron, in another the young warrior, in still another the elderly scholar.

In view of what the psychoanalysts and the child psychologists have taught us about the processes of personality formation, it is not surprising that one or more patterns of personality are more frequent among the French than among the Chinese, among the English upper classes than among the English lower classes. This does not, of course, imply that the personality characteristics of the members of any group are identical. There are deviants in every society and in every social class within a society. Even among those who approximate one of the typical personality structures there is a great range of variation. Theoretically this is to be expected because each individual's genetic constitution is unique. Moreover, no two individuals of the same age, sex, and social position in the same subculture have identical life experiences. The culture itself consists of a set of norms that are varyingly applied and interpreted by each father and mother. Yet we do know from experience that the members of different societies will tend, typically, to handle problems of biological gratification, of adjustment to the physical environment, of adjustment to other persons in ways that have much in common. There is, of course, no assumption that "national character" is fixed throughout history.

It is a fact of experience that if a Russian baby is brought to the United States he will, as an adult, act and think like an American—not like a Russian. Perhaps the sixty-four-dollar question in the whole field of anthropology is: what makes an Italian into an Italian, a Japanese into a Japanese? The process of becoming a representative member of any group involves a molding of raw human nature. Presumably the newborn infants of any society are more like other infants anywhere in the world than like older individuals in their own group. But the finished products of each group show certain resemblances. The great contribution of anthropology has consisted in calling attention to the variety of these styles of behavior, to the circumstance that various kinds of mental disease occur with varying frequency in different societies, to the fact that there are some striking correspondences between childhood training patterns and the institutions of adult life.

It is all too easy to oversimplify this picture. Probably the Prussian tends to see all human relationships in authoritarian terms largely because his first experiences were set in the authoritarian family. But this type of family structure was supported by the accepted ways of behaving in the army, in political and economic life, in the system of formal education. The fundamental directions of childhood training do not derive from the inborn nature of a people; they look forward to the roles of men and women and are cast in the mold of the society's most pervasive ideals. As Pettit has said, "Corporal punishment is rare among primitives not because of an innate kindliness, but because it is antipathetic to the development of the type of individual personality set up as an ideal."

Childhood training patterns do not in any simple sense cause the institutions of adult life. There is, rather, a reciprocal relation, a relation of mutual reinforcement, between the two. No arbitrary change, divorced from the general emphases of the culture, in methods of child rearing will suddenly alter adult personalities in a desired direction. This was the false assumption that underlay certain aspects of the progressive education movement. In these schools children were being prepared for a world that existed only in the dreams of certain educators.

When the youngsters left the schools they either reverted naturally enough to the view of life they had absorbed in pre-school days in their families or they dissipated their energies in impotent rebellion against the pattern of the larger society. "Competition"—or at least certain types of competition for certain ends—may be "bad," yet American tradition and the American situation weave competition into the whole texture of American life. The attempt on the part of the small minority to eliminate this attitude by school practices results either in failure or in conflict or retreatism for the individuals concerned.

It is especially absurd to seize upon a single childhood discipline as the magic key to the whole tone of a culture. One vulgarization of a scientific theory on Japanese character structure traces the sources of Japanese aggression to early and severe toilet training. This has been deservedly ridiculed as the "Scott Tissue interpretation of history." The whole set of childhood disciplines is as insufficient to explain typical personality structure as is any list of culture traits without information as to their organization. One needs to know the interrelationships of all the rewards and punishments; when, how, and by whom they were administered.

Occasionally there is a highly probable connection between a particular aspect of the child's experience and a particular pattern of adult life. Divorce is extremely frequent among the Navaho. In part, this may well be related to the fact that the Navaho child's affection and emotional dependency is not so tied to the two parents. However, we know from the recent history of our own society that a high divorce rate can also be produced by other causes, though there is the difference that Navaho divorce is taken in much more matter-of-fact fashion, with much less emotional upset. This is related to the absence of the romantic love complex among the Navahos, which, again, presumably depends to some degree upon the childhood experience where there is less focus upon one mother and one father.

At any rate, the over-all pattern for personality can be understood only in terms of total childhood experience *plus* the situational pressures of adult life. It may well be, as the psychoanalysts claim, that maximum indulgence of the child in the preverbal period is correlated with a secure, well-adjusted personality. However, this can be regarded only as foundation—not as promise of fulfillment. The Navaho child receives every gratification in the first two years of life. But adult Navahos manifest a very high level of anxiety. This is largely a response to the reality situation; in terms of their present difficulties as a people they are realistically worried and suspicious.

These situational factors and cultural patterns are jointly responsible for the fact that each culture has its pet mental disturbances. Malayans "run amok"; certain Indians of Canada take to cannibalistic aggression; peoples of Southeast Asia fancy themselves possessed by weretigers; tribes of Siberia are prey to "arctic hysteria"; a Sumatran people goes in for "pig-madness." Differentiated groups within a culture show varying rates of incidence. In the United States today schizophrenia is more frequent among the lower classes; manic-depressive psychosis is an upper-class ailment. The American middle classes suffer from psychosomatic disturbances such as ulcers related to conformance and repressed aggression. Certain kinds of psychological invalidism are characteristic of American social climbers. Feeding problems are more frequent among children of Jewish families in the United States. The explanation of these facts cannot be solely biological, for American women once outnumbered men as ulcer patients. In some societies more men than women become insane; in others the reverse. In certain cultures stammering is predominantly a female affliction, in others male. Japanese living in Hawaii are much more prone to manic-depressive disorders than Japanese living in Japan. High blood pressure troubles American Negroes but is rare among African Negroes.

Anthropologists have studied not the uniqueness of each individual but rather personality as the product of the channeling of the desires and needs, both biological and social, of the members of social groups. To the extent that we become aware of the needs, not only economic and physical but also emotional, of other peoples, their actions appear less obscure, less unpredictable, less "immoral." There is a unifying philosophy behind the way of life of each society at any given point in its history. The main outlines of the fundamental assumptions and recurrent feelings have only exceptionally been created out of the stuff of unique biological heredity and peculiar life experience. They are usually cultural products. From the life ways of his environment the ordinary individual derives most of his mental outlook. To him his culture or subculture appears as a homogeneous whole; he has little sense of its historic depth and diversity.

Since cultures have organization as well as content, this intuitive reaction is partially correct. Each culture has its standard plots, its type conflicts, and type solutions. And so the culturally stylized aspects of nursing, the usual ways of dressing a child, the accepted rewards and punishments in toilet training are all equally part of an unconscious conspiracy to convey to the youngster a particular set of basic values. Each culture is saturated in its own meanings. Hence no valid science of human behavior can be built on the canons of radical behaviorism. For in every culture there is more than meets the eye, and no amount of external description can convey this underlying portion of it. Bread and wine may mean mere nourishment for the body in one culture. They may mean emotional communion with the deity in another. The bare fact in each case is the same, but its place in cultural structure—and therefore its significance for understanding the behavior of individuals—has changed.

Some sorts of behavior will be manifested by all human beings regardless of how they have been trained. There is an organic "push" in each different individual toward certain kinds of acts. But to each biologically given characteristic is imputed a cultural meaning. Moreover, each culture is successful to greater or lesser extent in "pulling" the variety of impulses in the same directions. Over and above the penalties attached to deviance, it is easier and aesthetically more satisfying to pattern one's own conduct in accord with preexisting forms that have been made to seem as natural and inevitable as the alternation of night and day.

The characteristics of the human animal which make culture possible are the ability to learn, to communicate by a system of learned symbols, and to transmit learned behavior from generation to generation. But what is learned varies widely from society to society and even in different sectors of the same society. The manner of learning also shows patterned and characteristic forms. The emotional tone of the parents and of other agents for transmitting the culture has typical and culturally enjoined modes. The situations in which learning takes place are differently defined and phrased in different societies. The rewards for learning, the "squeezes" in learning situations, the sanctions for failing to learn take many different forms and emphases. This is true not only for the culture as a whole but also for various subcultures within it. The formation of the American child's personality is affected by the particular social, economic, and regional subgroup to which the parents belong. The patterns for physical growth and maturation are about the same for Café Society and Lower East Side children, but the child training practices, preferred life goals and manners, rewards, and punishments belong to quite different worlds.

All animals exhibit certain limitations, capacities, and requirements as organisms. These must never be forgotten in enthusiasm over the determining powers of culture. Margaret Mead's well-known book *Sex and Temperament in Three Primitive Societies* has given many readers an impression that she is arguing that the temperamental differences between men and women are completely produced by culture. The one-line book review by a fellow anthropologist is a sobering corrective: "Margaret, this is a very brilliant book. But do you really know any cultures in which the men have the babies?"

The pressures of child training bring their influences to bear upon different biological materials. Metabolic needs vary. Digestion does not require precisely the same time in every baby. The first cultural disciplines are directed toward three very basic organic responses: accepting, retaining, and releasing. Cultures vary widely in the extent to which they place positive or negative stress upon one or more of these reactions. A potent source of individual variation within a society rests in the fact that the reaction to cultural training is modified by the child's relative degree of neurological maturity. Even apart from babies known to be born prematurely, the nervous equipment of newborn infants shows a sizable range.

Nevertheless there is still considerable leeway among the organically defined possibilities. The requirements of human animals for survival and gratification can be attained in more than one way through the given capacities. Especially in the case of a symbol-using animal like man, these are significant questions: what is learned? who teaches it? how is it taught? There is a continuous and dynamic interrelationship between the patterns of a culture and the personalities of its individual members. Though certain needs are universal, they receive different emphases in different societies. A society perpetuates itself biologically by means that are well known. Less fully realized is the fact that societies are constantly perpetuating themselves socially by inculcating in each new generation time-tried ways of believing, feeling, thinking, and reacting.

Like rats learning to run a maze that has food at its exit, children gradually familiarize themselves with the well-trodden but often devious intricacies of the cultural network. They learn to take their cues for response not merely from their personal needs nor from the actualities of a situation but from subtle aspects of the situation as culturally defined. This cultural cue says: be suspicious and reserved. That says: relax; be sociable. In spite of the diversities of individual natures, the Crow Indian learns to be habitually generous, the Yurok habitually stingy, the Kwakiutl chieftain habitually arrogant and ostentatious. Far from being always resentful at the walls of the cultural maze, most adults, and even children to some extent, derive pleasure from the performance of cultural routines. Human beings generally find it highly rewarding to behave like others who share the same culture. The sense of running the same maze also promotes social solidarity.

The extent to which personality is a cultural product has been obscured by a number of factors. The child's physical and cultural heritage comes from the same persons, and physical and social growing up go on side by side. Human learning occurs slowly; animal learning is more dramatic. There are also at least two psychological clues to the overemphasis upon biological factors. Education necessarily involves more or less conflict between teacher and learner. Parents and teachers are almost certain to experience some guilt when they behave aggressively toward children, so they tend to welcome any generalization that denies the significance of hostility in the process of personality formation. The theory that personality is merely the maturation of biological tendencies provides elders with a convenient rationalization. If a child will indeed become what he is destined to become on the basis of his genetic constitution, then one needs only to provide him with the simple physical necessities. If a child does not turn out to be as capable or attractive as one parent thinks he should be on the basis of the "good blood" on that parent's side of the family, the theory can always be vindicated by blaming the in-laws.

Granted that personality is largely a product of learning and that much of the learning is culturally determined and controlled, it should be pointed out that there are two kinds of cultural learning: technical and regulatory. Learning the multiplication tables is technical, whereas the learning of manners (*e.g.*, in our society, not to spit indiscriminately) is regulatory. In neither case does the child have to learn everything for himself; he is given the answers. Both of these types of education are socially desirable and necessary to the individual, although he is certain to resist them to some extent. The one type is intended to make the individual productive, socially useful, to increase the group's wealth and strength. The other type of education is intended to reduce the nuisance value of the individual within the group as much as possible, to keep him from disturbing others, creating in-group disharmony, etc. In this connection it is noteworthy that common speech makes this distinction in the two connotations of the word "good" when used as an attribute for a person. A person is said to be "good" either in the sense of being morally and socially amenable, or he is "good" in the sense of being unusually skillful, accomplished, etc.

In our society, the school is traditionally appointed for the development of technological training, the home and church for regulatory training. However, there is considerable overlapping, the home teaching some skills and the school also teaching certain morals and manners.

There are certain limitations both as to how far and how

rapidly technical and regulatory learning can proceed. The physical structure and organization of each human organism determines the limits; the physical maturity and the amount of prior learning determines the rate. For example, the child cannot acquire the skill of walking until the necessary connections between nerve tracts are completed. Instruction learning cannot occur to a very marked extent until language has developed. Each stage or age has its own special and characteristic tasks. Both the age limits and the tasks vary greatly in different cultures, but everywhere development is by steps, stages, degrees. One level of adjustment is attained only to be superseded by another and another. This is very explicit in many nonliterate societies, but the extent to which school grades and, in adult life, lodges and clubs carry out this same segmentation in our own society must not be overlooked. To some extent, this means that any adult personality is a succession of habit strata, even though the organizing principles of the personality probably achieve rather early a relative fixity which makes for continuity. Only in earliest infancy does a child appear to behave in a haphazard manner. Soon he seems to have a personality policy which, albeit in disguised forms, often supplies the directional trends for his whole life.

In other words, the adult personality is an architectural integration. There are integrating principles, but there also various levels and areas that are more and less central to the structure as a whole. If we study a personality by levels, we see how characteristic responses of one degree of complexity supersede or disguise any direct manifestation of reactions that are typical at a different degree of complexity. The same personality responds to different situations with differences which are sometimes very dramatic. Every personality is capable of more than one mode of expression. The particular mode depends upon the total psychological field and upon cultural phrasings. If one reaches for an object, the movement of one's hand is steered by its perceived position in perceived surroundings. Likewise, personality manifestations are regulated, in part, by the person's perception of himself and others within the cultural setting.

It is descriptively convenient to speak of nuclear and peripheral regions of personality. Changes in the nuclear region, though sometimes trivial in themselves, always modify the personality policy and are necessarily of the either-or variety. Changes in the peripheral region may be purely quantitative and may occur without altering other personality traits. The major stages (oral, anal, genital) require nuclear changes, but together with these are those more superficial adaptations to status and role which every culture expects of persons of a given age, sex, and office. In most cases the periphery is where there is relative freedom to make adjustments. There is always the question of interrelationship, of what the peripheral adjustments mean to the less yielding nucleus. Cultures have precisely this same architectural property.

The sequence of development, or personality growth, is not wholly spontaneous or self-determined. Most stages or aspects of stages will persist just precisely so long as they work for the organism. There will be as much continuity in any individual's life as there is serviceability in his value system. The child goes on as long as his private variant of the cultural value system works. But when his environment demands change to obtain satisfaction he will change. Thus personality growth is rather a product of the continuous and often tempestuous interaction of the maturing child and his older, more powerful mentors upon whom falls the responsibility of transmitting the culture and who in so doing convert him into a particular kind of human being.

The fact that personality development must proceed in this way carries with it two important complications: It means that education must be a prolonged process, costly from the point of view of both time and effort. It predisposes the individual to regression, *i.e.*, to a return to an earlier stage of adjustment if difficulty is encountered in a later stage. Since permitting an infant or child to make an adjustment on a lower level means that he becomes more or less "fixated" at this level and since this development by successive "fixations" predisposes him to the danger of regression, it might seem reasonable to try to circumvent both of these complications by not allowing any fixations to occur. Why should we not teach the child the ultimately correct type of behavior from the very outset, or, when this is patently impossible, allow him to learn nothing until he becomes capable of learning precisely what will be ultimately expected of him as an adult member of society?

No one has seriously advocated this sort of short-circuiting of the educational process in the technical sphere. Children have not been expected to do calculus without first having learned simple arithmetic. But in the realm of regulatory education, serious attempts have been made to make children conform from the very outset of their lives to the demands for renunciation which will ultimately be made of them as adults—in the spheres, notably, of sex, cleanliness, and respect for property. For reasons not yet fully understood, it appears that fewer maladjusted individuals will result if certain infantile impulses are allowed to run their course. Indulgence and reassurance during the period when the oral drive is strong seem to be the best guarantees that the individual will later be able to restrict the pleasures of the mouth willingly and without distortion. To attain basic security the infant needs to be safe both from the physical world (supported) and from the cultural world (excused). Certain forms of learning can be achieved with less injury after language has been acquired. Without speech, the infant has to learn by trial and error and by conditioning. With speech, he can profit from instruction. When one type of activity is forbidden, the child can be told how to achieve his goal by a different type of behavior. Speech itself has to develop in the slow, primitive fashion, but, once it is acquired, other learning is greatly speeded.

The customary turns of phrase used to bring a child into line bear a relationship to the typical forms of adult character. Sometimes, as in our own society at present, the dominant tendency is for parents to assume full responsibility in the eyes of the child and to emphasize a sharp line between "right" and "wrong." "Do it because I say it is right." "Do it because I say so." "Do it because I am your father and children must obey their parents." "Don't do it because it is nasty." "Do it or I won't buy you any candy." "If you aren't a good little boy, mamma will be unhappy"—or even—"If you aren't a good little boy, mamma won't love you." While the threat of shaming ("If you wet your pants people will make fun of you") which is the primary instrument of socialization in many primitive societies is also used by Americans, most socialization after the verbal period is built around the threat of withdrawal of parental love and protection. This can give the child a sense of unworthiness with lifelong consequences. The fear of not measuring up is with many Americans a principal driving force. A persistent need is felt to show the parents that, after all, the child was capable of constructive achievements.

This tendency is reinforced by other cultural goals. Parents try to make their children "better" than they; they become "ambitious for their children," want their children to accomplish what they did not. Parents are under social pressure and are judged by their children. They compete with each other through their children, not having security enough themselves to resist this pressure. By pressing their children for renunciation and accomplishment they can ease their own anxieties.

Having chafed in their lowly positions, many lower- and lower-middle-class parents are eager to see their children "rise." But this involves postponement and renunciation, which can be learned and made a stable part of one's character only if, from early childhood on, the individual has continuous opportunities to experience the advantages of working and waiting. And, if parents are economically unable to give their children this kind of training—compensation for renunciation and enhanced reward for postponement, their efforts are almost certainly doomed to failure. Physical punishment for indolence and indulgence, if not conjoined with experienced gains and advantages, will not ordinarily accomplish the desired end. Because of the inability of underprivileged parents to keep their children from experiencing want, such children tend to develop precocious self-sufficiency and emotional detachment. Why, after all, should a child remain dependent upon and obedient to parents who have not really supported and protected him? When the child thus becomes prematurely independent, socialization is ordinarily at an end. And when this emancipation is accompanied by feelings of deep hostility and resentment toward the parents, the stage is set for a criminal career.

In order to be socially well adjusted, an individual must not be too shortsightedly selfish, too headlong in his pursuit of comfort and pleasure; but there is likewise a limit to which a person can profitably take the "unselfish" view. An otherworldly orientation, for example, demands that mundane existence should consist solely of obedience, sacrifice, charity, self-denial, and austerity. People who can attain and sustain this mode of life are often nice to have around; some of them make few demands on others and render much assistance and help. But if the criminal, or undersocialized type of individual, may be said to exploit society, surely it is equally true that society exploits many of the oversocialized, too conscientious, too moral and self-denying. Modern psychiatrists all tell us that human beings, if they are to remain emotionally healthy, must have fun. The attempt to make the individual take an excessively long-term view of his life is itself a shortsighted social policy which must be dearly paid for in the end.

Two common observations concerning the behavior of individuals in our culture become intelligible from this perspective on punishment, anxiety, and conscience. Why should it be that human beings commonly accept punishment for a misdeed as "just," with no remonstrance whatsoever? The explanation is complex, resting partly on our Christian background and on the mutually reinforcing system of our cultural norms and socialization process. The peculiarity of the North European tradition must be realized. The "emphasis upon the importance of moral choice" is not, as we too readily assume, a universal human trait, for, as Margaret Mead points out:

> Comparative studies . . . demonstrate that this type of character in which the individual is reared to ask first not "Do I want it?" or "Am I afraid?" or "Is this custom?" but "Is this right or wrong?" is a very special development, characteristic of our own culture and of a very few other societies. It is dependent upon the parents' personally administering the culture in moral terms, standing to the child as responsible representatives of right choices, and punishing or rewarding the child in the name of the *Right.*

Americans also sometimes voluntarily "confess" to sins which might never have been discovered, or they may even do certain forbidden acts quite openly, apparently for no other reason than with the hope of being punished. On the basis of these and similar observations, clinicians have sometimes posited a "need for punishment" or a "masochistic instinct." An alternative and simpler postulate is that "guilty" persons willingly accept or even solicit punishment because this is the only means by which their conscience-anxiety can be reduced or eliminated. If punishment always coincided with the occurrence of a misdeed, then once a deed had been committed without punishment, there would be no need to feel guilty and no need for punishment.

Many fascinating problems lie in this sphere. What, for example, is the relation between conscience and the "reality principle," *i.e.*, learning to postpone immediate gratification for greater ultimate satisfaction? Again one sees the ultimate in this principle in the concept of reward after death. Here, as in the case of the renunciatory type of personality maximized by early and Medieval Christianity, earthly pleasures are postponed indefinitely. This is an extension of a general habit that is learned and rewarded during the course of life proper. Heaven becomes a place in which happiness is safe. On the earth it is dangerous to be happy. The problem is whether thinking of this kind would arise if punishments were not often postponed so that one would not know when one was safe ("guiltless") and when one was not.

Another puzzling question exists as to precisely what the relation is between guilt and aggression. Depression and related guilt states are often referred to as "aggression turned inward." Does this mean merely that the aggression caused by a frustrated impulse is in turn inhibited by anxiety and that the person feels anxiety instead of aggression?

Fenichel has written at length on what may be called the psychology of apology, taking the position that apologizing is a common and, in many cases, a socially acceptable way of reducing guilt. In making an apology, one punishes oneself in a certain sense, and thereby prevents the other person from doing so. This dynamism would seem to give a clue to excessive deference and obsequiousness as the habitual strategies of a personality.

That human beings, as a result of their social experiences during and after childhood, sometimes develop a relatively complete and stable form of asceticism, may seem to constitute a psychological dilemma. Experimentation with lower animals has consistently indicated that unless a given act, or habit, is at least occasionally rewarded, it will eventually deteriorate and disappear. And it has been similarly demonstrated that in order for rewards to have a reinforcing effect upon a particular response, they must not be postponed long after the occurrence of this response. How, then, are we to explain the unremitting toil and steadfastness of purpose of those human beings who apparently eschew all wordly rewards and satisfactions? It is easy to dismiss this problem, either by making an *ad hoc* assumption, or by drawing a categorical distinction between the psychological laws which govern man and beast. It is true that human beings have developed symbolic processes to a far greater extent than have any of the lower animals and that this fact sets man apart in certain important respects. However, there is a simpler explanation. It is known that for those animals high enough in the evolutionary scale to experience anxiety, a reduction in this disagreeable state of affairs is highly rewarding and will sustain even the most difficult habits for a surprisingly long time. Although the exact relationship between anxiety and the moral sense in man has not as yet been clarified, it is generally acknowledged that a relationship does exist. Freud, for example, has said that "our conscience is not the inflexible judge that ethical teachers are wont to declare it, but in its origin is 'dread of the community' and nothing else."

From these premises it is an easy step to the conclusion that those individuals whose lives and work are ostensibly devoid of reward in the usual sense of the term are nevertheless reinforced and sustained by the gratification that comes from reduction of conscience-anxiety, or guilt. Nicias, the Epicurean philosopher in *Thaïs*, expresses this conception with singular clarity when, in comparing the motives for his own behavior with those of the abstinent monk, Paphnutius, he says: "Ah, well, dear friend, in doing these things, which are totally different in appearance, we shall both obey the same sentiment, the sole motive of all human actions; we shall both of us be seeking a common end: happiness, impossible happiness!" In this way the apparent contradiction is solved and a naturalistic conception of reward is created which is broad enough to include both the reinforcing, vivifying effects of sensuous gratification and the solace and comfort of a clear conscience.

Closely related to "moral masochism" is what Freud has called "criminality from a sense of guilt." Not infrequently persons present themselves for psychoanalytic treatment who, as their analysis reveals, have committed, not only trivial transgressions, but also such crimes as theft, fraud, and arson. This is a surprising observation, for most criminals are not ordinarily neurotic, and do not become candidates for analysis. Society may wish to change them or they may wish to change society, but they rarely wish to change themselves. The answer which Freud has given is that the analysis of such persons has "afforded the surprising conclusion that such deeds are done precisely *because* they are forbidden, and because by carrying them out the doer enjoys a sense of mental relief. He suffered from an oppressive feeling of guilt, of which he did not know the origin, and after he had committed a misdeed the oppression was mitigated. . . . Paradoxical as it may sound, I must maintain that the sense of guilt was present prior to the transgression, that it did not arise from this, but contrariwise—the transgression from the sense of guilt. These persons we might justifiably describe as criminals from a sense of guilt."

This analysis of "criminality from a sense of guilt" carries an important warning, namely: that one cannot validly diagnose personality on the basis of isolated actions, taken out of their dynamic context and detached from the meanings they have and the ends they serve for the individual actor. Let us suppose that three youths, *A*, *B*, and *C*, mount bicycles which do not belong to them and ride away without the rightful owners' knowledge. In our society, this action, objectively identical in all three cases, is a violation of property statutes. But it may be that individual A performed the act because he knew that in so doing he would be rendering the owner a service of some kind. Since his "intent" was not to steal, he would not be legally culpable and could not, therefore, be called a criminal. Individual B's motive for taking the bicycle may have been, not that he wished to use it or profit from its sale, but that by performing this action and allowing it to become known, he would humiliate his father and perhaps, in addition, gratify an unconscious "need for punishment." Here we would say that distinctly neurotic mechanisms were operative. Only in the case of individual C, who took the bicycle for the relatively uncomplicated reason that he consciously wanted it more than he feared the consequences of taking it, can we say that a really criminal personality has been manifested. And even this verdict can be reached only if we are sure that C was sufficiently familiar with the culture to be aware of the accepted rules applying to such a situation. The same kind of inquiry into motives, satisfactions, and knowledge must, of course, be made before the true significance of acts which are ostensibly "normal" or ostensibly "neurotic" can be reliably identified.

The fact that there is thus no fixed relationship between particular overt actions and the underlying motives was necessarily a hindrance to the development of a sound understanding of personality structure and dynamics. And because of the phenomenon of repression, even introspection, as we now know, could not be safely relied upon to give a complete picture of one's wishes and inclinations. It is mainly for these reasons that the special techniques designed by Freud and his followers for investigating the *total* personality, including the unconscious as well as the conscious aspects, have proved so revolutionary and given us the first really comprehensive psychological system.

Even if the need for physical and moral sanctuary during childhood be recognized, the practical problems are not solved by a policy of leaving the child alone. During infancy the child will in any event be developing an "attitude toward life": confidence, resignation, optimism, pessimism. These attitudes will be largely determined by the kind and amount of "care" given. The connection between child care and personality has not been fully appreciated. But its importance is twofold: it is useful in helping the child develop basic skills which will be later useful when indulgence ends and the child has to venture out on its own; and it is especially useful to have positive attitudes toward parents and others when regulatory training starts.

For the emotional pattern toward parents or brothers and sisters often becomes the prototype of habitual reactions toward friends and associates, employers and employees, leaders and deities. In a society where the childhood experience is typically that of overstrong but unsatisfied dependency upon the father there is a fertile soil for the demagogue. On the other hand, a culture like that of the Zuñi Indians, where the child's attachments are spread among many relatives and where dependence is focused upon the group as a whole rather than upon particular individuals, is peculiarly resistant to leaders of the Hitler type. Where the mother is the true center of family life, divinities are apt to be portrayed in female form.

The same patterns for parental treatment of children produce different varieties of personality, depending upon the inherent disposition of the individual child and the responses preferred in the culture. If the parents deal many blows to the self-esteem of the child he can compensate by an exaggerated, defiant conformity to expectations, by accepting unimportance and dependence, by egotistic self-inflation. Different patterns of behavior, as has been said, often represent the same underlying psychological cause. Aggressive and shy individuals may be just different outward manifestations of a wounded image of the self. Wherever gratification is denied and adequate rewards or substitute pleasures are not provided, the child builds up new sources of adjustment: lying, stealing, concealment, distrust, sensitiveness, disbelief, varying degrees of defiant indulgence in forbidden activities.

In spite of our patterns of socialization, some Americans are relatively free of anxieties, and relatively free from the need to fight. Even if weaning is carried out early, the happy mother who is not driven by her own inner insecurities and compulsions can handle the event so that it is more a physiological break and less a break in tenderness and association. In this case weaning is unlikely to be so momentous as it was with a boy whom Margaret Fries studied intensively through a number of his early years:

> The prototype of Jimmie's reactions to life's frustrations was to be found in his reaction to weaning at five months of age, when he became passive, negative, and withdrawn from the world.

Whereas excessive feelings of guilt tend to arise from too early and too energetic measures in habit training, special circumstances play an important role. If the mother has been too well trained to react negatively to the smell of her own and others' feces, she herself will experience active anxiety in the course of the bowel training of her children and will probably be driven at some points to active aggression against the child.

In other societies methods for inhibiting the responses of children which may be either socially objectionable or personally dangerous give the parents more ways of avoiding personal responsibility. A greater number of persons, uncles, aunts, and other members of the extended family, share in the disciplinary actions so that there is a less intense emotional involvement between child and one or both parents. The mechanism of shaming makes possible some displacement beyond even the circle of the family. Dominant reliance upon this technique would seem to result in a quite different sort of conformity, characterized by "shame" ("I would feel very uncomfortable if anybody saw me doing this") rather than "guilt" ("I am bad because I am not living up to the standards of my parents"). Finally, the sanctions may be placed to greater or lesser extent outside the range of all living persons. Supernatural beings (including ghosts) may be the punishing and rewarding agents. The child is told that misconduct will be punished in accord with supernatural laws. Eventually, misfortune or accident overtakes the erring child, and his preceptors are careful to impress upon him the connection between his misdeeds and his suffering. Although this method has certain obvious advantages in promoting positive adjustments to other people, it also tends to keep the individual from coming to grips with the external world. If one is at the mercy of more powerful and perhaps capricious forces, if one can always blame supernatural agencies instead of oneself, one is much less likely to make the effort for realistic adjustments.

In our society it must also be noted that it is only in the preschool period that the child is primarily preoccupied with the relationship to the members of his own immediate family. The school period brings on increasing socialization at the hands of teachers, children of the child's own age group, and older children. In our culture there is often conflict between parental standards and age-group standards. Both the life goals of the parents and the means for attaining them may be partially rejected. This necessity of compartmentalizing behavior and of otherwise resolving the conflict between expectations greatly complicates the socialization of the child in a complex culture.

In every culture, however, success, or reward, is essential to all learning. If a response is not rewarded, it will not be learned. Thus all responses which become habitual are "good" from the organism's point of view; they necessarily provide some form of satisfaction. The "badness" of habits is a judgment that is attached to them by other persons; *i.e.*, a habit is "bad" if it annoys another person or persons. The great problem of personal adjustment to a social environment is that of finding behavior that is satisfying to the individual and also either satisfying to other persons or at least acceptable to them. All men learn the responses that are to them motivation-reducing, problem-solving, but one of the factors which determines which responses are motivation-reducing is the given social traditon. Culture also largely determines, of course, which responses other persons will regard as "good" or as annoying. Learning, as related to motivation, deals either with a change in needs or a change in the means of their satisfaction.

The common assumption has been that habits are eliminated only by punishment, *i.e.*, by making them followed by more suffering than satisfaction. It is true that habits can be "broken" in this fashion, but this is costly in that the punishing person often earns the distrust of the child. There is, however, another mechanism utilized by cultural systems, namely the mechanism of extinction. Just as reward is essential to the establishment of a habit, so is it essential to its continued function. If the satisfaction that an organism usually obtained from a given habitual response can be withheld, this habit will eventually disappear. Aggression may occur as the first response to nonreward, but if this aggression is neither rewarded nor punished, it, too, will soon give way to a renewal of exploratory, variable behavior, from which a new habit or adjustment may evolve.

Although extinction is a valuable device for getting rid of objectionable habits, it also operates to eliminate those habits in an individual which others may like, or call "good," if these habits are not continually rewarding also to the individual. Thus good behavior, either in the child or in the adult, cannot be taken for granted; it must be satisfying to the individual as well as to the others. These considerations show the inadequacy of the old notion that repetition necessarily makes a habit stronger. We now know that habits can be either strengthened or weakened by repetition. It is not repetition as such but reward that is the crucial factor in determining whether a habit will grow or wane with repetition.

The next important fact about the learning process is that just as a correct response tends to become more and more strongly connected to the drive which it reduces, so does this response tend to become connected with any other stimuli which happen to be impinging upon the organism at the time the successful response occurs. For example, in many societies physical nearness to the mother soon becomes to the child a promise of reward. Therefore, any renunciation such as that involved in toilet training becomes learned much more easily when the mother is present. We are inclined to exaggerate the specificity of innate responses. We tend to think of nursing behavior, for example, as something automatic. But it isn't simply a chain of reflexes, as anyone who has seen the clumsy and inadequate behavior of a newborn infant realizes. Reflexes are involved, but so are other organic conditions and also learning. Thus if a newborn baby is hungry, pressure on its cheek will elicit the response of quick turning—which can bring the breast into view. But this response can be produced only with great difficulty from a baby who has just been fed.

A culture directs attention to one feature of the stimulus situation and gives it a value. In this way the responses to even very basic organic drives may be determined as much by cultural values and expectations as by internal pressures. As Margaret Mead says:

> The evidence of primitive societies suggests that the assumptions which any culture makes about the degree of frustration or fulfillment contained in cultural forms may be more important for human happiness than which biological drives it chooses to develop, which to suppress or leave undeveloped. We may take as an example the attitude of the Victorian woman who was not expected to enjoy sex experience and who did not enjoy it. She was certainly in no degree as frustrated as are those of her descendants who find sex, which they had been told they would enjoy, very unsatisfactory.

The more energy which a culture channels into the expression of certain drives, the less is left, presumably, to go into satisfying other drives. Indeed it must be argued that the way in which a single drive is satisfied eventually changes the nature of the drive itself. The hunger of a Chinese is not precisely identical with the hunger of an American.

The comparative study by anthropologists of child rearing in various cultures has within the last few years had a profound influence upon pediatrics. Progressive physicians are more and more favoring self-demand as opposed to clock schedules for babies. They also see the connection between children who have a secure sense that their parents are consistently loving and citizens who are responsible and cooperative because they feel that the community is concerned with their welfare. The child who can build his character upon the foundation of trust in the consistent affection of his parents is less likely to be a suspicious adult, seeking and finding enemies within his own group and in other nations. His conscience is more likely to be steady and realistic rather than ever fear-inspiring and threatening. A stable world order that takes account of new, wider, and more complex relationships can be founded only upon individual personalities that are emotionally free and mature. So long as leaders and masses are unable to tolerate types of integrity different from their own, differences will be reacted to as invitations to aggression. Demagogues and dictators flourish where personal insecurity is at a maximum.

The modern mother who reduces contact with the child to a minimum and maintains a highly impersonal relation to it is depriving herself of a type of experience which it is hard to equal in other ways. The experience of many nonliterate societies where the mother's first obligation is to the child during its first two years of life suggests that the investment pays good dividends to the mother in the long run both in ensuring later loyalty and emotional support and in the creative satisfaction of producing happy, productive children.

While the dangers of a "child-centered" culture in the sense that *only* the needs and interest of infants and children are recognized must be freely admitted, the question must not be distorted into an all-or-none dilemma. Surely children must come to realize that there are other people in the world, and that there is intense competition for gratifications. The sensible questions, however, are: when? and how suddenly or how gradually? The competitive emphases of our culture reinforce the patterns of haste in demanding renunciation in the spheres of weaning, cleanliness training, sex-tabooing, and aggression control. The justifications put forward for our present mores of socialization seem largely rationalizations. For example, the assumption is widespread that if a child is fed or otherwise cared for irregularly it will "ruin his health." But primitive children may be nursed and fed whenever they cry, with no indications of ill effects. Other young mammals are similarly treated by their mothers and probably have fewer digestive disturbances than do scheduled babies, who are likely to become overhungry and then overeat.

It is also commonly believed that any latitude in the matter of sleeping will be similarly ruinous to the child's physical well-being, but if the child sleeps only after a period of crying and restlessness, sleep may acquire for him a lifelong connotation of anxiety. Moreover, in the case of somewhat older children, the most obvious net consequence of a rigidly fixed number of hours in bed is that the child has many wakeful periods when it is alone, without social support—a situation favorable to the development of anxiety fantasies. How many children are really put to bed to get rid of them? How many intuitively realize this?

Nor are these problems of child rearing indifferent to the pressing issues of our contemporary world. One, though only one, of the causes of war is the inhibited aggression engendered by the socialization process. Anger, openly expressed toward parents and other elders, does not ordinarily work very well. It is therefore repressed, providing a canker of hate and resentment that may release its energy in fighting the battles of a group, a social class, or a nation. Insecurity, suspicion, and intolerance may likewise have their roots in childhood experience. As Cora DuBois writes:

> The inconsistent and restrictive quality of discipline which pervades the child's life might well be expected to breed in it a sense of insecurity and suspicious distrust. It has at its disposal only one weapon with which to meet frustration and that is rage. The alternative idea of being good in order to gain one's ends is not presented to the child. But that rage is an ineffectual weapon is learned at very latest during the first decade of life.

When, as a result of competition between two individuals for the same goal, one individual assaults the other, such action is commonly termed a crime. When the competition is between different social classes, minorities, or the like, the resulting antagonisms are likely to be called prejudice or persecution. And when the competition is between nations, the resulting aggressions and counteraggressions are, of course, known as war. No effective way of dealing with international competition and aggression has yet been devised, nor is one likely to be so long as repression and retaliation remain the standard devices for dealing with the in-group aggressions of individuals or minority elements. It is true that a certain transitory success can be achieved in inhibiting aggression by means of punishment, but this is not a basic solution to the problem. Intimidation and subjugation, while producing temporary outward conformity, merely increase the amount of pent-up resentment and hostility, which will erupt sooner or later, either as direct counteraggression against the subjugator, or as displaced aggression, or in some other irrational form of behavior.

Some sources of insecurity arise from national and international economic and political disorder. These sources and those arising from socialization are more closely intertwined than might appear at first glance. As long as the aggressions of children and of individual adults are met primarily by retaliation, this will remain the dominant pattern for dealing with interclass, interracial, and international aggressions. Likewise, so long as no security exists for nations, just so long will insecurity and frustration exist for the individuals comprising those nations. The sources of personal and of social disorganization are fundamentally the same and inextricably interrelated. In our American culture we must fiercely compete with each other and yet outwardly remain the best of friends. If a nation's intragroup aggressions become so serious that there is danger of disruption, war, by displacing aggression against another group, is an adjustive response from the point of view of preserving national cohesion.

The ideal of the gentle man and the gentle woman can never be fully realized without a world order which provides for safety and liberty of gentle nations. Retaliation and passive acceptance of aggression are not the only two alternatives for nations any more than they are for children. Nations, like children, need to be socialized. By parallel, an extension of dependency among nations would seem to be the right direction in which to move. In so far as nations recognized their mutual interdependence they would be willing to submit to the renunciations which socialization inevitably involves. In individuals, all character is a kind of delayed obedience. Most people behave socially to the extent that only a small part of the population has to act as a police force. So also the international police force could be small if international dependence were systematically cultivated. This presupposes a division of economic resources and tasks. The ideal of self-sufficiency, whether in the personal or political sphere, has important limitations which should be clearly recognized and evaluated. The principle of "collective security" through which the group makes itself stronger than any single individual (person or nation) and is thereby able to provide protection for even the weakest member of the group is the prime condition for curtailing the need for individual aggression.

A theory of personality is simply a set of presuppositions about "human nature." Emphasis must be laid—because of the findings of psychoanalysis, anthropology, and the psychology of learning—upon human *potentialities*. Nothing can be further from the truth than the shibboleth that "human nature is unalterable," if by human nature is meant the specific form and content of personality. Any theory of personality which rests upon such a basis is necessarily weak, for personality is preeminently a social product and human society is ever on the march. Especially at the present moment do new and momentous changes in international organization seem imminent whose implications for individual personality can be seen but vaguely.

An absolute, culture-bound view of human nature not only holds no conception of what future developments may be but actively stands in the way of those efforts that can be rationally made to hasten the realization of possible levels of personal, social, and international integration. It is true that among all peoples habit and custom die hard. The millennium will not come suddenly. Nevertheless, as men of all nations struggle to adjust themselves to the new demands of the international situation, they steadily modify their conceptions of themselves and of others. Slowly but surely, a new social order and new personality trends will emerge in the process.

Each culture must build upon what it has—its special symbols for arousing emotional responses, its distinctive compensations for the deprivations imposed by cultural standardization, its peculiar values which justify to the individual his surrender of a measure of his impulse life to cultural control. Gregory Bateson has well written:

> If the Balinese is kept busy and happy by a nameless, shapeless fear, not located in space or time, we might be kept on our toes by a nameless, shapeless unlocated hope of enormous achievement. We have to be like those few artists and scientists who work with this urgent sort of inspiration, that urgency that comes from feeling that great discovery or great creation (the perfect sonnet) is always just beyond our reach or like the mother of a child who feels that, provided she pay constant enough attention, there is a real hope that her child may be that infinitely rare phenomenon, a great and happy person.

CHAPTER IX

An Anthropologist Looks at the United States

Suppose that archaeologists five hundred years hence were to excavate the ruins of settlements of various sizes in Europe, in America, in Australia, and in other regions. They would properly conclude that American culture was a variant of a culture of world-wide occurence, distinguished by elaboration of gadgets and especially by the extent to which these were available to all sorts and conditions of men. Careful studies of distribution and diffusion would indicate that the bases of this civilization had been developed in northern Africa, western Asia, and Europe. The shrewd archaeologist would, however, infer that twentieth-century American culture was no longer colonial. He would see that distinctive features in the physical environment of the United States had made themselves perceptible in the warp of the American cultural fabric and that large-scale cultural hybridization and native inventions were continuing to produce a new texture and new patterns in the weft.

Unfortunately, the social anthropologist of 1948 cannot develop this picture much farther and remain in the realm of demonstrated fact. The anthropological study of American communities was initiated in *Middletown* (1928) and *Middletown in Transition* (1937). Since then we have had a series of monographs on *Yankee City*; two books on *Southerntown*; *Plainville, U.S.A.*; brief studies of six different communities by the Department of Agriculture; Margaret Mead's popular book

And Keep Your Powder Dry; and a score of scattered papers. Very recently Warner and Havighurst have published a study of class structure and education, *Who Shall be Educated?* Walter Goldschmidt has given us *As You Sow,* a report on California agricultural communities; and the publications on a Middle Western town, *Jonesville, U.S.A.,* have begun to appear. Yet contrast this total handful with the countless valuable volumes that have been published on the history, government, geography, and economy of the United States. Of this culture in the anthropological sense we know less than of Eskimo culture.

This book has thus far rested on well-documented data and on theory that has proved its predictive power. In treating American culture one must resort to an analysis that goes only a shade beyond impressionism. There is the special danger, considering the small quantity of recent field work, of describing American culture more as it has been than as it is. Yet a sketch of characteristic thought patterns, values, and assumptions may help us a little to understand ourselves and thus to understand other peoples better. One can assemble points of agreement in the anthropological studies that have been made, in the testimony of astute European and Asiatic observers, in personal observations. This has been a business civilization—not a military, ecclesiastical, or scholarly one. The brevity of our national history has made for this dominance of the economic as well as for the stress upon the potential as opposed to the actual society. Lacking the inertia of a deeply rooted culture pattern and given the high standard of living, American customs have changed rapidly under the influence of automobiles, radio, and moving pictures. There are many culture traits which are too obvious to require a massing of evidence: love of physical comfort, a cult of bodily cleanliness, finance capitalism. Certain values, such as fair play and tolerance, are generally agreed to but represent modifications of our British heritage rather than anything distinctively American. Rather than cataloguing traits exhaustively, however, this chapter will treat selectively some related traits that appear best to bring out the underlying organization of the culture.

American culture has been called a culture of paradoxes. Nevertheless national advertising and a national moving-picture industry would be impossible were there not certain terms in which one can appeal to the vast majority of this capturable people. Though sectional, economic, and religious differences are highly significant in some respects, there are certain themes that transcend these variations. Some life goals, some basic attitudes tend to be shared by Americans of every region and of all social classes.

To start with the commonplace: even the most bitter critics of the United States have conceded us material generosity. In spite of the romanticism of "public-spirited disinterestedness" most Americans are outgoing and genuinely benevolent. Sometimes, to be sure, American humanitarianism is linked with the missionary spirit—the determination to help others by making the world over on the American model.

Perhaps no huge society has ever had such generalized patterns for laughter. In older civilizations it is commonly the case that jokes are fully understood and appreciated only by class or regional groups. It is true that it is some distance from the sophisticated humor of *The New Yorker* to the slapstick of popular radio programs. But the most widespread formulas reach all Americans. Some of the most characteristic of these are related to the cult of the average man. No one becomes so great that we cannot make fun of him. Humor is an important sanction in American culture. Probably the ridicule of Hitler did more than all the rational critiques of Nazi ideology to make the man in the street contemptuous of Nazism.

All European travelers are struck by American attitudes toward women. They often note that "Americans spoil their women," or that "America is dominated by petticoats." The truth is more complicated. On the one hand, it is clear that a very large number of American women of privileged economic position are freed by labor-saving devices from much household drudgery—particularly after their few children have entered school. Their abundant leisure goes into women's clubs, community activities, "cultural" organizations, unhealthy devotion to their children, other mildly or seriously neurotic activities. It is also true that many American men are so wrapped up in pursuit of the success goal that they largely abdicate control over their children's upbringing to their wives. The responsibility of American women for moral and cultural questions is tremendous. On the other hand, it is too often forgotten that in 1940, 26 out of every 100 women of working age worked outside the home, that almost every girl who graduates from high school or college has had some job training. We interest women in careers but make it difficult for them to attain a full life in one. In a culture where "prestige" is everything we have felt it necessary to set aside Mother's Day as a symbolic atonement for the lack of recognition ordinarily given to domestic duties.

In Japan a year ago Japanese of many classes complained to me that it was difficult to understand American democracy because Americans seemed to lack an explicit ideology that they could communicate. The Japanese contrasted the Russians who could immediately give a coherent account of their system of beliefs. Various Americans have remarked that what the United States needed more than a good five-cent cigar was a good five-cent ideology. Such explicit ideology as we have derives largely from the political radicalism of the late eighteenth century. We repeat the old words, and some of the ideas are as alive now as then. But much of this doctrine is dated, and a new latent ideology inherent in our actual sentiments and habits is waiting for popular expression.

Particularly since the drastic disillusionment that followed the fine Wilsonian phrases of World War I, Americans have been shy at expressing their deepest convictions and have been verbally cynical about Fourth of July oratory. Yet devotion to the American Way has been none the less passionate. It is significant that aviators in this past war who were under narcotics in the course of psychotherapy would not only talk freely about personal emotional problems but were equally articulate on the ideological reasons for American participation in the war.

The pattern of the implicit American creed seems to embrace the following recurrent elements: faith in the rational, a need for moralistic rationalization, an optimistic conviction that rational effort counts, romantic individualism and the cult of the common man, high valuation of change—which is ordinarily taken to mean "progress," the conscious quest for pleasure.

Mysticism and supernaturalism have been very minor themes in American life. Our glorification of science and our faith in what can be accomplished through education are two striking aspects of our generalized conviction that secular, humanistic effort will improve the world in a series of changes, all or mainly for the better. We further tend to believe that morality and reason must coincide. Fatalism is generally repudiated, and even acceptance seems to be uncongenial—though given lip service in accord with Christian doctrine.

The dominant American political philosophy has been that the common man would think and act rationally. The same premises are apparent in typical attitudes toward parental responsibility. The individual, if "let alone" and not "corrupted by bad company" will be reasonable. If a child does not turn out well, the mother or both parents tend to blame themselves or to explain the failure by "bad blood"—as if action-guided-by-reason could of itself always produce well-adjusted children when the biological inheritance was adequate.

While many Americans are in some senses profoundly irreligious, they still typically find it necessary to provide moral justifications for their personal and national acts. No people moralizes as much as we do. The actual pursuit of power, prestige, and pleasure for their own sakes must be disguised (if public approval is to be obtained) as action for a moral purpose or as later justified by "good works." Conversely, a contemplative life tends to be considered "idleness."

The American mother offers her love to her child on the condition of his fulfilling certain performance standards. No conversational bromides are more characteristically American than "Let's get going"; "Do something"; "Something can be done about it." Although during the thirties there was widespread devaluation of present and future and though pessimism and apathy about the atomic bomb and other international problems are certainly strong currents in contemporary national thinking, the dominant American reaction is still —against the perspective of other cultures—that this is a world in which effort triumphs. A recent public opinion study showed that only 32 per cent of Americans were concerned about social security—for themselves.

Countless European observers have been impressed by "enthusiasm" as a typically American quality. During the war military analysts noted repeatedly that the British were better at holding a position but the Americans at taking one. As Margaret Mead has observed, the British cope with a problem; Americans start from scratch and build completely anew.

Americans are not merely optimistic believers that "work counts." Their creed insists that anyone, anywhere in the social structure, can and should "make the effort." Moreover, they like to think of the world as man-controlled. This view about the nature of life is thus intimately linked with that conception of the individual's place in society which may be called "romantic individualism."

In the English-speaking world there are two principal ideologies of individualism. The English variety (which may be tagged with the name of Cobden) is capitalistic in its basic outlook. American individualism has agrarian roots and may be associated with Jefferson. To this day Americans hate "being told what to do." They have always distrusted strong government. The social roles most frequently jibed at in comic strips are those that interfere with the freedom of others: the dogcatcher, the truant officer, the female social climber (Mrs. Jiggs) who forces her husband and family to give up their habitual satisfactions. "My rights" is one of the commonest phrases in the American language. This historically conditioned attitude toward authority is constantly reinforced by child-training patterns. The son must "go farther" than his father, and revolt against the father in adolescence is expected.

However, as de Tocqueville pointed out, Americans are characteristically more interested in equality than in liberty. "I'm as good as the next man," seems at first a contradiction of the American emphasis upon success and individual achievement within a competitive system. It is true that there are relatively few places at the top in a social pyramid—*at any one time.* But the American faith that "there is always another chance" has its basis in the historical facts of social mobility and the fluidity (at least in the past) of our economic structure. "If at first you don't succeed, try, try again." The American also feels that if he himself does not "get a break," he has a prospect for vicarious achievement through his children.

American individualism centers upon the dramatization of

the individual. This is reflected in the tendency to personalize achievement, good or bad. Americans prefer to attack men rather than issues. Corporations are personified. Public power projects were advertised as much as a means of beating the Utility Devil as a way of getting better and cheaper service.

The less opportunity the greater the merit of success. "You can't keep a good man down." Conversely, failure is a confession of weakness, and status distinctions and even class lines are rationalized on such grounds as, "he got there by hard work," "it's his own fault that he didn't get on." Such attitudes—and the idealization of the "tough guy" and the "red-blooded American" and the fear of "being a sucker"—derive both from the Puritan ethic and from the American pioneer era. Aggressive activity and rapid mobility were effectual in the rapid development of a new country, and it made sense then that the rewards in money and status should be high.

The worship of success has gone farther than in any known culture, save possibly prewar Japan. This is reflected in countless staple phrases such as "bettering yourself," "getting ahead," and "how are you getting on?" The opposition to Roosevelt's proposal for a taxation program that would limit net income to $25,000, attests to the depth of feeling for slogans like "the sky's the limit." But the striving for money is not simply the pursuit of purposeless materialism. Money is primarily a symbol. The deeper competition is for power and prestige. "Aggressive" is, in American culture, a descriptive adjective of high praise when applied to an individual's personality or character. "You have to be aggressive to be a success." The obvious crudities of aggression are, as Lynd says, explained away by identifying them with the common good.

But there is a defensive note in this aggressiveness which is also symptomatic. Competitive aggressiveness against one's fellows is not just playing a part in a drama. The only way to be safe in American life is to be a success. Failure to "measure up" is felt as deep personal inadequacy. In a phrase, the American creed is equality of opportunity, not equality of man.

The cult of the average man might seem to imply disapproval of outstanding individuals of every sort. Certainly it is true that a great deal of hostility is directed upward. However, under the influence of the dramatic and success aspects of the "romantic individualism" orientation, the typical attitude toward leaders may best be described as one of mixed feelings. On the one hand, there is a tendency to snipe at superior individuals with a view to reducing them to the level of their fellows. On the other hand, their very success is a dramatic vindication of the American way of life and an invitation to identification and emulation.

The cult of the average man means conformity to the standards of the current majority. To de Tocqueville this was "enfeeblement of the individual." A more recent observer, Fromm, who also looked at the American scene from a European viewpoint, likewise finds this conformity repressive to self-expression. But he fails to see that the American is not a passive automaton submitting to cultural compulsives like European provincials. The American voluntarily and consciously seeks to be like others of his age and sex—without in any way becoming an anonymous atom in the social molecule. On the contrary, all the devices of the society are mobilized to glamorize the individual woman and to dramatize every achievement of men and women that is unusual—but still within the range of approved aspirations of the conforming majority. "Miss America" and "the typical American mother" are widely publicized each year, but an announced atheist (no matter of what brilliance and accomplishment) cannot be elected President.

American devotion to the underdog must be linked to this attitude. As Lynd points out, we worship bigness yet we idealize "the little man." "Griping" is a characteristic American trait, but the griping of American soldiers against the officer caste system is to be understood in terms of American egalitarian notions and especially of the cult of the average man. The fact that officers and enlisted men did not have equal access to various facilities for recreation and transportation enraged what were felt to be the most basic sentiments in the American code. To some extent this aspect of the cult of the average man doubtless represents a refuge for those who fail "to rise," a justification for envy of those who do.

Because of the cult of the average man, superficial intimacy is easy in America. People of every social class can talk on common topics in a way that is not so easy in Europe where life is based more on repetition of patterns of early family routines that are differentiated by class. However, American friendships tend to be casual and transitory.

Thanks to our expanding economy and to national folklore created by various historical accidents, the nineteenth-century faith in "progress" became intrenched in the United States as nowhere else. As Lovejoy and Boas have pointed out, America's golden age has been located mainly in the future rather than in the past. To some extent, to be sure, the future has been brought into the present by installment plan buying, the philosophy of "spend, don't save," etc. But the basic underlying notions have been well made explicit by Carl Becker.

> By locating perfection in the future and identifying it with the successive achievements of mankind, the doctrine of progress makes a virtue of novelty and disposes men to welcome change as in itself a sufficient validation of their activities.

Western Europeans and Americans tend to be fundamentally different in their attitudes toward conforming. Americans believe in conforming only to the standards of one's own age group and change-in-time is a strong value; Europeans believe—or have believed—in conforming to a past society and have found security in traditional behavior; yet conformity to a contemporary society is only incidental and not a value. There are, to be sure, wide disparities in American hospitality to change. We take pride in material change but are, on the whole, more hostile than contemporary Europeans to changes in our institutions (say the Constitution or the free enterprise system). In some ways the conformity of middle-class Englishmen, for instance, is more rigid than that of Americans—but in other ways it is less so. American attitudes toward change make generational conflicts more serious. These very generational conflicts, however, make certain types of social change possible. As Mead points out, children can be more "successful" than their parents, hence "better."

Americans publicly state that having a good time is an important part of life and admit to craving "something new and exciting." In terms of this ideology we have created Hollywood, our Forest of Arden type of college life, our National Parks, Monuments, and Forests. Leaders of our entertainment industry are the best paid men and women in the United States. In 1947 the American people spent nearly twenty billion dollars for alcoholic beverages, theater and movie tickets, tobacco, cosmetics, and jewelry. We spend as much for moving pictures as for churches, more for beauty shops than for social service. However, because of the Puritan tradition of "work for work's sake," this devotion to recreation and material pleasure is often accompanied by a sense of guilt—another instance of the bipolarity of many features of American culture. The pleasure principle attains its fullest development in American youth culture. Youth is the hero of the American Dream. Most especially, the young girl ready for marriage is the cynosure of American society.

We have borrowed ideas and values from countless sources. If one takes single features, one can match almost every instance in a dozen or more cultures, including the primitive. For example, during the last war many of our soldiers carried magic amulets, such as a miniature wooden pig which was said to have raised fogs, smoothed out a high sea, commuted an execution, or cured assorted cases of illness. But if one looks at the total combination of premises and attitudes one sees a pattern that has its own special flavor, even though this description is too brief to take account of regional, class, ethnic group, and generational variations.

An anthropological snapshot of the American way of life cannot catch all the details, but, with other cultures in the background, it should highlight some meaningful interplay of light and shadow. And the attempt is needed. No amount of knowledge of Russian or Chinese culture will avail in the solution of our international problems unless we know ourselves also. If we can predict our own reactions to a probable next move in the Russian gambit and have some clues as to why we shall react in that manner, the gain to self-control and toward more rational action will be tremendous. Because of our tradition of assimilating immigrants and because of our overweening pride in our own culture it is particularly difficult to get Americans to understand other cultures.

Seen in the perspective of the range of human institutions, the following combination of outstanding features define the American scene: consciousness of diversity of biological and cultural origins; emphasis upon technology and upon wealth; the frontier spirit; relatively strong trust in science and education and relative indifference to religion; unusual personal insecurity; concern over the discrepancy between the theory and the practice of the culture.

"The melting pot" is one of the surest catchwords that has ever been applied to the United States. Probably much of the vitality of American life and the increased stature and other evidences of physical superiority for new generations of Americans must be attributed to the mingling of diverse cultural and biological strains as well as to dietary and environmental factors. The "Ballad for Americans" triumphantly proclaims our manifold origins. Newspapers during the war proudly referred to the fact that Eisenhower was a German name but he was an American, to the fact that another general was an Indian, to the variety of names in American platoons and in American graveyards oversees. The distinguished record of Japanese-Americans in the armed services was used to document the success of the American Way.

Heterogeneity has, in fact, become one of the organizing principles of American culture. Ripley's "Believe it or Not," "Quiz Kids" programs, "Information Please," and other formal and informal educational devices are evidence that Americans value disconnected pieces of information and feel that people must be prepared to live in a world in which generalizations are hard to apply.

If one looks at a culture as a system in which traits mainly received by borrowing are being patterned in response to situational factors and organic needs our American position at present bears a few compelling resemblances to that of Europe in perhaps the twelfth century. It was only then that a quasi-permanent integration had been attained in the European cultural melting pot. Pagan and Christian, Greco-Roman and Germanic culture elements had seethed in troubled opposition during the centuries of the movements of people. Our mass movements stopped only a generation ago with the closing of the frontier. During the tenth and eleventh centuries in Europe forests were cleared and swamps were drained; cities were built in large numbers in Northern Europe, and there came to be some fixity in the distribution and density of population.

Because of the very fact that diversity is an explicit theme of American culture one must be careful not to overemphasize the threats of the admitted contradictions in our way of life. Those who look longingly back to the good old days of a fancied homogeneity in American values forget that the Tories almost equaled the Patriots in number, do not remember the details of the situation that demanded the Federalist papers, neglect the two radically opposed sets of values that led to the War between the States. Actually, we must agree with Frank Tannenbaum that the harmony best suited to a democratic society "is one which comes from many-sided inner tensions, strains, conflicts, and disagreements." Though the stability of a culture depends on how much the conflicts it engenders can be supplied adequate outlets, still the strength of the democratic process is that it not only tolerates but welcomes difference. Democracy is based not upon a single value but upon a subtle and intricate multiple of values. Its strength rests in the balance of social institutions.

Although the definition of an American as a person who is endlessly catching trains is a caricature, the phrase of G. Lowes Dickinson "contemptuous of ideas but amorous of devices" remains uncomfortably correct as a characterization of all save a tiny minority of Americans. And while we indignantly met the Fascist label of "plutocracy!" by pointing to our humanitarian organizations, our numerous foundations dedicated to the spending of untold millions for lofty aims, and the generosity of individual citizens, it remains true that not only are we the wealthiest nation in the world but that money comes closer with us than with any other people to being the universal standard of value.

This is why the level of intellectual ability is very much

higher in the Harvard Law School than in the Harvard Graduate School of Arts and Sciences. The ablest undergraduates in Harvard College do not always receive the highest honors. The energies of many are often, realistically enough, consecrated to "making contacts" through "activities," through a sedulous campaign to acquire membership in a "final club." This is not necessarily because they are congenitally uninterested in ideas, but because they have been effectually conditioned by family pressure and by certain schools. They have considerable intuitive insight into the structure of our culture. They know that intellectual endeavor will lead them to little "recognition" and less salary. They know how vital is "success" to security in our society. Brilliant young men voluntarily condemn themselves to lives of cutthroat competition and narrow slavery.

Our economy is a prestige economy to a pathological extent. The wife must buy fur coats and drive an expensive automobile because she too is an item of conspicuous consumption. Even in the supposedly uncommercial halls of learning the awed whisper is heard, "Why, he is a $15,000-a-year professor." The numerical system of grading, an unmistakably American invention, is simply another projection of our conviction that all attainments can be expressed in figures.

Suppose that an intellectual Australian aborigine, who was also a trained anthropologist, were to write a monograph on our culture. He would unequivocally assert that machines and money are close to the heart of our system of symbolic logics. He would point out that the two are linked in a complex system of mutual interdependence. Technology is valued as the very basis of the capitalistic system. Possession of gadgets is esteemed as a mark of success to the extent that persons are judged not by the integrity of their characters or by the originality of their minds but by what they seem to be—so far as that can be measured by the salaries they earn or by the variety and expensiveness of the material goods which they display. "Success" is measured by two automobiles—not by two mistresses as in some cultures.

Could our aboriginal anthropologist introduce some time perspective into his study, he would note that this value system has shown some signs of alteration during the last two decades. However, against the background of all known cultures, American culture would still stand out for its quantitative and materialistic orientations.

Americans love bigness—so far as things and events are concerned. Their constant overstatement appears to others as boasting. Americans love to speak in numbers. They like to "get down to brass tacks" and "want the lowdown." Europeans are usually content to rate students according to categories corresponding to "high honors," "honors," "pass." Only Americans think that the relative standing of students in a course can be measured on a continuous scale from zero to 100. This emphasis on the quantitative must not be too easily taken as proof of a thoroughgoing materialism. But Americans do tend to get very excited about things as opposed to ideas, people, and aesthetic creations. "Virtuous materialism" has tended to be part of the American creed.

Status in the United States is determined more by the number and price of automobiles, air-conditioning units, and the like owned by a family than by the number of their servants or the learning and aesthetic skills of family members. In fact, Americans usually are scared out of being artists. There is reverence only for the man who "does *things* in a big way." Most Americans do subscribe to the current Einstein legend, but *Time* has recently pointed out that many did not take this very seriously until they were told that Einstein's "theories" had made the atomic bomb possible. It is significant that Edison is a household name, whereas only the professors have heard of Willard Gibbs.

John Dewey says that American thinking is characterized by a "lust after absolutes." By this he does not, of course, mean a hankering for the "absolutes" of religion and philosophy. He refers to the tendency to think that, because simple questions can be posed, there exist simple answers, which classify ideas and individuals as all black or all white. For this reason "compromise" has an unfavorable connotation in American English. Worship of the external and quantitative leaves little patience for the infinite shadings and variations of direct experience. Doubtless the vastness of the American scene and the impermanence of social place create a need to generalize. Europeans are ordinarily more sensitive to the complexity of situations.

Our phrase "pioneer of industry" is not a haphazard combination of words. The patterns of the American Way were set during that period when the United States was on the skirmish line of civilization. The frontier has been a predominant influence in the shaping of American character and culture, in the molding of American political life and institutions; the frontier is the principal, the recurring theme in the American symphony. Whatever distinction we have as a people, whatever differentiates us from the other branches of Western European civilization we owe in large part to the presence of the frontier—its unappropriated wealth, its dangers and challenges.

Unfortunately, many of the responses which made for survival under those conditions are singularly unsuited to our present situation. To some considerable degree, frontier virtues are the intolerable vices of contemporary America. To extemporize and not to plan "paid off" then. Unhappily, we have tended to see these qualities as absolutes rather than from the perspective of cultural relativity. Aggressive and childish young Mickey Rooney was recently the hero of a population which ought to have grown up. A reactionary comic strip which portrays the triumphs Orphan Annie and Daddy Warbucks attain by stubborn clinging to pioneer attitudes and habits is still the inspirational reading of millions of Americans. Egoistic individualism remains long after the economic place for it has passed.

This same frontier spirit, however, affords the spiritual sources which can swiftly bring about potential reforms. If we Americans are restless, unanchored in our ideas as in our habitations, if also we may boast a certain freedom, a flexibility in our thinking and a vigor and independence in our action, it is in some degree traceable to the constant flux of American life, always westward, always away from old and permanent things. The American tempo has not become a sophisticated dignified one, measured in harmony with the persisting splendor of ancient palaces, and the symmetry of great parks carpeted with lawns such as only centuries of tending could produce. We have not evolved a splendid system of common law out of the crude folk code of the German forest by a millennium of patient and slow change. Our political institutions did not grow deep in the shadow which the *imperium Romanum*, the *pax Romana*, the *instituta Gaii* have always cast over the ideas of the men of Western Europe. We on this continent have not upreared under the goad of a common ecstasy and mighty aspiration a sky-striving shrine for Our Lady of Chartres, nor a great temple for the Three Kings of Cologne. We share, to be sure, in all the achievements of Western Europe because we have a common ancestry in blood and in ideas with the men of Western Europe, but we share more distantly, more and more differently. The common ecstasy of our great-grandfathers went toward the conquest of a vast and magnificent, a sometimes pitiless and terrible land; our grandfathers were born beside covered wagons in mountain passes, on the prairie, on the desert; the Vigilantes administered the laws in many of our early communities. If our whole economic development as a nation was conditioned by the fact that for more than a century there was always free land in the West for the man who had lost his job in the East, it is equally true that this terrible struggle for survival against the Indian and against the land itself begot in our forefathers not a slow, ordered, conventionalized response to a given stimulus but a quick tense reaction to fit each differing need: the temper of American life to this day.

Assembly-line factories and skyscrapers must, in part, be understood in terms of the frontier. Our so rapid development in invention and technique, our gigantic financial and industrial systems—in general, the fact that we adjusted so completely and quickly, albeit so inharmoniously, to the Technical Age is to be traced to the absence of an ancient order of society and the presence of the frontier where we had to adapt ourselves to vastness with decision, speed, and skill. In an old culture there is a belief in the established order, a rooted opposition to change, a constitutional imperviousness to new ideas which would involve radical alteration in the mode of life. The frontier liberated the American spirit. It developed generosity and radiant vitality, together with a restlessness which was both good and ill, but did certainly bring with it a resiliency of mind, fluidity of idea and of society, a willingness for bold experiment.

Mass education, like mass suffrage and mass production, is a leading trait of our code. During the last generation education has supplanted the frontier as a favorite means of social mobility, for we have continued to define success in terms of mobility rather than in terms of stability. Our educational system has recently been built upon a kind of watery intellectualism. We have too often naïvely assumed that, if people were "well informed" and taught to reason in accord with accepted canons of logic, their characters would take care of themselves, and they would automatically acquire the point of view requisite in the citizen of a great society. Meanwhile, the toughening influences of frontier conditions were becoming steadily more dilute. Children of the economically dominant classes were being brought up in relative luxury. Parents failed to condition their offspring to rigorous standards of conduct because they were themselves confused. Actually many educative functions formerly carried out by the family have been surrendered to the school. The existing educational system is hopelessly irresolute on many fronts. It vacillates between training girls to be housewives or career women; it is torn between conditioning children for the theoretically desirable cooperative objectives or to the existing competitive realities. In spite of the terrific demands made upon them, elementary and high-school teachers are underpaid and lack social status. Psychiatrists are agreed that the elimination of social disorganization, as well as of personal disorganization, can be furthered only by more consistent educational practices both in the home and in the school because automatic actions based on the habits of early life are the most stable.

The anthropologist must also characterize our culture as profoundly irreligious. More than half of our people still occasionally go through the forms, and there are rural and ethnic islands in our population where religion is still a vital force. But very few of our leaders are still religious in the sense that they are convinced that prayer or the observance of church codes will affect the course of human events. Public figures participate in public worship and contribute financially to a church for reasons of expediency or because they know that churches represent one of the few elements of stability and continuity in our society. But belief in God's judgments and punishments as a motive for behavior is limited to a decreasing minority. Feelings of *guilt* are common but the sense of *sin* is rare.

The legend of Jesus lives in men's hearts and the Christian ethic is far from dead. As Bridges reminds us: "They who understand not cannot forget, and they who keep not His commandments call Him Master and Lord." But, in the opinion of many acute observers, American Protestantism is vital today primarily as an agency of benign social work. Relatively few Protestants, except in a few sects and in some rural areas, manifest deep religious feeling. The Roman Church certainly retains vigor, and parts of the encyclicals of recent Popes are not the least impressive of utterances upon contemporary life. To more than a few intellectuals of recent years the Catholic Church has appeared as the one firm rock in a sea of chaos and decay. To others it seems that the authoritarian Church, for all the social wisdom she has shown, for all the subtlety of her doctors, has purchased peace of mind in their time for her communicants by identifying ephemeral cultural expedients with immutable human nature. A system of beliefs, profoundly felt, is unquestionably necessary to the survival of any society, but an increasing number of Americans debate the extent to which the dogmas of any organized Christian Church are compatible with contemporary secular knowledge.

Much of this debate reflects the shallowness of certain aspects of American culture. The alternative of science *or* religion is fictitious once it be granted that the functions of religion are primarily symbolic, expressive, and orientative. Every culture must define its ends as well as perfect its means. The logical and symbolic expressions of the ultimate values of a civilization cannot arise directly from scientific investigation, though it is fair to demand that they should not rest upon premises contrary to known fact or proven theory. A mechanistic, materialistic "science" hardly provides the orientations to the deeper problems of life that are essential for happy individuals and a healthy social order. Nor does a political philosophy such as "democracy." Men need tenets that do not outrage the brain but are meaningful to the viscera and the aesthetic sensibilities. They must be symbolized in rites that gratify the heart, please the ear and eye, fulfill the hunger for drama.

Observers agree on the poverty of American ceremonial life. American ceremonialism is too overwhelmingly that of Shriner conventions and labor rallies. If such national sentiments as we possess are to be maintained at a degree of intensity sufficient to preserve them, they must be given collective expression on suitable occasions. If the conduct of the individual is to be regulated in accord with the needs and purposes of the society, the society's sentiments must be periodically reinforced in the individual by gatherings in which all classes assert in symbolic form: "we are one people." *

Mass economic upheaval following upon unprecedented economic growth; lack of attention to the human problems of an industrial civilization; the impersonality of the social organization of cities; the melting pot, transitory geographical residence, social mobility, weakening of religious faith—all of these trends have contributed to make Americans feel unanchored, adrift upon a meaningless voyage. The American family system is in process of settling into a new type of organization and such a phase does not make for psychic ease. Why are Americans a nation of joiners? In part this is a defense mechanism

* These statements may seem to imply an exaltation of nationalism or at least an acceptance of its inevitability for all time. Nothing of the sort is intended. I am primarily interested in calling attention to the empirical fact of the connection between means and ends. Also, I believe that certain American sentiments have a value to us and to the world—at least until the millenium of a world society arrives.

against the excessive fluidity of our social structure. Weary of the tension of continual struggle for social place, people have tried to gain a degree of routinized and recognized fixity by allying themselves with others in voluntary associations.

The smooth working of all societies depends upon individuals not having to think about many of their acts. They can carry out their specialized functions better if much of their behavior is a more or less automatic reaction to a standardized situation in a socially appropriate fashion. A man meets a woman acquaintance on the street. He raises his hat. Such small acts bind a society together by making one's behavior intelligible to one's neighbors and give the participants a sense of security. Because one knows what to do and knows what the other person will do everything seems to be under control. Such patterns likewise release energy for the activities in which the individual is really interested. The trouble in our society is that the cluster of meanings upon which such an expective, repetitive way of behaving must depend is sadly disorganized. The cultural dislocation of emigrant groups, the rapid and disorderly expansion of cities, and many other factors have all contributed to the disorientation of individuals from a cohesive social matrix. Technicians have applied science to industry without either management, unions, or the state making more than feeble attempts at the indispensable compensatory adjustments in social structure.

A disproportionate technological development has given tempo to American life but denied it rhythm. It has provided the constant overstimulation necessary to throw many of us into a perpetual state of neurotic indecision. The disparity between our ingenuity in solving mechanical as opposed to human problems is a grave question. It would be infantile, of course, to say "away with the machine!" Obviously, it is not machines but our lack of scientific attention to the problems they raise which is evil. It is a legitimate hope that machines may free the majority of humans from drudgery and thus afford an escape from industrial feudalism. Further, as Mumford has urged, machines and the rapid transportation and distribution of goods which they make possible, create an international reciprocity and dependency such as to make the peace and order of nations more nearly a condition which *must* be attained rather than a pious desirability.

In rural areas and small towns, quick and direct response of neighbors can make for great personal security and for other values enriching to life. In cities, however, the economy is so finely organized and specialized that the dependency of one individual upon another, though actually more acute, is not felt in warm personal terms. People miss a network of relationships linking the job, the family, the church and other institutions. They feel the lack of personal appreciation of the products of their labors and of nonutilitarian creativity. Edward Sapir has well contrasted our psychological position with that of the primitive:

> So long as the individual retains a sense of control over the major goods of life, he is able to take his place in the cultural patrimony of his people. Now that the major goods of life have shifted so largely from the realm of immediate to that of remote ends, it becomes a cultural necessity for all who would not be looked upon as disinherited to share in the pursuit of these remoter ends. Nor harmony and depth of life . . . is possible when activity is well-nigh circumscribed by the sphere of immediate ends and when functioning within that sphere is so fragmentary as to have no inherent intelligibility or interest. Here lies the grimmest joke of our present American civilization. The vast majority of us, deprived of any but an insignificant and culturally abortive share in the satisfaction of the immediate wants of mankind, are further deprived of both opportunity and stimulation to share in the production of non-utilitarian values. Part of the time we are dray horses; the rest of the time we are listless con-

sumers of goods which have received no least impress of our personality. In other words, our spiritual selves go hungry, for the most part, pretty much all of the time.

Most thoughtful Americans are concerned about the fact that the theory and the practice of our culture are hopelessly out of line. It is well established that while cultural content often changes rapidly, cultural forms often have extraordinary permanency. Thus it is only the *tradition* of economic independence which truly survives. For all our talk of free enterprise we have created the most vast and crushing monopolies in the world. Although the fable that every boy can become president has been repeatedly scoffed at in recent years, parents and children still act upon the ruling motivation that hard work, training, and aggressiveness can overcome almost all limitations. The result is of course, countless disgruntled or bitter men and women, for as Veblen has shown, in a capitalistic economy the number of places at the top is disappointingly few. A cramping constriction will be felt by individuals so long as our ideal pattern is proclaimed as equality of opportunity for all. "Freedom" likewise has become fertile of disillusioned cynicism because of increasing realization of the truth of Durkheim's words, "I can be free only to the extent that others are forbidden to profit from their physical, economic, or other superiority to the detriment of my liberty." And much of the exultation in our "high standard of living" is, as Norman Thomas contends, "ludicrously beside the point. What the workers have a right to demand of the machine age is not that it will give them more bath tubs than Henry VIII had for his troublesome domestic establishment; they have a right to ask that machinery will conquer poverty rather than increase insecurity."

A society may indeed be viewed as a structure of expectancies. Neuroses have been produced experimentally in laboratory animals by causing the relation between stimulus and proper response to be irregular and haphazard. It follows that if the expectancies which are generated by the cultural ideology are notably unrealistic, mass frustration and mass neurosis are the inescapable consequences.

The diversity of ethnic origins in our forming nation provided strong psychological reinforcement of the doctrines of human equality which were the gospel of the Age of Enlightment and of the Romantic Movement. Had not a belief in mystic equality become part of the official ideology of American culture and offered psychological security to non-Anglo-Saxons, these divergent groups might well have remained tight little islands of transplanted Europeans. But the contrast between this legal and political theory and the private theories and practices of too many American citizens (as symbolized in labels like "wops" and "greasers," in Jim Crow laws and lynchings) constitutes one of the severest strains undermining the equilibrium of the American social system. The Negroes and, to only a slightly lesser extent, the Spanish-speaking Americans constitute caste groups—that is, normal intermarriage does not occur between them and the rest of the population. Segregation in housing and discriminatory practices in our armed services stand out as intolerable contradictions in the institutions of a free society.

In the last fifteen years anthropologists have presented evidence that, in contrast to our official beliefs, a class structure has even now considerably crystallized in at least some parts of the United States. Lloyd Warner and his associates distinguish a six-class system: upper-upper, lower-upper, upper-middle, lower-middle, upper-lower, lower-lower. These groupings are not solely economic. In fact, members of the top class ordinarily have less money than those of the lower-upper group.

Nor does stratification correspond entirely to occupational lines. Physicians, for example, are found in all of the first four classes. In Warner's sense a class consists of persons who visit in one another's home, belong to the same social clubs, exchange gifts, and show awareness of themselves as a group set apart from others, and in a subordinate or superior position to others.

Whether the six-class system is generally valid or whether a larger or smaller subdivision better represents the facts in some communities is a factual question that cannot be answered until there have been more studies. The division of labor in a complex society makes some form of class stratification almost inevitable. It just so happens that in American culture recognition of the facts is repugnant to the American creed. Public-opinion polls indicate that 90 per cent of Americans insist that they are "middle class" despite wide variations in income level, occupation, and social habits. One study shows that 70 per cent of low-income groups claim middle-class social position. Warner, however, places 59 per cent of the people in one New England town in the two lower classes.

Under the influence of the depression and of Marxian theories discussion of class in the United States has increased greatly in the past twenty years. When class position is grudgingly recognized, it is often with anger—as something un-American and hence wrong. Some students of American class structure have failed to examine the significance of values—adhered to by almost all Americans—which operate to deny and tear down class divisions. Except possibly in limited areas of the eastern seaboard, the South, and the San Francisco area, the lines are still relatively fluid and everyone hopes to rise. The statement that American culture is dominantly a middle-class culture is something more than an acceptance of popular ideology which glosses over the sometimes ugly facts of differentiation. Hence "class," though a real phenomenon, does not have precisely the sense that it does in Europe. Certainly Americans are increasingly conscious of status, but the ranking of individuals and their immediate families is often still divorced from that of their close relatives. And the place of the whole body of kin in the smaller communities is frequently based primarily on length of residence there. Our society remains in important respects an open society.

Nevertheless the facts indicate that rapid rise through sheer ability and industry is much more difficult than it was a generation or two ago. Status is harder to achieve by one's own initiative and easier to acquire through family connections. In Washington during the war it was noted that considerable communication and power flowed through channels that were not only nonofficial but not those of political or other normal American interest groups. For the first time since the Age of Jackson an upper class appeared to be operating without much reference to regional or political lines. The class problem is also manifesting itself in the schools. Teachers, themselves usually of middle-class position, discriminate against lower-class children. The children sense that they are punished for following the cultural patterns of their parents. If effort and ability are not rewarded, the way to delinquency or stolid escapism is inviting. In short, class typing rather than individual typing has become one American mode of granting or denying recognition to other people.

Americans are at present seeing social change of a vastness difficult to comprehend. Concretely, social change has its origins in the strains and dissatisfactions felt by specific individuals. When personal insecurity is sufficiently intense and sufficiently widespread, new patterns are germinated in the few creative individuals, and there will be willingness to try them out on the part of larger numbers. Such is the present condition of American society. If a society be regarded as a system in equilibrium, it may be said that in the decade following 1918 the prewar equilibrium was precariously reattained. But the depression and World War II appear to have destroyed the old equilibrium beyond repair. At the moment Americans are in the tortures of attempting to reach a new and differently based equilibrium. The devastating appropriateness of the phrase, "the neurotic personality of our time," is both the condition and the result of this circumstance.

The basis of social life is the sensitivity of human beings to the behavior of other human beings. In a complex society the need for correct interpretation and response to the demands of others is especially great. But in American culture the first experiences of the growing child tend so to emphasize prestige (especially economic prestige) needs that the ego requirements of our adults are often too tremendous for them to follow any other pattern. As Horney says, "the striving for prestige as a means of overcoming fears and inner emptiness is certainly culturally prescribed." Such a device, however, like the intemperate devotion to the pleasure principle, is but a feeble palliative. The popular motto, "every man for himself," was less socially dangerous when firm and generally held beliefs in the afterworld provided some check upon rampant individualism.

The frontier code of sturdy individualism needs tempering and modification the more because it is seldom possible of attainment in the present situation. As Sirjamaki says, "The culture posits individualism as a basic social value but places overwhelming burdens upon its realization." In most aspects of social life American demands for conformity are too great. After the passing of the frontier, individualism was expressed mainly in the economic part of the culture. Today the United States is almost the only country in the world in which large numbers of people cling to laissez-faire principles in economics and government. In its extreme form this is utterly unrealistic, a fixation upon a vain phantasm of our past.

Some acceptance of planning and of stability as a value would decrease the envy and strife that go with incessant mobility. In a society where everybody is either going up or going down there is an excessive psychological necessity to cherish the familiar. This exaggerated stress upon conformity plus our business externalism has created what Fromm has recently termed "the personality of the market place" as the most frequent type in our culture. Given the pressures to conformity, personality fulfillment is denied to many, perhaps most, of our citizens.

America's claim to greatness thus far is not through its Whitmans and Melvilles, nor its Woods and Bentons, nor its Michelsons and Comptons. Still less does it consist in its having added to the contemplative or religious treasures of mankind. Emerson, Thoreau, James, and Dewey are distinguished thinkers, but that they are of the stature of many other ancient and modern philosophers is doubtful. Mary Baker Eddy, Joseph Smith, and other leaders of cultist or revivalistic sects represent all that is characteristically American in religion.

Americans have, however, been inventive in more than one sphere. Admirable and useful as are those material inventions which have made "the American standard of living" an international byword, American social inventions are the most distinctive contributions made by the United States to world culture. The cult of the average man is an even more characteristically American invention than the assembly line. Philosophers of many nations had dreamed of a state guided by a skillfully trained but small group of the good and wise. The United States, however, was the first country to dedicate itself to the conception of a society where the lot of the common man would be made easier, where the same opportunities would be available to all, where the lives of all men and women would be enriched and ennobled. This was something new under the sun.

We cannot rest upon the laurels of past achievement. E. H. Carr has bluntly stated the alternatives:

> The impact of the Soviet Union has fallen on a western world where much of the framework of individualism was already in decay, where faith in the self-sufficiency of individual reason had been sapped by the critique of relativism, where the democratic community was in urgent need of reinforcement against the forces of disintegration latent in individualism, and where the technical conditions of production on the one hand, and the social pressures of mass civilization on the other, were already imposing far-reaching measures of collective organization. . . . The fate of the western world will turn on its ability to meet the Soviet challenge by a successful search for new forms of social and economic action in which what is valid in individualist and democratic tradition can be applied to the problems of mass civilization.*

All advocates of government by an élite, from Plato to Hitler and Stalin, have ridiculed the competence of average citizens to form rational opinions upon complex issues. There is no doubt that many nineteenth-century utterances absurdly exalted rationality. Yet the best anthropological evidence, as Franz Boas pointed out, is that the judgment of the masses is sounder than the judgment of the classes on broad questions of policy where sentiments and values are concerned. This doctrine must not be perverted into a claim for the common man's expertness on technical or artistic matters. Nor does contemporary thought refer to the individual citizen's judgments. Rather, it

* From E. H. Carr, *The Soviet Impact on the Western World.* Copyright 1947 by The Macmillan Company and used with their permission and that of the author.

refers to collective decisions arrived at in group interaction and dealing with "matters of common concern which depend upon estimates of probability." As Carl Friedrich continues:

> This concept of the common man salvages from the onslaught of the irrationalist revolt those elements in the older doctrine which are essential to democratic politics. It seeks a middle ground between the extreme rationalistic ideas of an earlier day and the denial of all rationality by those who were disappointed over its limitations. . . . Enough common men, when confronted with a problem, can be made to see the facts in a given situation to provide a working majority for a reasonable solution, and such majorities will in turn provide enough continuing support for a democratic government to enforce such common judgments concerning matters of common concern.

What is the prospect for American culture? Let one anthropologist, though bearing in mind the principles of his science, speak unashamedly in terms of his own American sentiments. Given our biological and material wealth, given the adaptive genius which is the constructive heritage of our peculiarly American frontier spirit, it will be the fault not of angels but of ourselves if our problems are not in large part resolved. The decisive factor will be the extent to which individual Americans feel a personal responsibility. This, in turn, depends upon an intangible: their total philosophic attitude. James Truslow Adams in *The Epic of America* urges that the meaningful contribution which the United States has made to the totality of human culture is "the American Dream," "a vision of a society in which the lot of the common man will be made easier and his life enriched and ennobled." It was in the ideological field that America made its first and can still make its greatest contribution to the world. In the New World, peopled by robust men and women who had the courage to emigrate and many of whom were impelled by the active vision of a nobler society,

Americans enlarged the meaning of freedom and gave it many new expressions.

It is this prospect for American culture which we must cherish and believe in. Nor is there anything in science which indicates that the dreams of man do not influence, nay sometimes determine his behavior. While choice is most often a flattering illusion, while antecedent and existent hard-sense data usually shape our destinies, there are moments in the careers of nations, as well as in the careers of individuals, when opposing external forces are about equally balanced, and it is then that intangibles like "will" and "belief" throw the scales. Cultures are not altogether self-contained systems which inevitably follow out their own self-determined evolution. Sorokin and other prophets of doom fail to see that one of the factors which determines the next step in the evolution of a system is precisely the dominant attitudes of people. And these are not completely determined by the existent culture. John Dewey has shown us that in "judgments of practice" the hypothesis itself has a crucial influence upon the course of events: "to the extent that it is seized and acted upon, it weights events in its favor."

Even that erstwhile pessimist, Aldous Huxley, has seen that the discoveries of modern psychology have been perverted to bolster a false determinism. If responses can be conditioned, they can by the same token be deconditioned and reconditioned—though neither individuals nor peoples change suddenly and completely. We are now released from the dominantly external and material demands which frontier conditions made upon our society. Intelligent planning can ease the hostile tensions of national anarchy by providing both security and socialized freedom for the individual. Ideals of flourishing freshness that adapt to changed conditions and to what is sound and creative in the distinctive American Way are the only sure antidote for our social ills. Only those ideals will spread and be accepted which correspond to the culturally created emotional needs of the people. Scientific humanism is such an ideal. Rooted in the tradition of Americans to value scientific achievement highly, scientific humanism can actualize the American Dream. As our culture has come from all the world, so must we give back to all the world not that technological materialism which is science cheapened and debased but the scientific attitude woven into the stuff of people's daily lives. This is a vision of humility in the face of the complexity of things, of the joyous pursuit of ideas of which there is no exclusive possession. This is science not as the provider of the agencies of barbarism but science as revealing the order in experience, as heightening the sense of our precarious dependence one upon the other, as the surest and most powerful of internationalizing forces.

Scientific humanism should be the sturdy creed of the future. Despite uncritical worship of invention and technology, the masses are still, in Carlson's expression, "innocent of science, in the sense of the spirit and the method of science as part of their way of life. . . . Science in this sense has as yet hardly touched the common man or his leaders." An effective working majority of our citizens need no longer base their personal security upon expectation of future life or adult dependency upon the projected images of parent-persons. The scientific vision is the vision which Plato saw in the *Symposium*, a security system which is depersonalized but humanized rather than dehumanized. To try to make such a vision real, offers American men and women that common nobility of purpose which is the vitalizing energy of any significant culture. The venture demands a courage analogous to religious faith, a courage undismayed by the failure of any specific experiment, a courage ready to offer the renunciations of waiting long, a courage which recognizes that even negative knowledge means growth, a courage realizing that the general hypotheses underlying the venture will be proved only if diminished anxiety and greater gusto in day-to-day living transform the lives of us all.

CHAPTER X

An Anthropologist Looks at the World

THE TEMERITY of this title frightens the anthropologist who is accustomed to working upon a small canvas with careful attention to factual detail. Moreover, the recipe for action that must be drawn from applied anthropology thus far is that of caution, of modest expectations as to what can be accomplished by planning, of humility as to what may be predicted with present instruments for observing and conceptualizing, of preference for *vis medicatrix naturae* in many social situations.

Indications are not lacking that some anthropologists, exhilarated by newly discovered skills and intoxicated by the fact that for the first time men of affairs are seeking their advice on a fairly extended scale, are encouraging hopes which their science is not mature enough to fulfill. To restrain anthropologists from irresponsible pronouncements, the profession may need to develop sanctions comparable to those which law and medicine have created to control charlatanism and malpractice.

Anthropology has attained some practical utility. It has serviceable techniques for getting information necessary to diagnose and interpret human behavior. There is a body of slowly built up generalizations which statesmen, administrators, and planners would be foolish not to heed. Anthropology can lay bare the internal logics of each culture. It can sometimes show how the economic theory, the political theory, the art forms, and the religious doctrine of each society are all expressive of a single set of elementary assumptions. In certain cases anthropologists have proved that they can forecast the social weather with some accuracy. But it is one thing to be able to make some useful predictions as to what is likely to happen—and by thus foreseeing to be able to make useful preparations. It is quite another thing to interfere, willfully to introduce new complications into an already tortuous social maze. At least when it comes to big situations, the anthropologist would do well to abide by what has proved a helpful rule in many medical cases: "Sit tight. Watch. Prepare for probable developments but do not interfere with natural forces making for recuperation until you are sure action will be helpful, or, as an absolute minimum, do no harm."

On the other hand, as Walter Lippman has observed, "The controlling principle of our time is that the peoples of the world will not let nature take its course." The participation of social scientists in these decisions, if not overambitious or arrogant, can add a much needed leaven of specialized knowledge. Because social science deals with the facts of everyday life, many statesmen and men of affairs feel that they can become their own sociologists without training. A prevalent attitude toward professional social scientists is unreasonable in that too little is asked and too much is expected. As Scroggs has written:

When we find a charlatan vending snake-oil we don't find fault with doctors; instead, as the spirit moves us, we either pity or despise the rascal's gullible victims. Medicine and its allied sciences have attained a status which is so clearly defined and so well understood that they are not attacked when physicians do not work miracles or when quacks prostitute a noble calling to base ends. Economics and all the social sciences, on the other hand, are still in the making. In some respects they are like Kipling's ship before she found herself. Owing to the complicated character of the materials with which these sciences are concerned, their development cannot be hurried and their application is unavoidably limited. Those who are impatient with the ailments of human society demand too much when they expect social science to diagnose the malady, write a prescription, and soon have the patient on the road to recovery.

The anthropologist cannot be at once a scientist, expert framer of national policies, and infallible prophet. But if he is to make a truly scientific contribution to the solution of public problems his highly technical studies in basic science must be supported on a more substantial scale. There is vague public acceptance of the necessity for the natural scientist to conduct recondite experiments, some of which end in blind alleys. There tends, however, to be contempt or lack of patience with the endless detail devoted by the anthropologist to the analysis of a kinship system, for instance. Yet sound conceptions of human behavior must be based upon as exhaustive a study of minutiae as has been given to organic compounds in chemistry.

Present anthropology has recognizable limits. There is a wide gap between program and accomplishment. The greatest strength of anthropology rests in its asking some of the right questions rather than in supplying the answers. Anthropological knowledge needs to be fused with that of the other human sciences. In particular, more attention to individual variation must supplement the study of group variation. One of the wise things which Reinhold Niebuhr says in *The Nature and Destiny of Man* is that the contemporary world overestimates the powers of the "collective will" and underestimates those of the individual will.

Yet, in spite of all these deeply felt cautions and qualifications, the anthropologist as citizen is morally obligated to look at the world. For the essence of democracy is that each individual offers to the thinking of the group those insights that derive from his special experience and training. Contemporary understanding of international relations stands about where knowledge of the workings of small societies did when anthropologists began their field work among nonliterate cultures. The anthropologist has, not a solution, but an indispensable contribution to make to the appraisal of the total world scene. He will be under no delusions as to the adequacy of his empirical data. But he will be confident of the applicability of his principles. During the last ten years anthropologists have not only written a good deal about American and British culture. David Rodnick has described *Post-war Germans* as dispassionately as an Indian tribe. Ruth Benedict's and John Embree's books on Japan, those of various Chinese and foreign anthropologists on China have given a new outlook to our understanding of the Far East.

Historians, economists, and political scientists frequently say, "Anthropological methods work well enough when applied to simple peoples. But they are useless for dealing with a diverse, stratified, segmented society." This reasoning rests upon a misapprehension, though there are significant differences between tribal, peasant, and fully industrialized populations. The problems of a modern civilization are undoubtedly more complicated. The quantity of data needed is much greater. For certain purposes each subculture must be investigated separately. For other purposes, however, regional and class variations are relatively external, superficial, and unimportant. Though multicultural states like Jugoslavia present their special complications, no nation can exist for long as a nation unless there is some discoverable core of common purposes. These basic goals may be expressed in a confusing variety of forms, but they are held by the vast majority of members of all groups in the society. Ruth Benedict has provided a telling illustration:

The wealthy industrialist and the laborer or peasant, in a nation or area of Western civilization, hold many attitudes in common. The attitude toward property only in part depends upon whether one is rich or whether one is poor. Property may be, as in Holland, something which is an almost inseparable part of one's own self-esteem, something to be added to, kept immaculately, and never spent carelessly. This is true, whether the individual belongs to court circles or can say in the words of a proverbial expression: "If it's only a penny a year, lay it by." Alternatively, the attitude toward property may be quite different, as in Roumania. An upper-class person may be, or become, a pensioner of a wealthy man, without loss of status or self-confidence; his property, he says, is not "himself." And the poor peasant argues that, being poor, it is futile for him to lay anything by; "he would," he says, "if he were rich." The well-to-do increase their possessions by other means than thrift, and the traditional attitude toward property differences associates wealth with luck or exploitation, rather than with assured position as in Holland. In each of these countries, as in other European nations, many of which have deeply embedded special attitudes toward property, the specific nature of these assumptions can be greatly clarified by study of what is required of the child in his handling and ownership of property, and under what sanctions and conditions expanding opportunities are allowed in adolescence, and at his induction into fully adult status.

Attitudes toward authority are similarly localized. A Greek, whether he belongs to the upper classes, or whether he is a peasant villager, has a characteristic opposition to authority from above, which permeates daily conversation and influences his choice of a means of livelihood quite as much as it colors his political attitudes.

Just as anthropologists maintain that some themes crosscut complex cultures, so also they insist that there are known and knowable principles of human behavior which are universal. For this reason also a restriction of the applicability of anthropology is false. All human societies, from the "most primitive" to the "most advanced" constitute a continuum. Industrialization poses different problems but also some of the same ones to Navaho Indians, Polish peasants, Siamese rice farmers, and Japanese fishermen.

Anthropology grants the same amnesty to cultural variations that the psychoanalyst gives to incestuous wishes. In neither case, however, is approval implied. The barbarity of a concentration camp is not good by virtue of being one element in the Nazi design for living. The anthropologist and the psychiatrist accept what is only to the extent of asserting that it is meaningful and cannot be ignored. Fantasies of incest may play some part in the psychological economy of a certain personality. They are symptoms of underlying causes. If symptoms are prevented expression, the causes will still be operative and produce another disorder. If a tribe's customary outlet for aggression in war is blocked, one may predict an increase in intratribal hostility (perhaps in the form of witchcraft) or in pathological states of melancholy resultant upon anger being turned inward against the self. Culture patterns must be respected because they are functional. If a pattern is destroyed, a socially desirable substitute must be provided or energies must be purposefully channeled in other directions.

Respect does not mean preservation under all conditions. Sicilian folkways do not make much sense in Boston, however much color they may give to the North End. Chinese habits are out of place in San Francisco even if they appeal to tourists as "quaint." Anthropologists have sometimes been justly accused of wanting to keep the world a cultural museum, of striving to maintain aborigines in so many zoological parks. Some of the talk about the values of American Indian and Spanish-American cultures in the United States has been sentimental. It is significant that anthropologists have studied these exotic cultures almost to the exclusion of generalized American culture. We have sometimes confused the right to be different with a demand for the perpetuation of differences.

The best anthropological position takes a middle ground between sentimentality and the Philistine type of "modernization." When any culture is totally obliterated there is an irreparable loss to mankind, for no people has failed to create something worthwhile in the course of its experience. The anthropologist prefers evolution to revolution because a gradual adaptation means both that there are no lost generations and that whatever is of permanent value in the older way of life is poured into the total stream of human culture.

The anthropological outlook demands toleration of other ways of life—so long as they do not threaten the hope for world order. Satisfactory world order, however, cannot be brought about by the reduction of cultural diversity and the creation of a world-wide gray sameness. Those rich diversities of form that cultures assume from distinct histories, distinct physical environments, distinct contemporary situations—and that are not in conflict with modern technology and science—are invaluable assets for good life in the world. As Lawrence Frank says:

> To believe that the English-speaking or Western European peoples can impose upon all others the parliamentarism, the peculiar economic business practices, the esoteric creeds and religious rituals, and all the other idiomatic features of their Western European patterns, is the initial misconception and blindness in so much of present-day thinking and planning . . . Every culture is asymmetrical, biased, and incomplete, making a virtue of its deficiencies and its anesthesias. Each culture in grappling with the same problems has created patterns of action, speech, and belief, of human relationships and values that have accentuated certain potentialities of human life and have ignored or repressed others. Each culture seeks to represent itself by its aspirations, emphasizing its lofty ethical or moral goals as its essential character, and usually ignoring its shortcomings and its often destructive features. . . .
>
> No single culture can be accepted as the final and best for all peoples; we must recognize the unhappiness, the degradation, the

misery, the incredible brutality, cruelty, and human wastage in all cultures which each tends to ignore while stressing lofty ethical aims and moral aspirations. . . . We may view cultures as we view the arts of different peoples as esthetically significant and artistically meaningful, each in its own context or setting.

Our age is hostile to nuances. Increasingly, people of all continents are being forced to choose between the extreme right and the extreme left. Yet the scientific study of human variation indicates that experience is a continuum, that any extreme position represents a distortion of reality. To admit as good only what is American or English or Russian is unscientific and unhistorical. Americans have generally accepted diversity as a condition, but only some Americans have embraced it as a value. The dominant note has been that of pride in destroying diversity through assimilation. The significance of anthropological knowledge is that any particular way of life belongs to a greater phenomenon (the total culture of humanity) of which any one culture is one temporary phase. The anthropologist urges that each specific world problem be treated within a framework including the human species as a whole.

Order is bought too dearly if it is bought at the price of the tyranny of any single set of inflexible principles, however noble these may appear to be from the perspective of any single culture. Individuals are biologically different, and there are various types of temperament which reappear at different times and places in the world's history. So long as the satisfaction of temperamental needs is not needlessly thwarting to the life activities of others, so long as the diversities are not socially destructive, individuals must not only be permitted but indeed encouraged to fulfill themselves in diverse ways. The necessity for diversity is founded upon the facts of biological differences, differences in situation, varying backgrounds in individual and cultural history. The oneness of the world must be negative only in so far as violence is restrained. Positive unity will need to be firmly based upon universal adherence to a very general, very simple, but also very limited moral code. It can flower triumphantly only to the degree that the fullest and most various potentialities of the human spirit are realized. The healthiest kind of society would create citizens who wanted to express themselves in ways that were both personally and socially useful. The highest morality in the best society would allow fulfillment of all personality needs, limiting only the manner, place, time, and object of expression.

The paradox of unity in diversity was never so meaningful as today. The Fascists attempted an escape from "the frightening heterogeneity of the twentieth century" by a return to primitivism where there is no harassing conflict, no disturbing choice because there is but a single rule and that unquestioned. The Communists likewise promise escape from freedom through the individual's surrender of his autonomy to the state. The democratic solution is that of orchestrated heterogeneity. One may compare a symphony. There is a plan to the whole and a relation of parts which must be maintained. But this does not mean that the delicious contrast of themes, of tempos, is lost. The first movement is distinct from the fourth. It has its own value and significance—though still its full meaning is dependent upon an orderly and articulated relation to the rest.

So the world must be kept safe for differences. Knowledge of the problems of others and of alien ways of life must become sufficiently general so that positive toleration becomes possible. Also necessary to respect for others is a certain minimum of security for oneself. Certain inequalities of opportunity between peoples must be leveled out, even if at some apparent sacrifice on the part of nations now more fortunate. A secure and happy world can be built only from secure and happy individuals. The roots of individual and of national and international disorganization are in part the same. Lippit and Hendry well say:

> A civilization is a thing that kneads and molds men. If the civilization to which we belong was brought low by the failure of individuals, then our question must be, why did our civilization not create a different type of individual? We must begin by recovering the animating power of our civilization which has become lost. We have been taking advantage of democracy's tranquillity, its tolerance, its warmth. We have become parasites upon it. It has meant to us no more than a place where we were snug and secure like a passenger on a ship. The passenger makes use of the ship and gives nothing in return. If the members of our civilization have degenerated, against whom can we lodge a complaint?

When Copernicus showed that the earth was not the center of our universe, he forced a revolution in the thinking of natural scientists and philosophers. Thinking in the United States about international affairs still rests upon the false premise that Western civilization is the hub of the cultural universe. The Harvard report on general education, published in 1945, is in many respects a wise and indeed a noble document. Yet not one word is said of the need of the educated citizen to know something of Asiatic history and philosophy and art or of the natural resources of Africa or of non-European languages. History begins with the Greeks and the significant achievements of human culture are limited to the Mediterranean Basin, Europe, and America. A peaceful revolution must dethrone such parochialism.

Small wonder that we continue to interpret non-Western thought and action in terms of the categories of the West. We project our dominant concepts of the recent past—economics and politics and biology—instead of trying to grasp the more fundamental cultural patterns of which a given type of economic activity is merely one expression. It is these basic conceptions and the images a people has of itself and of others which anthropology can especially help to illumine. The anthropologist has had experience in penetrating the barriers of language, ideology, and nationality in order to understand and to persuade. He realizes that any piece of unfamiliar behavior is an expression of another people's total cultural experience.

It is fatal to all hopes for peace when Americans see every evidence of other nations' different cultural assumptions as examples of their moral perfidy. The alternatives are not to agree or to reject; it is possible to accept other assumptions in the sense of facing the fact of their existence and understanding them. To the extent that both policy makers and public realize that the values of any two societies in conflict cannot be suddenly altered by supposedly logical demonstration of their invalidity, the danger of pathological suspicions on each side is lessened. Reciprocal misunderstandings grow by mutual stimulation unless each party will substitute the question "reasonable in terms of their premises?" for "reasonable?" (meaning: compatible with our own premises which have never been thought through or even brought to the light of consciousness). The genuine conflicts of interests between two or more powers could often be resolved through compromise were not irrational emotional forces mobilized through culture-bound misinterpretations of motives. Relative to one group, the other appears unreasonable, unable to see the logical consequences, folly, and immorality of its own actions, and acquires the character of an evil force that must be attacked.

Of course, the realization on the part of the two nations that they are operating upon different premises does not always lead to sweetness and light. It is only a useful first step that cannot fail to diminish the power of the irrational. But premises may be different yet not incompatible or they may be different and incompatible. In the case of the conflicting ideologies of the

Soviet Union and the Western democracies, it may well be, as Northrop has suggested, that no stable equilibrium is possible unless one culture destroys the other or, more probably, a new set of cultural assumptions is evolved which absorbs and reconciles what is permanently valuable to the human animal in both opposing ways of life. Even now there is common ground which could well be brought nearer the center of bitter political discussion. For example, both the American people and the peoples of the Soviet Union are remarkable among the nations of the world for their faith in man's capacity to manipulate his environment and control his fate.

The shrinking of the world makes mutual understanding and respect on the part of different peoples imperative. The subtle diversities in the view of life of various peoples, their expectancies and images of themselves and of others, the differing psychological attitudes underlying their contrasting political institutions, and their generally differing "psychological nationality" all combine to make it more difficult for nations to understand each other. It is the anthropologist's duty to point out that these "mental" forces have just as tangible effect as physical forces.

The prime problem of the century is indeed whether world order is to be achieved through domination of a single nation that imposes its life ways upon all others or through some other means that does not deprive the world of the richness of different cultures. World uniformity in culture would mean aesthetic and moral monotony. The anthropologist's solution is unity in diversity: agreement on a set of principles for world morality but respect and toleration for all activities that do not threaten world peace. The anthropologist regards the attainment of this course as tremendously difficult but not impossible. Anthropology can aid by criticizing the formal machinery for keeping the peace, by insisting that this take account of peoples' sentiments, customs, and nonrational life rather than being thought of along purely legalistic lines. Anthropology can also help in education in the broadest sense. It can provide material for debunking potentially dangerous stereotypes of other peoples. It can assist in training experts in each country who have really fundamental knowledge of other countries, knowledge that goes beyond that of externals and permits the expert to interpret correctly the behavior of other nations to his own people. In many ways, direct and indirect, anthropology can influence public opinion in scientifically sound and practically healthy directions. Not least significant will be its demonstration of the basic unity of mankind, in spite of arresting and interesting superficial divergence.

Anthropology does not by any means have all the answers, but a public whose thinking has been clarified by anthropological knowledge will be somewhat better fitted to perceive the proper directions for national policy. Only those who are both well informed and well intentioned will have the understanding necessary for the building of bridges between different ways of life. A unifying survey of all cultural contributions and of all peoples will, in turn, influence the general mentality of men. By studying world cultures in this comparative setting, anthropologists hope to promote a better understanding of the cultural values of other nations and other times, and thus help to create something of that spirit of tolerant understanding which is an essential condition of international harmony.

If one looks at the record of human events from a perspective which is sufficiently wide in space and sufficiently long in time, there can be no doubt that there are certain broad, over-all trends in history. One of these persistent tendencies is for the size and spatial extent of societies to be ever greater. The anthropologist will hardly question that, eventually, there will be, in some sense, a world society. The sole argument will be over the questions, how soon? after how much suffering and bloodshed?

To draw the detailed blueprints for the political and economic instruments which might implement a world order is not the province of the anthropologist. Obviously, the sustained collaboration of economists, political scientists, lawyers, engineers, geographers, other specialists, and practical men of affairs from many lands will be required to devise the machinery with which men might build the new world. But inductions from anthropological data suggest certain basic principles which the social inventions must meet if they are to be workable. From their experience in studying societies as wholes, from experience with sharply contrasting peoples and cultures, the anthropologist and other social scientists have proved a few theorems which the statesman and the administrator will disregard at peril to the world.

Under the necessity of being at once a student of economics, technology, religion, and aesthetics, the anthropologist has perforce learned the intricate interdependence of all segments of a peoples' life. Although as a Jack-of-all-trades his work is usually crude, the anthropologist is at least tough-minded about academic abstractions. He knows at firsthand the fallacy of the "economic man," the "political man," etc. Because his laboratory is the world of living people at their ordinary daily tasks, the results of the anthropologist are not stated with the statistical refinements of the brass-instrument psychologist, but he perhaps has a more lively sense of the complications arising from an uncontrolled variety of stimuli—as opposed to the selected ones of the laboratory.

For all these reasons, the anthropologist will insist upon the stupidity of any policy that emphasizes political or economic factors at the expense of cultural and psychological factors. He will agree that geographical position, natural resources, present degree of industrialization, illiteracy rate, and countless other factors are of importance. But he will maintain that an approach which is purely geographical or economic is doomed to breed new confusion. No mechanical scheme for world government or an international police force will save the world. Something more than policemen have been found necessary for the maintenance of order in all social organizations.

The anthropologist will suspect that not only some of his fellow specialists but also the general American public will view the problems too exclusively in the light of reason. One of the most abiding traditions of this country is faith in reason. This is a glorious tradition—so long as people do not ludicrously overestimate how much reason can accomplish in a given limited time. When one minutely scrutinizes one's own behavior, one invariably sees how large a proportion of one's acts are determined in accord with the logic of the sentiments. If all men everywhere shared precisely the same sentiments, the great role of the nonlogical elements in action might not lead into great difficulty. But the sentiments of men are determined not only by those great dilemmas which face all humanity but also by the peculiar historical experience, the peculiar problems posed by the varying physical environments of each people.

As a result of the accidents of history, every people not only has a sentiment structure which is to some degree unique but also a more or less coherent body of characteristic presuppositions about the world. This last is really a borderland between reason and feeling. And the trouble is that the most critical premises are so often unstated—even by the intellectuals of the group.

And so more than the external facts about a nation must be taken into account. Their sentiments and the unconscious assumptions which they characteristically make about the world, are also data which must be discovered and respected.

These will all of course be tied in with religion, aesthetic tradition, and other more conscious aspects of the cultural tradition of the people. To understand all of these intangibles, and to cope with them in planning, the student must have recourse to history. It is not enough for science to explain the world of nature. Education must include the "intangible" environment in which we live.

The problem of how to minimize and to control aggressive impulses is in many ways the central problem of world peace. This problem must be approached from every possible angle. One, though only one, way of preventing wars is to lessen the irritants making for tension within each society. This means, first of all, assuring a certain minimun of economic well-being and of physical health to all populations in the world. Assuredly, however, the task does not end here. A people can be ever so prosperous and yet seething with hostility. Norway was poorer than Germany in 1939, yet had no war-minded groups.

Some things are now known about the sources and dynamics of hostility. Psychological bases in the individual for potential aggression are created by the deprivations incident to socialization. No society fails to beat the child's ears in at some point, though they differ greatly in the manner and the timing. Some childhood disciplines are probably exaggerated or needless. Others are carried out with avoidable brutality. To quote Lawrence Frank again:

> As long as we believe that human nature is fixed and unchangeable and continue to accept the theological conceptions of man as one who must be disciplined, coerced, and terrorized or supernaturally assisted into being a decent human being and a participating member of society, so long will we continue to create warped, twisted, distorted personalities, who continually threaten, if they do not frustrate and break down, all our efforts toward social order.

Some frustration and deprivation is inevitable in the production of responsible adults. But the resultant tensions can be drained off more effectively than most human societies have done in the past through socially useful competition, through socially harmless releases for aggression, as in sports, and in other, as yet undiscovered, ways.

Those who are insecure themselves manifest hostility toward others. It will be by diminishing both the realistic and unrealistic causes for anxiety in the world that the psychological bases for war can be controlled. Of course, war is not the only direction which violence can take. Ordinarily, aggression release within a society is inversely proportional to outlets outside. Many measures will merely shift the currents of hostility—not eliminate them. Nor is aggression, whether overt or masked, the only possible adjustive response to anxiety. Withdrawal, passivity, sublimation, conciliation, flight, and other responses are sometimes effective in reducing the strains of those who have been deprived or threatened. Some cultures, at their flowering, have been able to channel most of their free-floating hostility into socially creative channels: literature and the arts, public works, invention, geographical exploration, and the like. In most cultures, most of the time, the greater part of this energy is diffused into various streams: into the small angry outbursts of daily living; into constructive activities; into periodic wars. The destructive aggression, which seems to appear with some regularity after a major catastrophe to a society, breaks out only after an interval. Facism did not arise immediately after Caporetto nor Nazism immediately after the treaty of Versailles. Finally, it should be noted that, since it takes two or more nations to make a war, a psychological climate of uncertainity, confusion, and apathy can endanger peace as much as dammed up hostility.

War is a power struggle, but not simply for the control of

markets and manufacturing processes. Economic and social welfare do not, as the popular conception would have it, depend always upon political power. The standard of living in Switzerland and Denmark was higher than that in many of the great powers in the interval between the wars. War must also be thought of as arising from points of view, ways of looking at the world, for all deep-seated motives express themselves indirectly in biasing or loading the personal outlook. The quest for power, the preferred character forms of a group, its economic productivity, its ideology, its patterns of leadership are all so closely interwoven that a change in any one of these factors means an alteration in the others. The best perspective from which present world confusion can be viewed is the cross-cultural one. From this vantage point one may see both the characteristic illusions of every civilization and the fertilizing value of contrasting cultures.

Although imbedded in the past, this network of sentiments and assumptions looks to the future. Morale, whether individual or national or international, is largely a structure of expectancies. The nature of expectations is almost as crucial as the external facts in predicting consequences. In wartime patriotic citizens will undergo major privations with little complaint. In peacetime the same deprivations may lead to riots or widespread social unrest. The external facts are the same but the expectations are different. Much of what is happening in Europe and Asia depends not upon food shortages, the precise form of newly instituted political arrangements, the rebuilding of factories or other conditions as such, but rather upon the goodness of fit between these conditions and the anticipations of the people in question.

As the anthropologist puzzles the cross-cultural record, he can hardly fail to be struck by the importance of the time factor. Capacity for cultural change, indeed for sharp reversals, on the part of the same biological group seems almost unlimited. The mistake of many well-meaning social reformers has not always been limited to that of attempting sumptuary legislation. Sometimes the measures have been wise enough for the group intended, but all has been lost through undue haste. Make haste slowly is usually a good motto for those who wish to institute or direct social change. Because of the enormous tenacity of nonlogical habits, the hasty attempt to alter intensifies resistance or even produces reaction. Plans for the new world must indeed be vast and bold, but there must be great patience and tireless practicality in carrying them out.

This is a note of caution but not of pessimism. For perhaps the greatest lesson which anthropology can teach is that of the boundless plasticity of "human nature." The exuberant variety of solutions which have been devised to the same problem (say "sex" or "property") is truly amazing and makes one eternally sceptical of any argument couched in the form, "That would never work—it is contrary to human nature." However, some of the more enthusiastic exponents of cultural determinism and of education forget how many generations and indeed millennia have gone into the experiments in human living carried out by various societies. *Homo sapiens* will, under the right conditions, eventually do almost anything—but the time required before a particular result is achieved may be very long indeed.

Is prolonged collaboration between different peoples possible? Anthropology knows of no definitive evidence to the contrary. Certainly there are isolated instances of peaceful and sometimes long-continued cooperation between groups speaking different languages and, less frequently, between groups of different physical appearance. Nor have these invariably involved relationships of subordination.

This book has tried to steer a middle course between "economic determinism" and "psychological determinism." In recent times one group of students of human affairs has loudly proclaimed that everything is due to situational factors, especially technology and economic pressures. Another group—which has lately become increasingly fashionable—says in effect: "Tools and economic systems are but the expression of human personalities. The key to the world's problems lies not in new techniques of distribution nor in more equitable access to raw materials, or even in a stable international organization. All we need is a saner method of child rearing, a wiser education." Each of these "explanations" by itself is one-sided and barren. Probably the tendency to oversimplification in these two directions corresponds to what we find in contrasting schools of historians who, ever since Greek times at least, have seen history either as the process of impersonal forces or as a drama of personalities. Either conception has a strong appeal to human beings who crave simple answers to complex questions, but neither alone tells the whole story; we need both.

Both the external and the more internal aspects of the problem are tremendous. When disaster threatens, when experience is felt ever menacing, men may do one of two things or both. They may change the situation—the external environment—or they may change themselves. The first path, broadly speaking, is the only one which has been taken to any appreciable extent by Western European peoples in recent centuries. The second path, broadly speaking, is the one which has been taken by Asiatic peoples and our American Indians. Neither path, by itself, leads to a balanced good life for the majority of men. To act on the unstated premise that either one or the other will save us is the tragic consequence of our habituation to the Aristotelian mode of thought which thinks in terms of mutually exclusive alternatives. Both roads are necessary and open. To have democracy we must have personalities that are able to be free. However, no scheme of socialization or formal education which makes for freedom of the personality can guarantee organisms which are free from the need to fear and the need to fight unless the social and economic structure makes these orientations realistically rewarding.

The internal change must arise from the development of a faith which should give meaning and purpose to living but which could be believed in by a reasonable man familiar with what we have learned of our world by scientific methods. As wide an induction as anthropology can offer is that every society desperately needs morality in the sense of common standards, and religion in the sense of orientations toward such inescapable problems as death, individual responsibility, and other ultimate value attitudes. Religion in this sense is absolutely necessary to promote social solidarity and individual security by affirming and symbolically enacting a system of common purposes. In my opinion, a faith is required which would not force intellectual reservation or conflict or compartmentalization. Such a faith cannot today, I believe, successfully be based upon supernatural premises. It must needs be a secular religion. There is nothing whatsoever in the sciences of human behavior which denies the existence of "absolutes" in and for human conduct. However, a humanistic science does assert that these absolutes can and must be validated by empirical observation rather than by documents pretending to supernatural authority. Charles Morris, in *Paths of Life*, has pioneered the quest for a secular world religion. Others are beginning to think along not dissimilar lines. The difficulties are many; the need overwhelming. A "secular religion" does not neccessarily mean "atheism" in the proper meaning of that word. Many scientists who prefer the naturalistic to the supernaturalistic point of view believe in God as described by the philosopher, Whitehead, in *Process and Reality*. They are convinced that the universe is orderly and, in some sense, a moral universe. Their quarrel with the supernaturalists is as to how man can discover and live by the divine order.

Man must humbly but with courage accept responsibility for the destiny of mankind. Any other postulate is a frightened retreat and, in the long run a retreat which leads to the blank wall or the precipice of chaos unthinkable. Man may be able to understand and control himself as much as he has demonstrably understood and controlled nonorganic nature and domestic animals. At least it is worth the trial. This is the great emotional adventure, the second half of the twentieth century, that "rife idea of transcendent might" which must make all forms of exploitation seem commonplace or, rather, vulgar and uninteresting. To this adventure the "study of man" can contribute not only some of the guiding directions, but likewise the techniques for amassing much of the information which is as essential as principle and concept.

The development of a flourishing science of man will wait upon fuller public understanding of the need for anthropology and its kindred sciences and adequate support. The emphasis upon material things in American culture and the stupendous success of physical science have tended to draw the best brains into law, business, and natural science. Even if the average anthropologist were as smart as the average physicist, significant research among human beings takes a sizable number of people, time, and money. One can never do with even the best corporal's guard what one can do with an army. Yet American society spent more for a single telescope at Mt. Wilson than was spent in three years on all studies of human life (excluding medicine). In prewar years Americans spent ten times as much each year in collecting zoological and botanical specimens as in collecting irreplaceable data concerning the human cultures that are rapidly disappearing before the spread of European civilization. Yet, as Mortimer Graves has observed:

The essential fact is that man's major problems are not at all in the natural sciences but in such areas as race relations, labor relations, the control of organized power for social purposes, the establishment of the philosophical bases of life, the modernization of social and political structure, the coordination of efficiency with democracy—all the problems raised in man's adjustment to the scientific, social dynamic world in which he lives. Public health, for example, is not primarily a problem of learning more about disease in the strictly biological sense—it is primarily a problem in social science, a problem of putting effectively to work in the lives of men what is already known about medicine. At the technological level there is probably already enough known to give everybody a job with a full dinner pail. What is needed is not more physical science but better social organization. What is necessary is to force some of the medieval superstition out of social and political customs, and there is no sign that this will be done in the laboratories of physics and chemistry. Mere advance in these and similar sciences without concomitant solution of more important social, emotional, and intellectual problems can lead only to more maladjustment, more misunderstanding, more social unrest, and consequently more war and revolution.

There must be bold experiments in social living and a search for fresh integrating principles appropriate to a world which communication and economic interdependence have made one —for the first time in human history. If we are to do more than keep a finger in the dike, if we are to build upward out of the flood as well as stemming the tide of human misery and frustration, we must inject the study of human behavior, of the individual and his society, into the social process. This study must include the objective investigation of human values. People are not just driven by situational pressures; they are also pulled by the idealized goals set by their culture. As Ralph Barton Perry has said, if ideals make any difference at all in human life there must be certain occasions in which they make all the difference.

Contrasting human needs, in so far as they are characteristic of whole groups rather than of specific individuals, arise primarily from variant value systems. As has been said so often, the crisis of our age is a crisis of value. There is little hope of creating new social entities which shall be more stable than the old until new, wider, and more complex relationships can be built upon values that are not only generally recognized and deeply felt but that also have some scientific warrant.

No tenet of intellectual folklore has been so damaging to our life and times as the cliché that "science has nothing to do with values." If the consideration of values is to be the exclusive property of religion and the humanities, a scientific understanding of human experience is impossible. But it is absurd to claim a logical necessity for such an abdication. Values are social facts of a certain type which can be discovered and described as neutrally as a linguistic structure or the technique of salmon fishing. Those values that are instrumental in character can be tested in terms of their consequences. Are the means, in fact, effective in reaching the designated ends?

When it comes to intrinsic or "absolute" values, it must be admitted that methods and concepts are not yet available for rigorously determining the varying extent to which these are congruent with the facts of nature as scientifically established. This is, however, because until very recently scientists have uncritically accepted exclusion from this field. In principle, a scientific basis for values is discoverable. Some values appear to be as much "given" by nature as the fact that bodies heavier than air fall. No society has ever approved suffering as a good thing in itself—as a means to an end, yes; as punishment, as a means to the ends of society, yes. We don't have to rely upon supernatural revelation to discover that sexual access achieved through violence is bad. This is as much a fact of general observation as the fact that different objects have different densities. The observation that truth and beauty are universal, transcendental human values is as much one of the givens of human life as are birth and death. It is the great merit of F. C. S. Northrop to have pointed out the essential generalization: "The norms for ethical conduct are to be discovered from the ascertainable knowledge of man's nature, just as the norms for building a bridge are to be derived from physics."

To work out this problem in detail will require, at very least, a generation—if the best minds in many countries will give themselves to the task. There are endless complications and possibilities for distortion, especially through oversimplification. The key question is that of the universal human values. Justification for other values will turn upon the matter of appropriateness to particular sorts of individuals or to specific cultures. Some values (for instance, whether I prefer cabbage or spinach) involve taste only and are socially indifferent. The discovery and ranking of the universal values can never rest simply upon counting and placement in an assumed scale of cultural advancement. The facts are very complex. We are part of one of perhaps twenty literate cultures. However, one of our ideal patterns, monogamy, though practiced by only about one-fourth of described cultures, is shared with some of the most "backward" tribes of the earth. Nevertheless, in spite of all the difficulties, the methods of scientific analysis can be applied to human values with enormous hope of success.

Anthropology is no longer just the science of the long-ago and far-away. This very perspective is uniquely valuable in investigating the nature and causes of human conflict and in devising means for its reduction. Its all-embracing character gives anthropology a strategic position for determining what factors will create a world community of distinct cultures and hold it together against disruption. It has methods for revealing the principles that undergird each culture, for deciding to what extent a culture possesses people. It is singularly emancipated from the sway of the locally accepted. When asked how he happened to discover relativity, Einstein replied, "by challenging an axiom." As a consequence of their cross-cultural research anthropologists are freer to disbelieve something that appears, even to their fellow scientists of the same culture, necessarily true. In the present stage of world history the apparently unbridgeable gap between several powerful and competing ways of life can be surmounted only by those who can constructively doubt the traditionally obvious.

As Lyman Bryson concludes in *Science and Freedom:* "man's toughest problem is himself." The danger of atomic and other new weapons lies not in the weapons themselves but in the will to use them. It is the sources of this will, as varyingly conditioned by different cultures, that must be investigated, understood, and controlled. Science must create a climate in which it can, itself, operate without widespread destruction. The science of man, by applying to human behavior those standard procedures that have proved so successful in dealing with other aspects of nature, might produce some of the ingredients necessary to the creation of such a climate. It cannot do it alone, even if anthropology joins forces with psychology, sociology, and human geography. It cannot make its own full contribution unless public understanding and support add greatly to its resources in manpower and funds. If reliable answers are to be joined to right questions, the research that has been carried out is to the research that needs to be done as the film of atmosphere is to the full thickness of this planet.

Edwin Embree has eloquently answered the most usual objection to this program:

> Many people think it visionary to try to improve our own lives and relationships. They feel they have closed the whole subject with "You can't change human nature."

Well, we haven't changed the nature of the physical universe, but by understanding it we have turned it in myriad ways to our service and our convenience. We didn't set aside the force of gravity when we learned to fly. We didn't have to amend the laws of stress and strain, we only had to understand them, in order to build bridges and skyscrapers or to drive engines a hundred miles an hour. We didn't change the climate, yet by central heating we make ourselves comfortable through the coldest winters and by air-cooling devices we are beginning to have equal comfort in the hottest summers. We didn't alter the laws of biology to breed fleet horses and fat hogs, to grow corn and wheat of far finer quality than anything known in a wild state, even to devise such serviceable hybrids as mules and grapefruit.

So with human nature it is not a matter of "changing" the fundamental drives and instincts; it is simply a matter of understanding these forces and turning them to more constructive and wholesome channels than the strifes and frustrations that make up so much of life, even in the midst of our material plenty.

The new stage of development of the social sciences, still largely unrealized by the general public, may prove to have consequences as revolutionary as those of atomic energy. However, it would be fantastic to anticipate any immediate molding of world civilization to human desires and needs. Cultures and beliefs, attitudes, and feelings of men change slowly even in the accelerated modern tempo. It makes for sanity to consider some historical facts. As Leslie White reminds us, only about 2 per cent of human history has elapsed since the origin of agriculture, .35 per cent since the invention of the first alphabet, .009 per cent since the publication of Darwin's *Origin of Species*. Contemporary social science is merely a lusty infant, howling loudly because the world is still deaf. Still, he promises much if he be neither starved nor spoiled.

Present ignorance and the crudity of social-science methods and theories must not be glossed over. Humanity which is gradually abandoning the hope of the kingdom of heaven should resist the blandishments of cheap messiahs preaching an easy achievement of the kingdom of earth over night. To some degree cultures make themselves. From the short-range point of view man is still more or less at the mercy of irreversible trends he did not willfully create. Nevertheless, in longer range, social science offers the possibility of understanding and of prediction, of speeding up desired trends, of greatly increased opportunities for successful adjustment if not of control.

Human life should remain as a home of many rooms. But the world with all its variousness can still be one in its allegiance to the elementary common purposes shared by all peoples. Those boundaries that block mutual understanding will be worn dim by much international traffic in ideas, in exchange of goods and services. Within each society the use of scientific methods in the study of human relations can adjust our culture patterns to the changes brought about by technology and world-wide economic interdependence. This can happen. It probably will happen. But when?

Appendix

THE BRANCHES OF ANTHROPOLOGY AND THE RELATION OF ANTHROPOLOGY TO OTHER STUDIES OF MAN

To some people with neat academic minds the fields of knowledge dealing with human beings are laid out like a series of formal gardens with walls between. According to a recent article in a professional journal, the territories cultivated by the various social sciences are as follows:

sociology:	the relatedness of human beings
psychology:	human behavior under controlled conditions
social psychology:	human behavior under actual life-conditions
history:	unique events and their connections through time
economics:	subsistence behavior, its forms and processes
political science:	control behavior, its forms and processes
anthropology:	basic anatomical and cultural likenesses and differences

Such a map of these gardens of learning is useful in describing the theoretical layout as it developed historically. Some scholars indeed visualize these high, tight walls as actually existing and defend their frontiers against all poachers. But in actual practice some walls were never built or were so low they were easily leaped over by the more intrepid students; others have crumbled in the past decade or two. But, just because some students of man have believed in the reality of these walls, some of the most precious flowers in the gardens have failed to bear fruit. Moreover, some rich lands were never fenced in because their ownership was in dispute. So they have been little cultivated, for the hardy scholar who ventured to follow his problem outside the walls of his own territory was punished by the suspicion and indignation of his more conservative colleagues. Hence, between and beyond the boundaries of the several social sciences, there is a vast no man's land.

The unstated assumption has been that human behavior took place in a series of watertight compartments. Hence the economist must study "economic man," the political scientist "political man," the sociologist "social man," etc. To the anthropologist, accustomed to working among primitive groups where trading is often a religious procedure and "government" inseparable from the rest of social life, such distinct and separate categories have appeared to result from the rigidity of academic organization. To him such classification appears to impede the following of the problem wherever it leads. Scholars in other fields also have become increasingly dissatisfied with carrying their investigations only so far as the conventional boundaries and abandoning them upon an intellectual dumping ground.

As to what students of man actually do, the tight distinctions are disappearing. Already there are scientists of whom it is arbitrary to say "he is a social psychologist" rather than "he is a sociologist" or "he is an anthropologist." The department of Social Relations at Harvard merges the fields of social anthropology, sociology, social and clinical psychology. A few psychiatrists can as well be called anthropologists. A number of men are almost equally "human geographers" and anthropologists. Certain physical anthropologists teach human anatomy in medical schools.

There are still, however, distinctions in both theory and practice which are relevant to an understanding of anthropology's role in the contemporary scene. The division of labor between anthropology and other studies of human life, as well as between the different branches of anthropology, is determined by the "what," on the one hand, and by the "how," on the other.

The most obvious division of territory is indicated by saying that anthropologists investigate the biology, history, language, psychology, sociology, economics, government, and philosophy of primitive peoples. The history of primitives is known only for the brief time spanned by the memories and oral traditions of men plus whatever scant references exist in European historical documents and the limited, though useful and important, evidence supplied by archaeology. The anthropologist must reconstruct history on the slender basis of the sequence of artifacts in time and their distribution in space. Because the anthropologist working with primitives can seldom take living subjects into a laboratory, he cannot perform the kind of experiments which are the hallmark of psychology and of medical research. Since primitives do not have written constitutions nor international cartels, certain fields of investigation of the political scientist and economist have remained outside the anthropologist's province.

A closer examination reveals that some groups conventionally allotted to anthropology are not primitive. The Maya of Middle America had a partly written language. The archaeology of China, the Near East, and Egypt has been considered almost as much the bailiwick of the anthropologist as of the Orientalist and Egyptologist. Moreover, anthropologists for at least a century have resisted as a matter of principle any attempt to restrict their domain to that of "higher barbarology." Though the study of European and American communities by anthropologists is less than twenty years old, and the anthropological exploration of modern industry still younger,

English and German anthropologists had invaded the sacrosanct territory of classical scholars considerably before 1900. Their point of view shed new illumination upon Greek and Roman civilization. By 1920, the French scholar, Marcel Granet, was examining Chinese civilization from the anthropological angle. In physical anthropology the restriction to primitives has been even less marked. Anthropometry (a standard technique for measuring human beings) was developed among and applied to Europeans on a grand scale.

From the point of view of subject matter, the sole feature which has distinguished every branch of anthropology and which has not been characteristic of any of the other human studies is the use of comparative data. The historian is ordinarily a historian of England or of Japan or of the nineteenth century or of the Renaissance. In so far as he makes systematic comparisons between the histories of different countries or areas or periods, he becomes a philosopher of history—or an anthropologist! A famous historian, Eduard Meyer, assigns indeed to anthropology the task of determining the universal features in human history. With a few exceptions, the sociologist has limited himself to Western civilization. The economist knows only the systems of production and exchange in societies where money and markets prevail. Although the study of "comparative government" has become fashionable, the political scientist still thinks in terms of constitutions and written laws. The horizons of the traditional linguist have been bounded by Indo-European and Semitic languages. Only of late, under the influence of anthropology, have psychologists and psychiatrists seen that the standards of normal and abnormal "human nature" are in part relative to time, place, and people. To the physician, human anatomy and physiology have meant the structures and functionings of modern white Euro-Americans.

But the anthropologist long ago took *all* mankind for his province. The physical anthropologist studies the hair form of Negroes only to compare it with that of Chinese and whites. The archaeologist never reports upon an excavation without making comparisons, and in writing his report he arranges his data with a view to other archaeologists using these data for comparative purposes. To the anthropological linguist the description of an unusual sound or grammatical form is not an end in itself but the establishment of a point in a range of variation. The ethnologist is interested in a specific type of clan organization as one link in a chain of evidence that indicates connections between two or more peoples at some past time. The social anthropologist analyzes witchcraft belief and practice to show how human beings handle the same fundamental problem in different ways or to demonstrate the universality of some social process.

Today psychology, some parts of medicine, sociology, human geography, and, to a lesser extent, linguistics, law, philosophy, and other sciences are using comparative data more and more. Psychologists study child rearing in primitive societies and comb anthropological literature for data of perception, learning, and aesthetics. Psychiatrists have developed great interest in the types of mental illnesses found in various non-European groups and in ways these people handle such aberrations. Other physicians find it profitable to discover what diseases occur in tribes that have had little contact with Europeans and what "racial" immunities exist. Sociologists, unlike human geographers, have done little field work among primitives, but the contemporary sociologist studies anthropological fact and theory as part of his training. The sociologist, psychologist,and psychiatrist pilfer the factual storehouse of the anthropologist to test a theory, to illustrate a point, or to find a new question that needs formulation and verification.

History, in the broadest sense, is the attempt to describe past events as accurately, concretely, and completely as possible; to establish the sequence of those events; to depict any patterns in the sequences. Thus history is as much a method as a separate science, and anthropology has its historical side. The course of human development, the dispersal of mankind over the face of the earth, and the evolution of cultures are historical inquiries.

Psychology and anthropology are the two main bridges between the life sciences and studies of human behavior. Physiology and medicine study man as an animal. Sociology, economics, and government study man's actions and their results. Only psychology, psychiatry, and anthropology unite the two approaches by being simultaneously interested in behavior and its biological foundation. Similarly, anthropology and human geography help bridge the gap between the physical sciences and the social sciences. The anthropologist and the geographer are both interested in man's adjustment to climate, natural resources, and location.

Of those who study man as an animal, the physical anthropologist stands out for his insistence on measurement and on dealing with a sizable number of cases. The student of extinct or fossil animals (the palaeontologist) often has only a few specimens to go on. Medical researchers, except in the field of public health, have only recently begun to see the necessity for statistical treatment. Anatomists, under the influence of physical anthropology, have begun to deal with graphs and curves of variation, but they still like to report on a dissection of one or a few cadavers. The anthropologist differs from the doctor in studying the well more than the sick.

The difference in outlook between psychologist and anthropologist arises primarily out of the fact that the psychologist has his eye upon the individual, the anthropologist upon the group and upon the individual as a member of a group. The contrast with the geographer is also one of focus and emphasis. The geographer cares about individuals only incidentally if at all. He looks to the technology that a people has developed and to the ways in which that people has altered the natural landscape by means of it. He deals with physiques and vital statistics only to the extent that these appear to reflect temperature extremes or soil qualities. For the rituals, the arts, and the linguistic habits which intrigue the anthropologist, he has only the faintest concern.

In view of the fact that they are ostensibly interested in many of the same problems, the extent to which sociologists and anthropologists have maintained fundamentally distinctive approaches is one of the more curious facts in the history of Western thought. The sociological attitude has tended toward the practical and present, the anthropological toward pure understanding and the past. Anthropology developed in the classes; sociology in the masses. A rich man's hobby can permit itself the luxury of aesthetic exultation in fascinatingly different and complex materials. The anthropologist has also been considered less socially dangerous by the conservative because he was "a gentleman" and preoccupied with the long ago and the far away.

Even today in a joint gathering it is comparatively easy to spot the two species. They talk differently; they even have a different look about them. This contrast may be traced to the differing origins of the two subjects, to the varying motivations that lead men and women to sociology or anthropology, and to the different intellectual affiliations of the two groups. Anthropology was created largely by individuals who had been trained in tough-minded empirical sciences like medicine, biology, and geology. Sociology stemmed from theology and philosophy where abstract reasoning reigns supreme. Sociologists have had many personal affiliations with social workers, reformers, and philosophers. On the other hand, the biases of anthropologists have been in the direction of pure observation. They are still, unfortunately, distrustful of talking much about concepts, methods, and theories. An unkind critic has said that sociology was "the science with the maximum of methods and the minimun of results." Anthropologists have often failed to see the forest for the trees, whereas one sometimes wonders if sociologists recognize that such a thing as a tree exists. These generalizations must be regarded, of course, as tendency rather than literal fact. While the word "sociologist" is often an epithet in the mouth of the anthropologist, the two have grown noticeably closer in recent years. The work of certain great European sociologists, such as Emile Durkheim, has long been so admired by anthropologists that they have tried to claim these men for their own.

The sciences are commonly divided into physical (physics, chemistry, geology, etc.); biological (botany, zoology, medicine, etc.); social (economics, sociology, etc.). Sometimes the physical and biological sciences are lumped as "natural sciences" with which the "social sciences" are usually contrasted unfavorably. Indeed some would say that the social studies are not and even cannot become sciences. This view is a curious reflection of the ignorance and prejudices of past centuries. It was once held that to study God's special creation, man, was impious, or that human behavior was in its essence unpredictable because all the data were "subjective." Any scientist, however, should know that data are never "subjective" or "intangible"—it is our ways of looking at them which may or may not be "tangible" and "objective." The social sciences are admittedly immature; this is understandable, for they are also young.

History is primarily one of the humanities, but it is also, to a growing extent, a social science. Government or "political science" is ordinarily considered a social science, but its resemblances to history and law are so striking that the assignment is disputable. Certainly firsthand observation has thus far played a very small role in this field. Some psychologists are biological scientists; some are social scientists. Anthropology cannot be forced into any one of the categories. The archaeologist to a considerable degree works and thinks like a geologist or a historian. The procedures of the anthropologist who is studying the physical environment of a certain tribe can scarcely be distinguished from those of the human geographer. The physical anthropologist is inevitably one kind of human biologist.

Something must also be said of the difference in approach of anthropology and the humanities. In general, the humanities look backward, whereas anthropology looks forward. The same questions are probed, but the methods are different. Art and science equally try to render experience intelligible. To the artist, however, Sitting Bull is the dramatic exemplification of the whole struggle of the Indians against the white man. For the anthropologist, Sitting Bull disappears in the mass of Plains Indian chieftains, to be understood in terms of all our knowledge of the role of the chief, of various situational factors at that time, as well as in terms of his own particular life history. The humanities approach general questions through particular persons or incidents. Anthropology deals with particulars in the framework of universals.

Many writers appear to be resentful of the encroachments of scientific students of man upon a territory that has been considered the property of dramatists, novelists, and lately, of journalists. It must be admitted at once that great novelists and dramatists, drawing upon the long traditions of their craft, are much more adept at laying bare the mainsprings of human action than are anthropologists. If a friend of mine wants to find out in a short time what makes rural Poles tick, I should certainly send him to Ladislas Reymont's novel *The Peasants* and not to the social-science classic *The Polish Peasant,* by Thomas and Znaniecki. Malinowski's best monographs on the Trobrianders are not in a class with Willa Cather's *My Antonia* or Rebecca West's *Black Lamb and Grey Falcon* so far as conveying with imaginative reality the inner workings of a society and the motivation of individual actors in that society.

But even the very greatest artists offer no way of checking their conclusions except that of subjective conviction. The fact that a novelist can profoundly stir the feelings does not prove that he is telling verifiable truth. Some famous dramatists are notably restricted to private worlds that are moving and interesting but narrow. The artist lays great weight on intuition and inspiration, while the anthropologist is grateful for his hunches but does not accept them until they have been tested by rigorous methods. By offering ways to scrutinize his conclusions, and by minimizing personal bias through the use of standard methods of investigation, the anthropologist presents insights which, though more abstract and hence less immediately gripping, have certain tough merits.

What is the difference in the approach of a good reporter, and a good field anthropologist? They have much in common —in the obstacles they must surmount to meet the people they want to meet, in the care they must take in choosing their informants, and in their regard for accurate recording of what was said and done. It is high praise for one anthropologist to say to another, "That was good reporting." The difference arises from the purposes for which the two accounts are intended. The reporter must be interesting. The anthropologist is obliged to record the tiresome along with the flashy. The reporter must always think of what will engage his audience, of what will be intelligible to them in terms of their life ways. The first responsibility of the anthropologist is to set down events as seen by the people he is studying.

The point is that writers and scientists have different ways of attacking the same problem, but it is no either-or matter. Both approaches are needed, for each has its limitations and each contributes its special enlightenments.

The usual major division of anthropology is into physical and cultural. Physical anthropology includes primate paleontology (the description of the extinct varieties of man and his close animal relatives); human evolution (the process of development of human types, beginning with man's nonhuman ancestors); anthropometry (the techniques of human measurement); somatology (description of living varieties of man, of sex differences, and of individual physical variations); racial anthropology (classification of mankind into races, racial history of man, race mixture); comparative studies of growth; and constitutional anthropology (the study of the predispositions of bodily types to certain kinds of diseases and behavior, for instance, criminal behavior). Cultural anthropology includes archaeology (study of the remains of past times); ethnography (the pure description of the habits and customs of living peoples); ethnology (the comparative study of peoples past and present); folklore (the collection and analysis of drama, music, and tales preserved by oral tradition); social anthropology (study of cultural process and social structure); linguistics (the study of dead and living languages); and culture and personality (the relation between a distinctive way of life and a characteristic psychology). Applied anthropology is a way of selecting and using the data from both the physical and cultural studies, for dealing with modern social, political, and economic problems such as colonial administration, military government, and labor relations.

Acknowledgments

A COMPLETE RECORD of the persons who have made it possible for me to write this book would include the long list of those who have given me so much, beginning with my parents, George and Katherine Kluckhohn, and my sister Jane Kluckhohn. I cannot mention them all, but I should like to set down certain obligations that are especially relevant. Evon Vogt of Ramah, New Mexico, was responsible for my original interest in anthropology. Some of my undergraduate teachers at the University of Wisconsin had an especially deep influence upon my whole intellectual development: Walter Agard, Eugene Byrne, Norman Cameron, Harry Glicksman, Michael Rostovtseff, Bertha and Frank Sharp, Ruth Wallerstein. I owe a similar debt to teachers at Oxford (R. R. Marett, T. K. Penniman, Beatrice Blackwood), Vienna (W. Schmidt, W. Koppers, Edward Hitschmann), and Harvard (Alfred Tozzer, Earnest Hooton, Lauriston Ward). Ralph Linton has taught me a great deal and provided me with professional opportunities. The members of the departments of Anthropology and Social Relations at Harvard have been instructors as well as colleagues. The number of professional friends to whom I am indebted is so large as to make any selection almost invidious. However, I am particularly conscious of profound obligation to the following (in addition to those already named above): Henry A. Murray, John Dollard, Talcott Parsons, Edward Sapir, Alexander and Dorothea Leighton, Alfred Kroeber, W. W. Hill, Paul Reiter, Ruth Benedict, O. H. Mowrer, Donald Scott, J. O. Brew, L. C. Wyman, Gregory Bateson, Leslie

White, Robert Redfield, Fred Eggan, Margaret Mead, and Lawrence Frank. To John Collier, Laura Thompson, Alexander Leighton, and George Taylor I am grateful for opportunities to participate in the application of anthropological knowledge to modern problems. Many students, graduate and undergraduate, have clarified my thinking and stimulated me to more nearly adequate presentation. My wife, Florence Kluckhohn, has given immeasurable help, both intellectual and personal.

The Rhodes Scholarship Trust, the Rockefeller Foundation, and the Carnegie Corporation have enabled me to study with unusual advantages. I owe an especial debt to Charles Dollard, president of the Carnegie Corporation. This book was written under a fellowship provided by the John Simon Guggenheim Memorial Foundation in 1945–1946. To the Foundation and to its secretary general, Henry Allen Moe, I am very grateful.

The organizations and individuals who have supported my technical researches have also contributed importantly to this book for the layman: the Peabody Museum of Harvard University and its director, Professor Donald Scott; the Laboratory of Social Relations and its director, Professor Samuel Stouffer; the Viking Fund and its director of research, Dr. Paul Fejos; the Milton Fund of Harvard University, and Provost Paul H. Buck; the American Philosophical Society; the Social Science Research Council; the Old Dominion Foundation.

From the McGraw-Hill Book Company, Inc., and Whittlesey House I received generous help and cooperation in the writing and preparation of this book. To many members of the McGraw-Hill staff and most especially to Mrs. Beulah Harris I express my warmest thanks. Mrs. Harris's contribution to this book is intellectually as well as stylistically a very meaningful one.

The following friends and colleagues have given all or a portion of the text the benefit of their criticism: W. C. Boyd, J. O. Brew, Edward Bruner, James B. Conant, JoAnn and Paul Davis, Clarissa Fuller, W. W. Hill, Earnest Hooton, Stuart Hughes, Jane Kluckhohn, Florence Kluckhohn, Alfred and Theodora Kroeber, Alexander and Dorothea Leighton, Paul Reiter, James Spuhler, Evon and Naneen Vogt, Lauriston Ward. Naturally, none of these must be blamed for errors in fact or judgment, for I have often stuck stubbornly to my original statement. To Mrs. Ernst Blumenthal and Mrs. Bert Kaplan I am indebted for their enormous help and care in typing the various drafts of the manuscript.

W. H. Kelly, Dorothea Leighton, Florence Kluckhohn, and O. H. Mowrer have generously allowed me to revise and use published and unpublished materials that we had written jointly. Columbia University Press has consented to the republication of certain passages by Dr. Kelly and me, from the paper "The Concept of Culture," in *The Science of Man in the World Crisis*, edited by Ralph Linton (1945). The Harvard University Press has permitted me to use some paragraphs that Dr. Leighton and I wrote for *The Navaho* (1946). These appear mainly in Chapter VI of the present book. The Harvard Press has likewise given me permission to rework some parts from my chapter in *Religion and Our Racial Tensions* (1945). The Conference on Science, Philosophy, and Religion has allowed the reuse of portions of an essay by my wife and myself that appeared in *Conflicts of Power in Modern Culture* (1947) and parts of an earlier essay by me which they published in *Approaches to World Peace* (1944). Professor John Crowe Ransom, editor of the *Kenyon Review*, has permitted me to draw from my article "The Way of Life" which appeared in the *Review* in 1941. All of the sentences and paragraphs taken from earlier writings have been substantially rearranged or rewritten for this book.

This book is dedicated to two men to whom I owe very much. R. J. Koehler, business associate of my grandfather, Charles Kluckhohn, was one of the most significant influences of my formative years and has been a lifelong friend. H. G. Rockwood, my father-in-law, has for the past sixteen years aided and inspired me in many ways. The character and sense of personal and social responsibility of these two men have much that is similar. Their lives testify more dramatically than any words to the best in the distinctive American virtues which I have attempted to sketch in Chapter IX of this book.

The following publishers granted me permission to quote from the articles and books credited: *

W. W. Norton & Company, Inc.: Franz Boas's *Anthropology and Modern Life*. Copyright 1928 by the publishers.

The *Philosophical Review*: Grace de Laguna's "Cultural Relativism and Science" (March, 1942).

Alfred A. Knopf, Inc.: Edward Sapir's chapter in *The Unconscious, a Symposium* (1928).

The Scientific Monthly and the Rutgers University Press: Lawrence Frank's "Science and Culture" which appeared in the *Scientific Monthly* in June, 1940, and is reprinted in *Society as the Patient* (1948).

Duell, Sloan & Pearce, Inc.: Wallace Stegner's *Mormon Country* (1942).

* Listed in the order in which they appear in this book.

C. A. Watts & Co., Ltd.: V. G. Childe's *Man Makes Himself* (1936).

The American Philosophical Society: A. V. Kidder's "Looking Backward" (*Proceedings,* American Philosophical Society, vol. 83, 1940).

The Scientific Monthly: A. L. Kroeber's "Structure, Function and Pattern in Biology and Anthropology" (February, 1943).

The New American Library: V. G. Childe's *What Happened in History* (1943).

Psychiatry: Ruth Benedict's "Continuities and Discontinuities in Cultural Conditioning" (vol. 1, January, 1938).

The Ronald Press Company: the poem from W. J. Humphreys' *Ways of the Weather.* Copyright 1942, The Ronald Press Company.

Charles Scribner's Sons: R. B. Dixon's *Building of Cultures* (1928).

The Scientific Monthly: T. Dobzhansky's "The Race Concept in Biology" (vol. lii, February, 1941).

The American Association for the Advancement of Science, and G. P. Putnam's Sons: E. A. Hooton's "Anthropology and Medicine" which appeared in *Science* (1935) and was reprinted in *Apes, Men and Morons* (1937).

Philosophy and Phenomenological Research: Morris Opler's "Fact and Fallacy Concerning the Evolution of Man" (June, 1947).

The *American Journal of Orthodontics:* E. A. Hooton's "The Evolution and Devolution of the Human Face" (vol. 32, 1946).

Doubleday & Company, Inc.: *The Heathens* by William Howells. Copyright 1948 by William Howells.

The British Association for the Advancement of Science and the Smithsonian Institution: Karl Pearson's "The Science of Man: Its Needs and Prospects" (Smithsonian Report, 1921).

The Columbia University Press: W. M. Krogman's "The Concept of Race" from *The Science of Man in the World Crisis*, edited by Ralph Linton (1945).

The Royal Anthropological Institute: J. B. S. Haldane's "Anthropology and Human Biology" from *Proceedings of the International Congress of Anthropological and Ethnological Sciences* (1934).

Science Education: S. L. Washburn's "Thinking About Race" (vol. 28, 1944).

The Teaching Scientist: Franz Boas's "Genetic and Environmental Factors in Anthropology" which appeared in *The Teaching Biologist* (November, 1939).

Human Biology: Gunnar Dahlberg's "An Analysis of the Conception of Race and a New Method of Distinguishing Race" (1942).

The Ronald Press Company: S. Rosenzweig's "Outline of Frustration Theory" which appeared in *Personality and the Behavior Disorders*, J. McV. Hunt, editor. Copyright 1944, The Ronald Press Company.

Asia and the Americas: Harry Shapiro's "Certain Aspects of Race" which appeared in *Asia* (June, 1944).

The University of California Press: A. B. Johnson's *Treatise on Language*, edited by David Rynin (1947).

Linguistic Society of America: Edward Sapir's "The Status of Linguistics as a Science" published in *Language* (1929).

Henry Holt and Company: Leonard Bloomfield's *Language* (1933).

Oxford University Press: S. de Madariaga's *Englishmen, Frenchmen, and Spaniards* (1929).

Yale University Press: Carl Becker's *Heavenly City of the Eighteenth Century Philosophers* (1935).

Child Study: Margaret Mead's "When Were You Born" (Spring, 1941).

Transactions of the New York Academy of Sciences: Margaret Mead's "The Application of Anthropological Techniques to Cross-National Communication" (February, 1947).

The Macmillan Company: Edward Sapir's "Language" in the *Encyclopedia of the Social Sciences*, (vol. ix). Copyright 1933 by The Macmillan Company.

The Columbia University Press: Felix Keesing's "Applied Anthropology in Colonial Administration" in *The Science of Man in the World Crisis*, edited by Ralph Linton (1945).

The United States Department of Agriculture: R. Redfield and W. Warner's "Cultural Anthropology and Modern Agriculture" which appeared in the 1940 *Yearbook of Agriculture*.

The Southwestern Journal of Anthropology: F. Hulse's "Technological Development and Personal Incentive in Japan" (1947).

The Conference on Science, Philosophy, and Religion: Lyman Bryson's "What Is a Good Society" which appeared in *Science, Philosophy, and Religion, a Symposium* (1943).

The Journal of Applied Anthropology: Eliot Chapple's "Anthropological Engineering" (January, 1943).

The American Anthropologist: John Embree's "Applied Anthropology and Its Relation to Anthropology" (1945).

The University of California Press: George Pettitt's *Primitive Education in North America* (1946).

The Journal of the National Association of Deans of Women: Margaret Mead's "Administrative Contributions to Democratic Character Formation at the Adolescent Level" (January, 1941).

William Morrow and Co., Inc.: Margaret Mead's *From the South Seas*. Copyright 1928, 1930, 1935, 1939 by M. Mead.

Professor Leslie Spier (chairman of the editorial committee for *Language, Culture and Personality*): Cora Du Bois's "Attitudes Toward Food and Hunger in Alor" (1941).

The Conference on Science, Philosophy, and Religion: Gregory Bateson's "Comment" on Margaret Mead's paper in *Science, Philosophy, and Religion, a Symposium* (1942).

The American Journal of Sociology: Edward Sapir's "Culture, Genuine and Spurious" (1924) and C. J. Friedrich's "The New Doctrine of the Common Man" (1944).

The Macmillan Company: E. H. Carr's *The Soviet Impact on the Western World.* Copyright 1947 by The Macmillan Company.

The Saturday Review of Literature: William Scroggs's "What's the Matter with Economics?" (November 11, 1939).

The New York Academy of Sciences: Ruth Benedict's "The Study of Cultural Patterns in European Nations" (June, 1946).

United Nations World and the Rutgers University Press: Lawrence Frank's "World Order and Cultural Diversity" which appeared in *Free World* (June, 1942) and has been reprinted in *Society as the Patient* (1948).

The Society for the Psychological Study of Social Issues: Lippitt and Hendry's contribution to *Human Nature and Enduring Peace* (1945).

Dr. Mortimer Graves: an unpublished memorandum.

The Institute for Psychoanalysis (Chicago): Edwin Embree's pamphlet "Living Together" (1941).

Living authors whose addresses were accessible have also been asked for permission, which has been graciously granted by each writer reached. I am very grateful to them also.

CLYDE KLUCKHOHN

Index

5 32